3rd Workshop on NLP for Computer-Assisted Language Learning 2014

(NLC4CALL)

NEALT Proceedings Series Vol. 22

Linkoping Electronic Conference Proceedings 107

Uppsala, Sweden
13 November 2014

Editors:

E. Volodina
L. Borin
I. Pilan

ISBN: 978-1-63439-637-0

Printed from e-media with permission by:

Curran Associates, Inc.
57 Morehouse Lane
Red Hook, NY 12571

Some format issues inherent in the e-media version may also appear in this print version.

Printed by Curran Associates, Inc. (2015)

For permission requests, please contact the Association for Computational Linguistics at the address below.

Association for Computational Linguistics
209 N. Eighth Street
Stroudsburg, Pennsylvania 18360

Phone: 1-570-476-8006
Fax: 1-570-476-0860

acl@aclweb.org

Additional copies of this publication are available from:

Curran Associates, Inc.
57 Morehouse Lane
Red Hook, NY 12571 USA
Phone: 845-758-0400
Fax: 845-758-2634
Email: curran@proceedings.com
Web: www.proceedings.com

Proceedings of the

third workshop on NLP for computer-assisted language learning

at SLTC 2014, Uppsala University

edited by

Elena Volodina
Lars Borin
Ildikó Pilán

Preface

Intelligent Computer-Assisted Language Learning (ICALL), i.e., the integration of Natural Language Processing (NLP) and Speech Technologies (ST) in language learning applications, is a rapidly developing area which has started to attract increased attention from the Language Technology (LT) – generally understood as encompassing both NLP and ST – community. ICALL research has generated a number of successful applications for alleviating a variety of (mechanical) tasks that teachers face daily in their work, for example grammar or spelling error marking, essay grading, preparation of text questions for reading activities, creating tests and exercises, etc.

However, reusing LT methods or tools (developed for other than pedagogical purposes) in pedagogical applications is not always straightforward since they need to be adapted to the educational tasks, e.g. readability measures for legal texts adapted to the second language learning context. Thus, LT researchers who intend to re-use their algorithms and techniques in CALL applications need new datasets, specifically designed corpora, databases, etc. to fine-tune their tools for new target groups, the design and compilation of which are both critical for achieving good results and time-consuming.

There are other challenges that the area of LT-based CALL faces: re-use and sharing of existing LT components, copyright issues, standardization of pedagogical framework, lack of collaboration with end-users, to name just a few. Probably the most significant challenge is to make sure that the research results reach the actual end-users in the form of tools which can become a part of the educational process, and which are both easy to use and have a pedagogically sound basis. The goal of the workshop was to bring together (computational) linguists involved in research aiming at integrating LT in CALL systems and exploring the theoretical and methodological issues arising in this connection, with the purpose of sharing experiences, achievements and setbacks, and to discuss potential ways of addressing the challenges that need to be overcome.

This year we invited submissions of papers and software demonstrations that would

- describe research directly aimed at ICALL
- demonstrate actual or discuss potential use of existing LT tools or resources for language learning
- describe ongoing development of resources and tools with potential usage in ICALL, either directly in interactive applications, or indirectly in materials, application or curriculum development, e.g. collecting and annotating learner corpora; developing tools and algorithms for readability analysis, selecting optimal corpus examples, etc.
- discuss challenges and/or research agendas for ICALL

with a special focus on Nordic languages. Out of 13 submissions, 10 papers have been accepted following the recommendations of two anonymous reviews per paper provided by the members of our Program Committee:

- Lars Ahrenberg, Linköping University, Sweden
- Lars Borin, University of Gothenburg, Sweden
- Antonio Branco, University of Lisboa, Portugal
- Simon Dobnik, University of Gothenburg, Sweden
- Robert Eklund, Linköping University, Sweden
- Katarina Heimann Mühlenbock, DART, Sahlgrenska Universitetssjukhuset, Göteborg, Sweden

Elena Volodina, Lars Borin and Ildikó Pilán 2014. Preface. *Proceedings of the third workshop on NLP for computer-assisted language learning.* NEALT Proceedings Series 22 / Linköping Electronic Conference Proceedings 107: i–ii.

- Thomas François, UCLouvain, Belgium
- Arne Jönsson, Linköping University, Sweden
- Sofie Johansson Kokkinakis, University of Gothenburg, Sweden
- Chris Koniaris, University of Gothenburg, Sweden
- Peter Ljunglöf, University of Gothenburg, Sweden
- Hrafn Loftsson, Reykjavik University, Iceland
- Montse Maritxalar, University of the Basque country, Spain
- Detmar Meurers, University of Tübingen, Germany
- Martí Quixal, University of Tübingen, Germany
- Mathias Schulze, University of Waterloo, Canada
- Joel Tetreault, Yahoo! Labs, US
- Trond Trosterud, Universitetet i Tromsø, Norway
- Cornelia Tschichold, Swansea University, UK
- Francis Tyers, The Arctic University of Norway, Norway
- Elena Volodina, University of Gothenburg, Sweden

The geography of accepted papers (i.e. author affiliations) covered Belgium, Canada, Germany, Norway, Russia, Spain, Sweden and USA. The resources and tools described in the papers in this volume are aimed at a range of languages: Swedish, Russian, Estonian, French, German, Spanish and English. The papers cover three main topic areas: *resources for development of ICALL applications* (learner corpora vs coursebook corpora), *tools and algorithms for the analysis of learner language* (focusing on collocations, reading tasks, cloze items, pronunciation, spelling, level classification of learner production), and *generation of learning materials* (e.g., exercise generators).

The workshop started off with short presentations of each paper, followed by discussions during the two poster sessions. The workshop concluded with an invited talk by Detmar Meurers on *A roadmap connecting NLP research and language learning* which developed into a free discussion on challenges and future prospects of ICALL.

The workshop organizers:
Elena Volodina
Lars Borin
Ildikó Pilán

WS website: `http://spraakbanken.gu.se/eng/Research/ICALL/3rdNLP4CALL`

Acknowledgements: Financial support for the organization of the workshop has come from the University of Gothenburg through its support of the *Centre for Language Technology*: `http://www.clt.gu.se`

Contents

Improving Collocation Correction by Ranking Suggestions Using Linguistic Knowledge

Roberto Carlini[1], *Joan Codina-Filba*[1], *Leo Wanner*[2,1]

(1) Natural Language Processing Group, Department of Information and Communication Technologies
Pompeu Fabra University, Barcelona
(2) Catalan Institute for Research and Advanced Studies (ICREA)

roberto.carlini@upf.edu, joan.codina@upf.edu, leo.wanner@upf.edu

ABSTRACT

The importance of collocations in the context of second language learning is generally acknowledged. Studies show that the "collocation density" in learner corpora is nearly the same as in native corpora, i.e., that use of collocations by learners is as common as it is by native speakers, while the collocation error rate in learner corpora is about ten times as high as in native reference corpora. Therefore, CALL could be of great aid to support the learners for better mastering of collocations. However, surprisingly few works address specifically research on CALL-oriented collocation learning assistants that detect miscollocations in the writings of the learners and propose suggestions for their correction or that offer the learner the possibility to verify a word co-occurrence with respect to its correctness as collocation and obtain suggestions for its correction in case it is determined to be a miscollocation. This disregard is likely to be, on the one hand, due to the focus of the CALL research so far on grammatical matters, and, on the other hand, due to the complexity of the problem. In order to be able to provide an adequate correction of a miscollocation, the collocation learning assistant must "guess" the meaning that the learner intended to express. This makes it very different from grammar or spell checkers, which can draw on grammatical respectively orthographic regularities of a language. In this paper, we focus on the problem of the provision of a ranked list of correction suggestions in a context in which the learner submits a collocation for verification and obtains a list of correction suggestions in the case of a miscollocation. We show that the retrieval of the suggestions and their ranking benefits greatly from NLP techniques that provide the syntactic dependency structure and subcategorization information of the word co-occurrences and a weighted Pointwise Mutual Information (PMI) that reflects the fact that in a collocation, it is the base that is subject of the free choice of the speaker, while the occurrence of the collocate is restricted by the base, i.e., that collocations are per se asymmetric.

KEYWORDS: CALL, collocations, miscollocation correction, syntactic dependencies, subcategorization, PMI.

Roberto Carlini, Joan Codina-Filba and Leo Wanner 2014. Improving collocation correction by ranking suggestions using linguistic knowledge. *Proceedings of the third workshop on NLP for computer-assisted language learning.* NEALT Proceedings Series 22 / Linköping Electronic Conference Proceedings 107: 1–12.

1 Introduction

The importance of collocations in the context of second language learning is beyond any doubt; see, among others, (Granger, 1998; Lewis, 2000; Nesselhauf, 2004, 2005; Lesniewska, 2006; Alonso Ramos et al., 2010) for studies in this respect. Orol and Alonso Ramos (2013) even show in their study that the "collocation density" in learner corpora is nearly the same as in native corpora, i.e., that the use of collocations by learners is as common as it is by native speakers. At the same time, they also find that the collocation error rate in learner corpora is about 32% (compared to about 3% by native speakers). That is, *Computer Assisted Language Learning* (CALL) could be of great aid to support the learners for better mastering of collocations. However, surprisingly few works address specifically CALL-oriented collocation learning assistants that detect miscollocations in the writings of the learners and propose suggestions for their correction or that offer the learner the possibility to verify using an interactive interface a word co-occurrence with respect to its correctness as collocation and obtain suggestions for its correction in case it is determined to be a miscollocation; cf. (Wanner et al., 2013) for an overview. This is likely to be, on the one hand, due to the focus on grammatical matters that CALL research had so far, and, on the other hand, due to the complexity of the problem. The problem envisaged by a collocation learning assistant is that in order to be able to provide an adequate correction of a miscollocation, it must "guess" the meaning that the learner intended to express. Thus, if the learner writes *assume an exam*, we do not know a priori (especially not when the learner uses an interface for the verification of *assume an exam* as an isolated word co-occurrence; cf., e.g., http://miscollocation-richtrf.rhcloud.com/ for illustration), whether she wants to say *take an exam* or *pass an exam*. This makes collocation checkers very different from grammar or spell checkers, which can draw on grammatical respectively orthographic regularities of a language.

In what follows, we focus on the problem of the collocation learning assistants of the verification of isolated word co-occurrences introduced by the learner with respect to their collocation status and the provision of a ranked list of correction suggestions in case a co-occurrence is considered to be a miscollocation. In the state-of-the-art proposals, the correction suggestions are ranked in terms of occurrence frequency or point-wise mutual information (PMI). Both measures do not take into account the essential linguistic features of collocations, and, in particular, their dependency structures and subcategorization and their asymmetric nature that results from the fact that the *base* element of a collocation is subject of the free choice of the speaker, while the occurrence of the *collocate* element is restricted by the base.

In the next section, we introduce the linguistic considerations on collocations that motivate our proposal. Section 3 presents how we draw upon these linguistic considerations to rank collocation correction suggestions. Section 4 outlines the experiments we carried out to verify our proposal, and Section 5 discusses the outcome of these experiments. In Section 6, a short summary of the related work is presented, before Section 7 draws some conclusions.

2 The Linguistic nature of collocations

The term "collocation" as introduced by Firth (1957) and cast into a definition by Halliday (1961) encompasses the statistical distribution of lexical items in context: lexical items that form high probability associations are considered collocations. It is this interpretation that underlies most works on automatic identification of collocations in corpora; see, e.g., (Choueka, 1988; Church and Hanks, 1989; Pecina, 2008; Evert, 2007; Bouma, 2010). However, in contemporary lexicography and lexicology an interpretation that stresses the idiosyncratic nature of collocations prevails. Thus, Benson (1989) states that "collocations should be defined not just as 'recurrent word combinations', but as 'ARBITRARY recurrent word combinations' ". "Arbitrary" as opposed to "regular" means that collocations are unpredictable and language-specific. For instance, in English, one *takes a walk*, while in French, German and Italian one 'makes' it: *faire une promenade, einen Spaziergang machen, fare una passeggiata*, and in Spanish one 'gives' it: *dar un paseo*. In English, one *gives a lecture*, in German and Italian one 'holds' it: *eine Vorlesung halten, tenere una lezione*, and in Russian one 'reads' it: *čitat′ lekciju*.

According to Hausmann (1984), Cowie (1994), Mel'čuk (1995) and others, a collocation is a binary idiosyncratic co-occurrence of lexical items between which a direct syntactic dependency holds and where the occurrence of one of the items (the *base*) is subject of the free choice of the speaker, while the occurrence of the other item (the *collocate*) is restricted by the base. Thus, in the case of *take* [*a*] *walk*, *walk* is the base and *take* the collocate, in the case of *high speed*, *speed* is the base and *high* the collocate, etc. It is this understanding of the term "collocation" that we find reflected in general public collocation dictionaries and that we follow since it seems most useful in the context of second language acquisition. However, this is not to say that the two main interpretations of the term "collocation", the distributional and the idiosyncratic one, are disjoint, i.e., necessarily lead to a different judgement with respect to the collocation status of a word combination. On the contrary: two lexical items that form an idiosyncratic co-occurrence are likely to occur together in a corpus with a high value of *Pointwise Mutual Information* (PMI) (Church and Hanks, 1989):

$$PMI = \log\left(\frac{P(a \cap b)}{P(a)P(b)}\right) = \log\left(\frac{P(a|b)}{P(a)}\right) = \log\left(\frac{P(b|a)}{P(b)}\right) \tag{1}$$

The PMI indicates that if two variables a and b are independent, the probability of their intersection is the product of their probabilities. A PMI equal to 0 means that the variables are independent; a positive PMI implies a correlation beyond independence; and a negative PMI signals that the co-occurrence of the variables is lower than the average. Two lexemes are thus considered to form a collocation when they have a positive PMI, i.e., they are found together more often that this would happen if they would be independent variables.

PMI has been a standard collocation measure throughout the literature since Church and Hank's proposal in 1989. It can be used not only for collocation detection, but also for ranking miscollocation correction suggestions: collocations of the base of the miscollocation retrieved from a reference corpus are ranked such that those with a higher PMI appear higher in the correction list than those with a lower PMI. Since for lexemes with largely different individual probabilities (the probabilities can be measured in terms of the number of sentences that contain these words) the PMIs cannot be compared in magnitude, a normalization has been suggested by Bouma (2009):

$$NPMI_{CB} = \frac{\left(\log \frac{P(a,b)}{P(a)P(b)}\right)}{-\log P(a,b)} \tag{2}$$

However, a mere use of PMI, $NPMI_{CB}$ or any similar measure does not consider two central linguistic features of collocations:

1. The lexical dependencies between the base and the collocate are not symmetric, while PMI is commutative, i.e., $PMI(a,b) = PMI(b,a)$.

2. Between the base and the collocate of a collocation, always a direct syntactic dependency holds whose sub-categorization structure depends on the base (as the semantic head of the collocation).

2.1 Lexical asymmetry of collocations

Collocations are lexically asymmetrical. Consider, for instance, the collocation *take an exam*. The base *exam* is far less frequent than the collocate *take*. Thus, if we suppose that in a collection of 10000 sentences *take* appears 1000 times, *exam* 10 times, and *take an exam* 5 times, we obtain:

$$P(take|exam) = 0.5 \gg 0,005 = P(exam|take)$$

with the PMI:

$$PMI = \log\left(\frac{P(take \cap exam)}{P(take)P(exam)}\right) = \log\left(\frac{P(take|exam)}{P(take)}\right) = \log\left(\frac{P(exam|take)}{P(exam)}\right) \quad (3)$$

$$PMI = \log\left(\frac{0.0005}{0.1 \cdot 0.001}\right) = \log\left(\frac{0.5}{0.1}\right) = \log\left(\frac{0.005}{0.001}\right) = \log(5)$$

On the other hand, analyzing the co-occurrence of *exam* with a less frequent verb such as *cheat*, and considering that in the same collection *cheat* appears 10 times and *cheat on an exam* 5 times, we obtain:

$$PMI = \log\left(\frac{P(cheat \cap exam)}{P(cheat)P(exam)}\right) = \log\left(\frac{P(cheat|exam)}{P(cheat)}\right) = \log\left(\frac{P(exam|cheat)}{P(exam)}\right)$$

$$PMI = \log\left(\frac{0.0005}{0.001 \cdot 0.001}\right) = \log\left(\frac{0.5}{0.001}\right) = \log\left(\frac{0.5}{0.001}\right) = \log(500)$$

In both cases, the PMI is positive, such that we can consider both co-occurrences to be valid collocations. However, the PMI of *take [an] exam* is much smaller than the PMI of *cheat [on an] exam*. This means that when using the PMI as criterion for ranking collocation suggestions, *take [an] exam* is ranked much lower than *cheat [on an] exam* — although *take [an] exam* is a very common collocation and should be ranked higher.

To address this inconvenience, Bouma (2009) normalizes in Eq. (2) the collocation PMI (i.e., for $PMI > 0$) with a neutral (or symmetric) $p(collocate \cap base)$. However, Eq. (2) does not compensate the penalization of highly frequent collocates: In general, it can be observed that when the collocate is a very common word, the $NPMI_{CB}$ is still penalized. This is because $NPMI_{CB}$ is symmetric with respect to the base and the collocate.

In order to account for this problem, we propose an asymmetric normalization that uses $p(collocate)$:

$$NPMI_C = \frac{PMI(collocate, base)}{-log(p(collocate))} \quad (4)$$

Normalizing with *p(collocate)* and replacing the PMI computed with conditional probabilities, as done in Eq. ((1)), we obtain:

$$NPMI_C = \frac{PMI(collocate, base)}{-\log(P(collocate))} \tag{5a}$$

$$= \frac{\log\left(\frac{P(collocate|base)}{P(collocate)}\right)}{-log(P(collocate))} \tag{5b}$$

$$= \frac{\log(P(collocate|base)) - \log(P(collocate))}{-\log(P(collocate))} \tag{5c}$$

$$= -\frac{\log(P(collocate|base))}{\log(P(collocate))} + 1 \tag{5d}$$

$$= 1 - \log_{P(collocate)}(P(collocate|base)) \tag{5e}$$

In Eq. ((5e)), we can observe that the $NPMI_C$ is the logarithm of the conditional probability, with the probability of the collocate as its base. Figure 1 shows that in the interval [0,1], $NPMI_C$ is always above $NPMI_{CB}$. Furthermore, $NPMI_C$ is much less influenced by high frequencies of the collocate. In the next sections, we will analyze how this changes the ratings of the collocation correction suggestions in some sample cases.

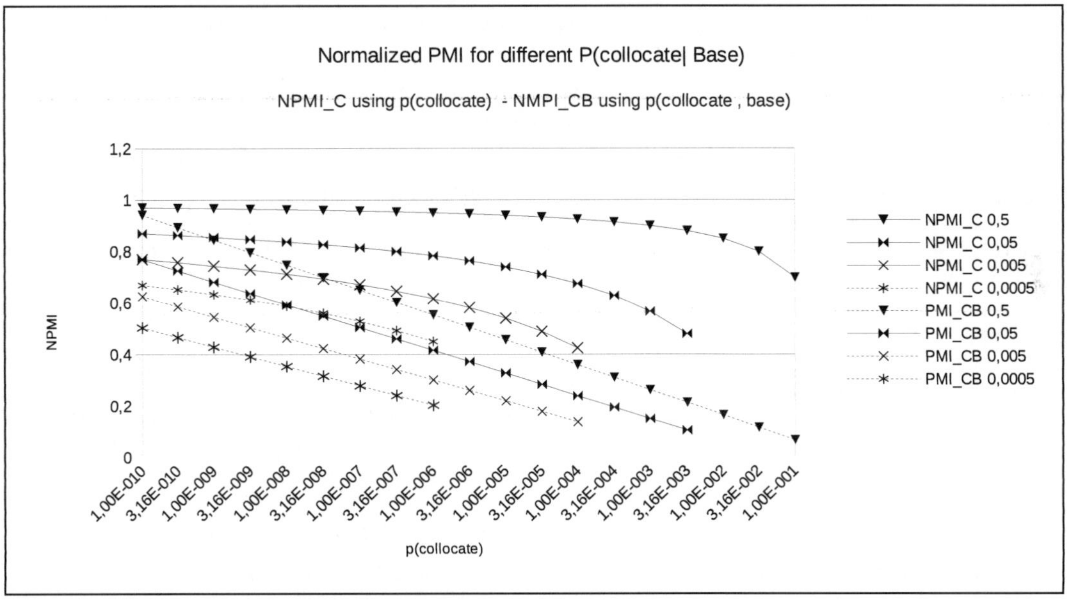

Figure 1: Graph showing the differences between the $NPMI_C$ (continuous line) and $NPMI_{CB}$ (dashed line). Each line shows the variation of the $NPMI$ for different values of $p(collocate|base)$ as the probability of the collocate changes, given a probability of the base of 10^-10.

2.2 Syntactic dependencies in collocations

As argued in lexicography (see the citations above), an essential feature of a collocation is that a direct dependency holds between the base and the collocate. Thus, in *take* [*a*] *walk* as in *I took a walk with Mary*, the base *walk* is the direct object of the collocate *take*. In contrast, in *Wexford followed him through the pleached walk and they entered the house by a glazed garden door*,[1] *pleached* is a participle modifier of *walk*. It may thus be considered as an adjective–noun collocation, but not as a verb–direct object collocation *pleach* [*a*] *walk* — as assumed by the MUST collocation checker.

In *I enjoyed the privacy during my walk with Mary*, *enjoy* and *walk* cannot form a collocation at all, even if they may have a rather high PMI, because there is no direct syntactic dependency between them.

Apart from syntactic dependencies, the sub-categorization information of the base must be considered. We say *apply for* [*a*] *job*, *apply to college* and *apply* [*a*] *theory*; *nominate for presidency*, and *nominate* [*the*] *candidate*; and so on. Governed prepositions must be clearly distinguished from semantically full prepositions; cf. *to* in *go to the concert* or *through* in *drive through the city*.

That is, when searching for correction suggestions for a given miscollocation, we need to be aware that a collocation is not a mere prominent co-occurrence of words, as argued in early works in the field; see, e.g., (Choueka, 1988; Church and Hanks, 1989). Rather, it implies dependency information that needs to be taken into account.

3 Ranking of Collocation Suggestions

The basic source that allows us to check a sequence of words provided by the user for its collocation status and to come up with corrections suggestions is a large reference dependency treebank. For each pair of POS-tagged tokens between which a relevant dependency relation holds, the PMI, $NPMI_{CB}$ and $NPMI_C$ are calculated; proper nouns, determiners, conjunctions, numerals, etc. are excluded. As “relevant", we consider relations that have been observed to hold between collocation elements; the most prominent of them are: direct object, indirect object, subject, modifier, and adverbial. When the noun is not a direct dependant of the verb because there is a preposition in between, the preposition is considered part of the relation.

In order to check the validity of a word combination introduced by the user as collocation and to propose correction suggestions for a miscollocation, the following procedure is followed:

1. Check the $NPMI_C$ value of the combination in the database:
   (a) If the combination is found in the reference corpus, the collocation is considered correct or wrong depending on whether the $NPMI_C$ value is positive or negative respectively.
   (b) If the combination does not exist in the reference corpus, we consider its elements as mutually exclusive and, accordingly, the combination as a miscollocation.[2]
2. If the collocation is considered wrong, we attempt to find candidate suggestions for its correction: any valid combination with the base or the collocate of the miscollocation that fits the dependency profile of the miscollocation are retrieved from the corpus.

[1]Example offered by the MUST collocation checker (http://miscollocation-richtrf.rhcloud.com/) on October, 1st 2014 for *pleach walk*, which has been proposed by MUST as one of the collocations the learner should consider along with *take* [*a*] *walk*.

[2]This criterion can be improved by checking whether the individual words exist in the reference corpus. If the collocate or the base are missing, we could pre-calculate PMI values using semantic information from EuroWordNet and search for the missing word using its hypernym.

3. Retrieved candidate suggestions are ranked according to their $NPMI_C$. Only the first items of the list are shown, but the user can ask to go down in the list. Also, the user can solicit sample sentences from the corpus in which the corresponding collocation occurs (as in the MUST collocation checker) to help them to understand the correct use of it.

4 Experiments

In order to validate our model, we carried out experiments on Spanish material, taking as starting point some miscollocations with the bases *siesta* 'nap' (Table 1), *meta* 'finish line , target, objective, goal, goalkeeper' (Table 3), *examen* 'exam' (Table 2) , and *teléfono* 'phone' (Table 4) from the learner corpus CEDEL2 (Lozano, 2009). As reference treebank, we use a treebank of Spanish newspaper material. The sentences of the treebank are indexed in a Solr (Lucene) index for more efficient access. The index allows us to retrieve directly the list of tokens, the list of lemmas and all the tokens related with another token by a given relation type. It is also used to retrieve examples to be shown to the user.

The table of each base lists the most common collocates, indicating the frequencies in the corpus, the PMI, $NPMI_{CB}$ and $NPMI_C$; for *meta* the table contains two parts, a list for *meta* acting as direct object and another for *meta* being the subject. That is, the tables can be considered as ranked lists of collocation suggestions.

collocate	$Freq_C$	$Freq_{CB}$	PMI	$NPMI_{CB}$	$NPMI_C$
dormir	612	69	3,611	0,716	0,881
echar	5847	42	2,415	0,459	0,775
hacer	165124	18	0,597	0,106	0,358
estar	13349	3	0,911	0,142	0,33
haber	149464	9	0,339	0,057	0,198

Table 1: Table of PMI and normalized PMIs for the base *siesta*.

collocate	$Freq_C$	$Freq_{CB}$	PMI	$NPMI_{CB}$	$NPMI_C$
pasar	23170	228	1,69	0,373	0,671
superar	19861	119	1,475	0,307	0,57
aprobar	12676	82	1,508	0,303	0,542
realizar	28999	99	1,231	0,252	0,508
suspender	6241	32	1,407	0,262	0,455
preparar	11526	35	1,18	0,221	0,418
someter	1927	11	1,454	0,249	0,404
hacer	165124	139	0,623	0,131	0,373
ordenar	6494	15	1,061	0,186	0,345
terminar	4906	11	1,048	0,179	0,328
efectuar	4909	11	1,048	0,179	0,328
practicar	5091	11	1,032	0,177	0,325
afrontar	8994	11	0,785	0,134	0,268

Table 2: Table of PMI and normalized PMIs for the base *examen*.

The miscollocations have been entered in sequence via an interface comparable to the MUST collocation checker (http://miscollocation.appspot.com/).

collocate	$Freq_C$	$Freq_{CB}$	PMI	$NPMI_{CB}$	$NPMI_C$
cruzar[1]	4608	223	2,442	0,538	0,758
alcanzar[1]	25412	227	1,708	0,377	0,689
fijar[3]	8803	43	1,446	0,275	0,492
batir[2]	2066	17	1,672	0,296	0,468
perforar[2]	217	5	2,12	0,343	0,466
lograr[2 3]	21357	50	1,126	0,217	0,441
conseguir	25486	50	1,05	0,202	0,423
regatear[2]	342	3	1,7	0,265	0,391
encarar[2]	1200	6	1,456	0,238	0,383
inquietar[2]	520	3	1,518	0,237	0,364
marcar[2]	15636	26	0,978	0,179	0,363
cumplir[3]	19295	26	0,887	0,162	0,341
perseguir[3]	3462	8	1,121	0,187	0,335
rebasar[3]	958	3	1,253	0,195	0,321
conquistar[3]	2033	5	1,148	0,186	0,321
collocate	$Freq_C$	$Freq_{CB}$	PMI	$NPMI_{CB}$	$NPMI_C$
ser[1,2,3,4]	784559	388	0,558	0,13	0,564
desviar[4]	532	6	1,917	0,314	0,461
parar[4]	1999	6	1,342	0,22	0,374
salvar[4]	2045	6	1,332	0,218	0,373
alcanzar[3,4]	11168	15	0,992	0,174	0,35
estar[1,2,3,4]	171062	80	0,534	0,107	0,323
fijar[3]	3394	5	1,033	0,167	0,308
tocar[4]	3227	4	0,958	0,152	0,284

Table 3: Table of PMI and normalized PMIs for the base *meta*. The upper part of the table captures the figures for *meta* as direct object and the lower part for *meta* as subject. Each collocate corresponds to a given sense of *meta*: '[1]' stands for 'the finish line' , '[2]' for 'goal' in football, '[3]' for 'objective' and '[4]' for 'goalkeeper'.

collocate	$Freq_C$	$Freq_{CB}$	PMI	$NPMI_{CB}$	$NPMI_C$
pinchar	403	77	2,789	0,558	0,652
descolgar	230	61	2,931	0,575	0,648
sonar	2218	105	2,183	0,449	0,617
coger	4627	123	1,932	0,403	0,6
intervenir	1294	55	2,136	0,415	0,566
colgar	1723	61	2,057	0,403	0,564
llamar	12957	111	1,44	0,298	0,519
desconectar	234	14	2,285	0,398	0,506
contestar	3066	41	1,634	0,31	0,481
atender	8563	57	1,331	0,259	0,451
usar	6286	46	1,372	0,263	0,444
habilitar	760	14	1,773	0,309	0,443

Table 4: Table of PMI and normalized PMIs for the base *teléfono*.

5 Discussion

In the tables, we can appreciate the differences produced by the different measures used to calculate the co-occurrence strength between the collocation elements. The main differences occur with verbs that are very common, such as *hacer* '[to] make' as collocate of *siesta* or *examen*. In both cases, $NPMI_C$ considers it more important than other verbs. Thus, PMI and $NPMI_{CB}$ rank *hacer* in co-occurrence with *examen* as lowest (0.623 respectively 0,131), while $NPMI_C$ keeps it in the middle of the table, ranking it higher than *efectuar* '[to] effect' or *afrontar* '[to] face', which are much less common (which makes the $NPMI_C$ ranking more appropriate).

In co-occurrence with the base *teléfono*, the verb *llamar* '[to] call' appears in the middle of the list when ranked by $NPMI_C$, while when ranked by PMI or $NPMI_{CB}$ it appears down in the least, even if it is almost the most common collocate of phone (5% of the cases).

Table 3 shows that the verb *ser* '[to] be' is the most common (33 of the cases) for *meta* as subject; the $NPMI_C$ upgrades it, ranking it higher, even if is a very common verb and has a low PMI. Looking at the list, we see that there is also *estar* '[to] be' with similar PMI. However, $NPMI_C$ does not promote it. Analyzing the data more deeply, we can observe that $p(meta|ser) \sim p(meta|estar)$, but $p(ser|meta) \gg p(estar|meta)$. That is, the penalization of *estar* by $NPMI_C$ is correct.

The tables show the relationship between the base and the collocate when the collocate is a verb and the base its direct object. When the base is subject (or a different kind of object), different collocations may appear. Table 3 shows that when the base *meta* has a different grammatical function in the sentence, it often also has a different sense. It tends to mean 'goal', 'finish line' or 'objective' when is the direct object, but when appears as subject it often stands for 'goalkeeper'.

There are some coincidences between the two lists of verbs in Table 3. This is because of their use as both passive and active. For the moment, we do not make any distinction between passive and active forms.

6 Related Work

A number of works deal with detection of miscollocations and collocation error correction in learners' writings. However, only a few allow for the validation of isolated word co-occurrences with respect to their collocation status and provide ranked lists of correction suggestions. One of them is (Chang et al., 2008). They check a V–N co-occurrence provided by a learner against a collocation list obtained before from a reference corpus. Co-occurrences not found in this collocation list are variegated in that their verbal elements are substituted by all English translations of their L1 (Chinese, in this case) counterpart in an electronic dictionary. The variants are again matched against the collocation list. The finally matching co-occurrences that contain the noun of a non-matching co-occurrence are offered as correction suggestions. The Mutual Reciprocal Rank (MRR) of the correction list is reported to reach 0.66.

Dahlmeier and Ng (2011), who deal with the detection of miscollocations in writings also exploits L1 interference in learners. They work with confusion sets of semantically similar words. Given an input text in L2, they generate L1 paraphrases, which are then looked up in a large parallel corpus to obtain the most likely L2 co-occurrences. For this strategy, they report a precision of 38%.

Futagi et al. (2008) target the detection of miscollocations in learner texts, leaving the correction aside. Unlike the above proposals, they are not restricted to V+N co-occurrences. But similar to (Chang et al., 2008), they extract the co-occurrences from a learner text, variegate them and then look up the original co-occurrence and its variants in a reference list to decide on its status. To obtain the variants, they apply spell checking, vary articles and inflections and use WordNet to retrieve synonyms of the collocate. Wu et al. (2010) use a classifier to provide a number of collocate corrections. The classifier takes the learner sentence as lexical context. The probability predicted by the classifier for each suggestion is used to rank the suggestions. According to the evaluation included in (Wu et al., 2010), an MRR of 0.518 for the first five correction suggestions has been achieved. Liu et al. (2009) retrieve miscollocation correction suggestions from a reference corpus using three metrics: (i) mutual information (Church and Hanks, 1989), (ii) semantic similarity of an incorrect collocate to other potential collocates based on their distance in WordNet, and (iii) the membership of the incorrect collocate with a potential correct collocate in the same "collocation cluster"'. A combination of (ii)+(iii) leads to the best precision achieved for the suggestion of a correction: 55.95%. A combination of (i)+(ii)+(iii) leads to the best precision of 85.71% when a list of five possible corrections is returned.

Ferraro et al. (2014) suggest a two stage strategy for correction of miscollocations in Spanish. The first stage is rather similar to the one proposed by Futagi et al. (2008): it retrieves the synonyms of the collocate in the miscollocation in question from a number of auxiliary resources (including thesauri, bilingual L1-L2 dictionaries, etc.) and combines them with the base of the miscollocation to candidate corrections. The candidate corrections that are valid collocations of Spanish are returned as correction suggestions. If none of them is, the second stage applies a metric to retrieve correction suggestions. Three metrics have been experimented with: affinity metric, lexical context metric and context feature metric. The context feature metric, which uses the contextual features of the miscollocation (tokens, PoS tags, punctuation, grammatical functions, etc.), performed best in that it achieved an MRR of the top five suggestions of 0.72.

However, none of the above mentioned works considers in detail the asymmetric nature of collocations as captured by $NPMI_C$ and none of them takes into account that the co-occurrence strength between tokens (as captured by the (normalized) PMIs) needs to be calculated differentiating between different dependency relations and different sub-categorization frames.

7 Conclusions

In this paper, we have shown that the asymmetric nature of collocations requires an "asymmetric" normalization of the commonly used PMI measure and that any co-occurrence measure should be applied to co-occurrences of the same syntactic profile, i.e., with the same syntactic dependency relation and the same sub-categorization frame. The consideration of these characteristics of collocations allows for a more accurate ranking of correction suggestions for miscollocations.

Acknowledgments

The work presented in this paper has been supported by the Spanish Ministry of Economy and Competitiveness under the contract number FFI2011-30219-C02-02 in the framework of the HARENES Project, carried out in collaboration with the DICE Group of the University of La Coruña.

References

Alonso Ramos, M., Wanner, L., Vincze, O., Casamayor, G., Vázquez, N., Mosqueira, E., and Prieto, S. (2010). Towards a motivated annotation schema of collocation errors in learner corpora. In *Proceedings of the 7th International Conference on Language Resources and Evaluation (LREC)*, pages 3209–3214, La Valetta, Malta.

Benson, M. (1989). The structure of the collocational dictionary. *International Journal of Lexicography*, 2(1):1–13.

Bouma, G. (2009). Normalized (pointwise) mutual information in collocation extraction. In Chiarcos, C., Eckart de Castilho, R., and Stede, M., editors, *Von der Form zur Bedeutung: Texte automatisch verarbeiten / From Form to Meaning: Processing Texts Automatically. Proceedings of the Biennial GSCL Conference*, pages 31–40. Gunter Narr Verlag, Tübingen.

Bouma, G. (2010). Collocation extraction beyond the independence assumption. In *Proceedings of the ACL 2010, Short paper track*, Uppsala.

Chang, Y., Chang, J., Chen, H., and Liou, H. (2008). An Automatic Collocation Writing Assistant for Taiwanese EFL learners. A case of Corpus Based NLP Technology. *Computer Assisted Language Learning*, 21(3):283–299.

Choueka, Y. (1988). Looking for needles in a haystack or locating interesting collocational expressions in large textual databases. In *In Proceedings of the RIAO*, pages 34–38.

Church, K. and Hanks, P. (1989). Word Association Norms, Mutual Information, and Lexicography. In *Proceedings of the 27th Annual Meeting of the ACL*, pages 76–83.

Cowie, A. (1994). Phraseology. In Asher, R. and Simpson, J., editors, *The Encyclopedia of Language and Linguistics, Vol. 6*, pages 3168–3171. Pergamon, Oxford.

Dahlmeier, D. and Ng, H. (2011). Correcting semantic collocation errors with L1-induced paraphrases. In *Proceedings of the 2011 Conference on Empirical Methods in Natural Language Processing*, pages 107–117, Edinburgh, Scotland.

Evert, S. (2007). Corpora and collocations. In Lüdeling, A. and Kytö, M., editors, *Corpus Linguistics. An International Handbook*. Mouton de Gruyter, Berlin.

Ferraro, G., Nazar, R., Ramos, M. A., and Wanner, L. (2014). Towards advanced collocation error correction in Spanish learner corpora. *Language Resources and Evaluation*, 48(1):45–64.

Firth, J. (1957). Modes of meaning. In Firth, J., editor, *Papers in Linguistics, 1934-1951*, pages 190–215. Oxford University Press, Oxford.

Futagi, Y., Deane, P., Chodorow, M., and Tetreault, J. (2008). A computational approach to detecting collocation errors in the writing of non-native speakers of English. *Computer Assisted Language Learning*, 21(1):353–367.

Granger, S. (1998). Prefabricated patterns in advanced EFL writing: Collocations and Formulae. In Cowie, A., editor, *Phraseology: Theory, Analysis and Applications*, pages 145–160. Oxford University Press, Oxford.

Halliday, M. (1961). Categories of the theory of grammar. *Word*, 17:241–292.

Hausmann, F.-J. (1984). Wortschatzlernen ist kollokationslernen. zum lehren und lernen französischer wortwendungen. *Praxis des neusprachlichen Unterrichts*, 31(1):395–406.

Lesniewska, J. (2006). Collocations and second language use. *Studia Lingüística Universitatis lagellonicae Cracoviensis*, 123:95–105.

Lewis, M. (2000). *Teaching Collocation. Further Developments in the Lexical Approach*. LTP, London.

Liu, A. L.-E., Wible, D., and Tsao, N.-L. (2009). Automated suggestions for miscollocations. In *Proceedings of the NAACL HLT Workshop on Innovative Use of NLP for Building Educational Applications*, pages 47–50, Boulder, CO.

Lozano, C. (2009). CEDEL2: Corpus escrito del español L2. In Bretones Callejas, C., editor, *Applied Linguistics Now: Understanding Language and Mind*, pages 197–212. Universidad de Almería, Almería.

Mel'čuk, I. (1995). Phrasemes in Language and Phraseology in Linguistics. In Everaert, M., van der Linden, E.-J., Schenk, A., and Schreuder, R., editors, *Idioms: Structural and Psychological Perspectives*, pages 167–232. Lawrence Erlbaum Associates, Hillsdale.

Nesselhauf, N. (2004). How learner corpus analysis can contribute to language teaching: A study of support verb constructions. In Aston, G., Bernardini, S., and Stewart, D., editors, *Corpora and language learners*, pages 109–124. Benjamins Academic Publishers, Amsterdam.

Nesselhauf, N. (2005). *Collocations in a Learner Corpus*. Benjamins Academic Publishers, Amsterdam.

Orol, A. and Alonso Ramos, M. (2013). A Comparative Study of Collocations in a Native Corpus and a Learner Corpus of Spanish. *Procedia–Social and Behavioural Sciences*, 96:563–570.

Pecina, P. (2008). A machine learning approach to multiword expression extraction. In *Proceedings of the LREC 2008 Workshop Towards a Shared Task for Multiword Expressions (MWE 2008)*, pages 54–57, Marrakech.

Wanner, L., Verlinde, S., and Alonso Ramos, M. (2013). Writing assistants and automatic lexical error correction: word combinatorics. In Kosem, I., Kallas, J., Gantar, P., Krek, S., Langemets, M., and Tuulik, M., editors, *Electronic lexicography in the 21st century: Thinking outside the paper. Proceedings of the eLex 2013 conference*, pages 472–487, Tallinn & Ljubljana. Trojina, Institute for Applied Slovene Studies & Eesti Keele Instituut.

Wu, J.-C., Chang, Y.-C., Mitamura, T., and Chang, J. (2010). Automatic collocation suggestion in academic writing. In *Proceedings of the ACL Conference, Short paper track*, Uppsala.

An analysis of a French as a Foreign language corpus for readability assessment

Thomas François
IL&C, Cental, Université catholique de Louvain
thomas.francois@uclouvain.be

ABSTRACT
Readability aims to assess the difficulty of texts based on various linguistic predictors (the lexicon used, the complexity of sentences, the coherence of the text, etc.). It is an active field that has applications in a large number of NLP domains, among which machine translation, text simplification, text summarisation, or CALL (Computer-Assisted Language Learning). For CALL, readability tools could be used to help the retrieval of educational materials or to make CALL platforms more adaptive. However, developing a readability formula is a costly process that requires a large amount of texts annotated in terms of difficulty. The current mainstream method to gather such a large corpus of annotated texts is to get them from educational resources such as textbooks or simplified readers.

In this paper, we describe the collection process of an annotated corpus of French as a foreign language texts with the purpose of training a readability model. We follow the mainstream approach, getting the texts from textbooks, but we are concerned with the limitations of such "annotation" approach, in particular, as regards the homogeneity of the difficulty annotations across textbook series. Their reliability is assessed using both a qualitative and a quantitative analysis. It appears that, for some educational levels, the hypothesis of the annotation homogeneity must be rejected. Various reasons for such findings are discussed and the paper concludes with recommandations for future similar attempts.

KEYWORDS: readability, FFL, corpus collect, reliability of difficulty annotations.

Thomas François 2014. An analysis of a French as a Foreign Language corpus for readability assessment. *Proceedings of the third workshop on NLP for computer-assisted language learning.* NEALT Proceedings Series 22 / Linköping Electronic Conference Proceedings 107: 13–32.

1 Introduction

Today, the market for foreign language learning is actively growing as a result of various factors, such as the E.U. enlargement and the increase in the number of languages represented in the Union, but also a greater mobility of its citizens. Faced with this increased interest in foreign language learning, teaching institutions are struggling to keep up with demand. In this context, the domains of CALL (Computer-Assisted Language Learning) and iCALL (Intelligent CALL) have a role to play (Nerbonne, 2003, 673). Various CALL and iCALL applications have been designed to enhance classroom practices or replace it, but they still lack some flexibility as regards the input and the feedback offered to the user (Klenner and Visser, 2003).

For instance, some adaptive programs are able to select, in an exercise database, an item tailored to the learner's level (Desmet, 2006). However, it requires the pre-annotation of all the items in terms of difficulty, which restricts the versatility of the user module. Being able to generate suitable exercises on the fly from a corpus appears as a better way to adapt to specific learner difficulties. The automatic generation of exercises has already been researched, mostly for English (Coniam, 1997; Brown et al., 2005; Smith et al., 2009; Chen et al., 2006; Heilman, 2011; Meurers et al., 2010), but also for French (Antoniadis et al., 2005; Selva, 2002). However, the majority of these systems either use excerpts whose difficulty has been manually annotated or excerpts extracted from a large corpus and thus lacking any difficulty annotations. In the first case, the system is able to adapt to the user's needs only within the limits of the available materials. In the second case, any type of exercise can be generated on the fly, but because there is no control of the difficulty of excerpts, the contextual complexity is likely to hinder the user's comprehension and his/her ability to perform the exercise.

Faced with this challenge, one solution is to use readability metrics in order to pre-select a subset of excerpts matching the user's proficiency level, as it is done in the *Lärka* platform (Pilán et al., 2013). Readability is a field that aims to assess the difficulty of texts in a reproducible way – which can therefore be automatized – based on various linguistic dimensions of the texts (e.g. lexicon, syntax, text structure, etc.). The first studies in the field date back to the 1920's (Lively and Pressey, 1923) and have traditionally been carried out by psychologists. However, readability has undergone recent developments. They result from the contact with two other fields: natural language processing (NLP) is used to extract more complex linguistic predictors, whereas artificial intelligence (AI) provides complex statistical algorithms to better exploit the regularities existing between text difficulty and the linguistic predictors. Recent work has been carried out mostly on English as a first language (L1) (Collins-Thompson and Callan, 2005; Feng et al., 2010; Vajjala and Meurers, 2012) or English as a second or foreign language (L2) (Heilman et al., 2007; Schwarm and Ostendorf, 2005), but also on other languages such as Swedish (Pilán et al., 2014), French (François and Fairon, 2012; Todirascu et al., 2013; Dascalu, 2014; François et al., 2014), or Arabic (Al-Khalifa and Al-Ajlan, 2010), among others.

Although the field is quite lively, there is only limited work specifically dedicated to the readability of L2 languages. Furthermore, attempts to integrate such L2 readability models within an automatic exercise generation system are even more scarce. In our view, this can be explained by the high cost needed to create a readability model, especially in terms of the corpus collection process. Moreover, a convenient readability model should be able to output predictions that are useful for users. In Europe, this means to be able to assess text complexity in terms of the Common European Framework of Reference for Languages (CEFR) (Council of Europe, 2001). This scale has now become the reference for foreign language education within

Europe. To our knowledge, only two research teams have currently designed a readability model compliant with the CEFR scale (François and Fairon, 2012; Pilán et al., 2014). We suspect that this is partly due to the efforts needed to collect the training corpus required to develop such readability formula.

In this paper, we detail the collection process of a readability-intended corpus that has been carried out for French as a foreign language (FFL), using FFL textbooks as a source for the labelled texts. We describe the various issues encountered during this collection, focusing mostly on the issue of the reliability of the difficulty annotations. In section 2, we first expose the various type of criteria that have been used in readability studies to get data annotated in terms of difficulty and we discuss the advantages and shortcomings of each of them. The section 3 then details our collection process and describes the resulting corpus. Finally, Section 4 investigates the quality of the collected data, using both a qualitative analysis and a quantitative analysis based on statistical tests to assess the homogeneity of the annotations across textbooks.

2 Criteria for readability annotation

This section discusses various techniques that have been used to measure the difficulty of texts for reading. This issue is influenced by the fashion we define the term "difficulty", which is an elusive concept corresponding to a multifaceted reality. A large corpus of studies in psycholinguistics have addressed this question (for a survey, see (Ferrand, 2007)), but there is currently no integrated model that precisely explains what causes reading difficulty. However, the pragmatic vision underlying readability studies cannot be satisfied with a fuzzy definition. It is therefore common in the field to use a single variable, easily measured and based on theoretical arguments from psycholinguistics, as an estimation of the reading difficulty of texts. This variable is called "criterion" and various ones have been used for readability purposes. We briefly discuss each of them and explain why collecting texts from textbooks is currently considered as one of the best criteria.

The first criterion used in readability was **expert judgements**. It dates back as early as the seminal work by (Lively and Pressey, 1923) and consists in gathering a small set of experts – supposed to share a good vision of the reading difficulties encountered by the population of interest – and ask them to judge the difficulty of a set of texts. Using a scale such as educational grades to label the texts, the experts need to project themselves into the mind of potential readers whose characteristics they know from their professional activity. However, the quality of this projection is variable. Gilbert de Landsheere (1978) had six texts annotated by twenty experts and noticed a high variation between their judgements. More recently, van Oosten et al. (2011) addressed this question with modern statistical techniques: 105 excerpts were assessed by pair (e.g. text A is more difficult than text B) by a group of experts. The experts were then grouped according to the similarity of their annotations via a clustering algorithm. Each expert group corresponded to a set of texts, which was divided into a training and a test corpus. Then, for each training corpus available, binary classification models were trained and their performance was assessed both on the test corpus from the same cluster (intra-cluster validation) and on test corpora from other clusters (inter-cluster validation). Interestingly, the performance of all models significantly deteriorates in the inter-cluster condition, leading the authors to question the possibility of reaching a satisfactory agreement between experts.

Carver (1974) and Singer (1975) adopted the reverse view, considering that the human annotation of text difficulty can be reliable under some conditions. Their method, called *levelling*, involves defining a small subset of passages, each of them being typical of a level.

Then, three experts compare the same text with this yardstick and the final label of the text corresponds to the average of the three judgements. Carver (1974) carried out two experiments using this technique and showed that it is slightly more valid than classic formulas such as (Dale and Chall, 1948) or (Flesch, 1948). Later, (Björnsson, 1983, 482) reached a similar conclusion:

> *Traditionally it has been thought that judges' ratings of absolute difficulty are unreliable. From our experience they are not, i.e., when they are made by a fairly large group of persons, when the passages are relatively long, and when the range in difficulty in the text battery is wide.*

Beyond this crucial and still opened question of the validity of experts' judgements, this criterion presents another shortcoming, namely the availability and cost of experts that limits the amount of data that one can collect.

The second criterion to be used in readability is **comprehension tests**. Faced with the questionable validity of experts' judgements, Dale and Tyler (1934) and Ojemann (1934) investigated another approach: testing the reading comprehension of subjects directly with tests. The difficulty level of a text therefore corresponds to the mean score obtained by all the subjects that took the test. This approach has the benefit of directly measuring the comprehension, taking into account the interaction existing between the text and the reader. This criterion appeared for some time as the best criterion for readability, even though it was more costly than expert judgements. However, a major shortcoming was soon stressed: the interaction existing between the difficulty of the text and the difficulty of the questions. Davis (1950, cited by de Landsheere (1978, 33)) confirmed this issue with the following experiment: he designed two versions of a test on the same text, manipulating only the frequency of the words used in the questions, and noticed a significant difference in the scores of the subjects between both conditions. Further issues with comprehension tests also arose: the order of the questions matters and comprehension tests are not able to focus on all parts of the texts. In spite of these problems, comprehension tests were largely used as a readability criterion between 1930 and 1960.

They were gradually abandoned to the advantage of a third criterion: the **cloze test**. Introduced by Taylor (1953), this test simply consists in deleting a word out of five in a text before asking subjects to fill those gaps. The amount of filled blanks is supposed to be correlated with the subject understanding of the text. Since there is no need to formulate questions, the main flaw of comprehension tests (the interaction between the questions and the text) is removed. Moreover, with such a simple design process, it is possible for two researchers to produce exactly the same test for a text. As a result of these advantages, the cloze test was quickly adopted by researchers in readability (Miller and Coleman, 1967; Aquino et al., 1969; Bormuth, 1969; Caylor et al., 1973; Kincaid et al., 1975). Bormuth (1969) also highlighted another advantage of this criterion: its ability to measure the difficulty of smaller units than a text, such as a sentence or even a word.

The main issue with cloze test is to determine what exactly is measured. Bormuth (1969, 365) believes that cloze tests "measure skills closely related or identical to those measured by conventional multiple-choice reading comprehension tests". Taylor (1957) compared the outputs of cloze tests and multiple-choice question (MCQ) tests and he obtained correlations between 0.51 and 0.92. Similarly, Jenkinson (1957, cited by Jongsma (1969)) compared cloze test scores with results at standardized reading tests and she got a 0.78 correlation with the section of this standard test that measures lexical knowledge and she got a correlation of 0.73 with the section measuring comprehension. However, Weaver and Kingston (1963) stand up for the opposite view, arguing that it is textual redundancy which is rather measured. They obtained weak correlations between the *Davis Reading Test* and cloze test.

Another critic addressed to the cloze test is that it is hardly necessary to use clues located beyond the local context of the current sentence to correctly fill one gap. Miller and Coleman (1967) investigated this issue with a protocol in which subjects had to guess 150 consecutive words from excerpts. It appears that the answers produced were not much constrained by the previous sentences. Shanahan et al. (1982) confirmed that sentential information is paramount to correctly perform a cloze task. This obviously appears as a major weakness of this criterion, especially for more advanced readers for whom reading problems are more global than local.

Other criteria also have been investigated, but only by a limited number of researchers. **Recall**, or more precisely the number of words memorized, was used by Richaudeau (1974). However, this criterion was criticized by Kintsch et al. (1975), since it does not match any psychological reality. Another criterion explored is **reading time**. Brown (1952) compared the time spent on two texts by subjects, the former being considered as difficult and the latter as very difficult. On the former, the average reading speed was 306 words/min. while it only reached 235 words/min. for the latter. This association between reading comprehension and reading speed has been later experimentally corroborated by Oller (1972) and supported by the theoretical model by (Just and Carpenter, 1980). Despite these favourable studies, reading speed has been very little used in readability. One of the problems is the necessity to ensure that the subjects read naturally, while the experimental cost is also an issue.

In view of all these considerations, there is no criterion that stands out as the most valid and practical. This fact led current approaches of readability to use a criterion convenient enough to collect the large amount of texts required by the NLP and IA techniques. This criterion consists in collecting texts from textbooks or simplified readers, provided that these books are labelled accordingly to an educational scale. Such approach relies on the assumption that the calibration of those texts have been carried out by experts, which amounts to use experts' judgements. This way of colecting labelled data has been widely used in readability. Most of the famous classic formulas (Lorge, 1944; Dale and Chall, 1948; Flesch, 1948; Gunning, 1952) have been trained on the McCall and Crabbs lessons. Spache (1953) trained, on a corpus of primary textbooks, a formula intended for primary schoolchildren that has been acknowledged as one of the most reliable for this specific population. However, it is with the advent of what François and Fairon (2012) call the "IA readability" that this criterion has somehow becomed the standard approach. This is also due to the fact that Si and Callan (2001) suggested to view text readability assessment as a classification task. It implies to assign training texts to a few number of classes, which may quite logically corresponds to educational levels.

Most of the recent readability formulas have adopted this approach (Schwarm and Ostendorf, 2005; Feng et al., 2009; François, 2009; Tanaka-Ishii et al., 2010; Vajjala and Meurers, 2012; Pilán et al., 2014), but, to our knowledge, none of them have systematically addressed the issue of their corpus homogeneity. Although textbooks are indeed written by experts and may even benefit from updates based on teachers' feedback, the criteria used to select texts are likely to differ from one author to another as well as from one textbook series to another. This is why we decided to investigate this problematic using a corpus of FFL textbooks, which is described in the next section.

3 A textbook corpus for French as a foreign language

3.1 The collect

With the intent of later training a readability formula, we have collected a corpus of texts from FFL textbooks. This choice was motivated by the following three requirements: (1) as said above, the size of our corpus must be large enough to allow the training of modern machine learning algorithms; (2) the difficulty labels used for annotation must be convenient for the end users of the readability model, and (3) the content and the genre of the texts should be as diverse as possible to ensure a better generability of the model. Therefore, extracting texts from FFL textbooks compliant with the the Common European Framework of Reference for Language (CEFR) appeared to be a good solution to these three constraints.

Released in 2001 by the Council of Europe, the CEFR "provides a common basis for the elaboration of language syllabuses, curriculum guidelines, examinations, textbooks, etc. across Europe" (Council of Europe, 2001, 1). The document has achieved a wide success in Europe, being translated into at least 20 European languages (Little, 2006) and being implemented in most of the institutions providing L2 education. One of the flagship features of the CEFR is its competency scale that has been described according to two dimensions: vertical and horizontal. The vertical dimension is the best known and describes six levels: A1 (Breakthrough); A2 (Waystage); B1 (Threshold); B2 (Vantage); C1 (Effective Operational Proficiency) and C2 (Mastery). This scale has been calibrated with a mixed methodology that combines experts knowledge with data from qualitative and quantitative studies on learners (Council of Europe, 2001, 150). As a result, the CEFR scale appears quite reliable and the large majority of textbooks posterior to 2001 bear a CEFR level. Unfortunately, the Council of Europe has not developed a system validating the adequacy between the self-declared level of textbooks and their actual content (Alderson, 2007). This lack of control is prone to generate some heterogeneity between textbooks series.

To investigate this potential issue, we collected 2,042 texts from 28 textbooks. Not all textbooks available on the market were selected, because they had to meet the three following criteria: (1) to be published after 2001 in order to bear a CEFR level, (2) to be intended for adults or teenagers learning FFL for general purposes and (3) not to be tailored for a public with a specific L1 background. These two last considerations were implied by the type of population that we wanted to model for our readability model: young adults and adults with varied L1 backgrounds. Furthermore, all extracted texts had to be related to a reading comprehension task. Each of the 2,042 collected texts was scanned and automatically transformed into a machine-readable format (XML) using an optical character recognition tool. We then manually revised and corrected the scanned texts, removed peripheral information such as instructions, images, tables, etc. and assigned to each text the level of the textbook it came from.

We met an unexpected difficulty during this last operation. Some textbooks cover more than one CEFR level and have a mixed tag (e.g. A1/A2). In this case, we had to analyse each textbook introductory comments, organisation and structure to gather enough information to distribute each text in one of the two levels [1]. The corpus collected at the end of the process is summarised at Table 1, which lists the series used and the amount of texts collected per level.

[1]The detailed description of this breakdown process by level is available in (François, 2011, 334-338)

	A1	A2	B1	B2	C1	C2
Activités CECR	/	/	80	50	63	8
Alter Ego	90	92	116	/	/	/
Comp. écrite	/	87	89	/	/	/
Connexions	60	/	/	/	/	/
Connexions : prep. DELF	11	12	/	/	/	/
Delf/Dalf	/	/	/	31	78	19
Festival	76	/	54	/	/	/
Ici	41	42	/	/	/	/
Panorama	58	98	113	41	/	/
Rond-point	22	13	40	76	/	/
Réussir Dalf	17	/	/	/	43	22
Taxi !	27	44	107	/	/	/
Tout va bien !	50	92	82	/	/	/
Total	452	478	681	198	184	49

Table 1: Number of texts per level, by textbooks series

3.2 Corpus characteristics

In this section, we further discuss some characteristics of our corpus, namely (1) the metadata used; (2) the distribution of text genres in the corpus, and (3) the distribution of texts per level.

As for the metadata, the tags were kept very simple since most of the contextual features of texts (such as instructions, images, figures, etc.) had been removed. We defined the six following tags:

Level: take one value among the six levels the CEFR scale (A1, A2, B1, B2, C1, and C2);

Lesson: the textbook lesson in which the text is studied. It was normalized as follows:

$$\text{Lesson localization index} = \frac{\text{number of the lesson}}{\text{total number of lessons in the textbook}}$$

This lesson localization index appeared propitious in case we would like to transform the CEFR ordinal scale into a continuous scale.

Source: the textbook name from which the text was extracted;

Page: the page(s) of the textbook from which the text comes;

Date: the publication date of the textbook;

Type of text: the genre of the text (see below for details),

Title: the title of the text.

Among those tags, the only one that required some manual classification was the genre of the texts. The following genres were distinguished: text (either narrative or informative), collection of disconnected sentences (mostly in A1 and A2 textbooks), dialogue (including interviews), mail, e-mail, advertisement (e.g. reproduction of leaflet), poem and recipe. As these types of texts can be quite easily identified thanks to stereotypical clues, the classification was performed by two humans annotators on the basis of simple guidelines. The distribution of texts and words across genres and levels is displayed in Table 2. For exposition purposes, we merged the rare genres (ads, songs, poems, and recipes) within the *Varias* category. It should also be mentioned that although the corpus does not seem very balanced across text genres and levels at first glance, we believe that these figures are pretty representative of the distribution of texts within the population of FFL textbooks.

Genre	A1	A2	B1	B2	C1	C2	Total
Dialogue	153 (23,276)	72 (17,990)	39 (11,140)	5 (1,698)	/	/	269 (54,104)
E-mail, mail	41 (4,547)	24 (2,868)	44 (11,193)	18 (4,193)	8 (2,144)	1 (398)	136 (25,343)
Sentences	56 (7,072)	21 (4,130)	12 (1,913)	5 (928)	/	/	94 (14,043)
Varias	31 (3,990)	36 (4,439)	23 (5,124)	14 (1,868)	1 (272)	/	105 (15,693)
Text	171 (23,707)	325 (65,690)	563 (147,603)	156 (63,014)	175 (89,911)	48 (34,084)	1,438 (424,009)
Total	452 (62,592)	478 (95,117)	681 (176,973)	198 (71,701)	184 (92,327)	49 (34,482)	2,042 (533,192)

Table 2: Number of texts and words per level and genre.

The distribution of texts per level at Table 2 is clearly unbalanced: A1 includes almost ten times more texts than C2. This situation is due to the fact that at the later stages of learning, L2 learners are able to read almost any authentic texts and the need for carefully calibrated texts thus decreases. As a consequence, there are not many textbooks available for higher levels, especially for C2. The problem of having unbalanced classes is that "classification is sensitive to the relative sizes of the (...) component groups and will always favour classification into the larger group" (Hosmer and Lemeshow, 1989, 147). In the next section, we will also further discuss this issue of unbalanced classes along with the main issue of this paper: the heterogeneity of the level annotations.

4 Analyses of the corpus

The previous section has related the collection process of our corpus and detailed some of its characteristics. It has also stressed two main issues regarding the corpus: (1) the possible heterogeneity of the difficulty annotations due to a lack of control in the adequacy between textbook contents with the CEFR scale and (2) the shortage of high level texts, which results into an unbalanced dataset likely to cause bias in any readability model trained on the corpus. In this section, we report analyses investigating both issues, starting with the latter.

4.1 The class imbalanced experiment

In order to determine whether having an unbalanced dataset would impact subsequent learning on that corpus, we applied the following methodology. We sampled two different datasets from the whole corpus. For the first (*Corpus6Apriori*), we simply applied a stratified sampling that respects the a priori probability of each class. This amounts to 66 texts for A1, 72 for A2, 99 for B1, 29 for B2, 27 for C1 and 7 for C2. For the second dataset (*Corpus6Equi*), we also applied a stratified sampling, but selected a fixed amount of texts in each class– about 50, which corresponds to the size of the least populated class (C2). Finally, we sampled 120 texts (20 per level) in the remaining texts[2] to be used as the test set.

Concerning the readability model, since the aim was not to reach the highest performance possible, we selected two simple and broadly-used linguistic features as predictors: the mean number of letter per words (NLM) and the mean number of words per sentence (NWS). They were combined with a proportional-odds model, also known as ordinal logistic regression (Agresti, 2002, 274-282). Their performance were assessed with the multiple correlation

[2]For the *Corpus6Equi*, there were no remaining texts for C2, so we had to use the same texts for the training and the test set. However, this does not seem to produce much overfitting, as shown in the subsequent analysis.

coefficient (R^2), estimated on the training set, the test set and using a bootstrap .632 procedure [3]. The results are detailed in Table 3.

	Training corpus	Bootstrap .632	Test corpus
Corpus6Equi	0,40	0,39	0,41
Corpus6Apriori	0,43	0,42	0,43

Table 3: R^2 estimated, for both datasets, on the training set, on the test set or with the bootstrap .632 procedure.

Surprisingly, the *Corpus6Apriori* model performs better in all of the three conditions (training, test and bootstrap). However, this apparent superiority must be qualified when we look more closely at the confusion matrix. Tables 4 and 5 show the confusion matrix for both models on the test set. It clearly appears that the high number of B1 texts in the *Corpus6Apriori* condition distorts the regression space (about 50% of the texts are predicted as B1). The model trained on *Corpus6Equi* presents a more balanced distribution that slightly favours the extreme classes (A1 and C2) [4]. Moreover, the *Corpus6Apriori* model is not able to classify any text as B2, which is a very critical flaw for a tool aiming to be used in real contexts by L2 learners or teachers. We conclude from this first experiment that a readability corpus should have, as much as possible, a balanced number of observations per class.

	Predictions					
Actual levels	1	2	3	4	5	6
1	15	4	1	0	0	0
2	5	7	1	4	1	2
3	3	4	3	3	3	4
4	0	4	5	1	4	6
5	3	0	3	3	3	8
6	0	1	2	0	4	13
Total	26	20	15	11	15	33

Table 4: Confusion matrix for the model trained on *Corpus6Equi*.

	Predictions					
Actual levels	1	2	3	4	5	6
1	14	5	1	0	0	0
2	6	8	5	0	0	1
3	1	5	13	0	1	0
4	1	1	16	0	1	1
5	0	3	13	0	4	0
6	0	0	11	0	9	0
Total	22	24	59	0	15	2

Table 5: Confusion matrix for the model trained on *Corpus6Apriori*.

[3]This procedure, described among others by Tufféry (2007, 369-370), estimates the model's performance as the average of 100 repeated experiments. In these, each training set is slightly different since it is obtained through a sampling with replacement of the texts.

[4]Similar effect was stressed by François and Fairon (2012) although they used a support vector model (SVM) instead of a logistic model.

4.2 Testing the homogeneity of the corpus

4.2.1 Methodology and hypotheses

For the reasons exposed in Section 3.1, the difficulty annotations in our corpus are likely to be more heterogeneous than expected. To investigate this issue, we applied the following methodology. First, we selected two readability indices whose relation with text difficulty has been confirmed by many studies in the literature: the mean number of letter per words (*NLM*) and the mean number of words per sentence (*NWS*). They are representative of the lexical and syntactic dimensions of the texts in our corpus, but we also wanted to have a semantic index, so we opted for the density of ideas in a text (*ConcDens*). The efficiency of this last feature is not as well-acknowledged as that of the two previous ones, but *ConcDens* has the advantage of taking into account textual dimensions that have been deemed critical for comprehension since the 1970's. However, parameterizing the density of ideas in a text is not as straightforward as counting the number of letters or the number of words. It underlies a more complex theoretical model, which also involves more complex NLP routines.

Our measure of the density of ideas is based on Kintsch et al. (1975)'s propositional model [5]. These authors showed that the number of propositions and the number of different arguments in a sentence influence its reading time and therefore, most likely, its comprehension. To implement Kintsch's model, we used the recently published French tool *Densidées* (Lee et al., 2010). This program draws from previous attempts for English: Snowdon et al. (1996) showed that it is possible to estimate the propositional density of a text from the number of verbs, adjectives, adverbs, prepositions, and conjunctions divided by the number of words, while Brown et al. (2008) implemented this approach using 37 rules. *Densidées* is based on a similar approach. It is able to estimate the mean number of propositions per word in a text using 35 rules making use of lexical and part-of-speech clues.

In a second step, we computed, for each of the three above variables, their means on all texts belonging to a given textbook and classified within one given level [6]. Then, these means were compared using a twofold approach: (1) a qualitative analysis of the tables 6, 7, and 8 first helped to detect irregularities, (2) then quantitative analyses were performed to determine whether these irregularities were large enough to conclude to the corpus heterogeneity. More precisely, we aimed to test the three following hypothesis:

1. the means of each variable per level (computed on all the texts of this level), which is shown at the last row of each table, should increase with the level of difficulty.
2. if the annotations within a given level are homogeneous, the means of each textbook from this level will not be significantly different from all other means from that level.
3. within the same textbook series, the mean of a given level will be greater than the means of all textbooks at a lower level.

The hypothesis (1) and (3) were investigated manually, while for the (2), the analyses were based on the analysis of variance (ANOVA), which takes in account each of the three predictors independently, and its multivariate variant (MANOVA), in which the effect of all three variables can be taken into account in a combined way.

[5]This model postulates that any text can be represented as a list of propositions, a proposition being defined as a predicate (for instance a verb or a noun) and a few number of arguments linked to this predicate.

[6]This precision is necessary since we saw that a textbook may include materials from two different levels.

4.2.2 Qualitative analysis

As regards the qualitative analysis of the three tables 6, 7, and 8, it first appears that the means by level indeed increase, as expected from the hypothesis (1). There are however a few exceptions: the lexical complexity of B2 textbooks is surprisingly lower than that of B1 textbooks, whereas *ConcDens* is not very efficient to distinguish between A2, B1 and B2 texts, as well as between C1 and C2. This could be due either to the fact that the content of textbooks series does not increase in terms of conceptual difficulty or to the fact that *ConcDens* is a less reliable predictor of difficulty than *NLM* and *NWS*. A manual skimming of sampled texts of various levels tends to let us discard the first explanation. To test the second one, we sampled 50 texts per level with a stratified sampling by textbooks and then computed Pearson correlations between each of our three features and these text annotations. It was obvious that **meanNWS** ($r = 0,62$) and **NLM** ($r = 0,52$) are better predictors than **ConcDens** ($r = 0,37$). This last feature is interesting for it takes higher textual dimension into account. However, it does not seem reliable enough to undertake a critical analysis of our corpus annotations. This is why we will not discuss it any further in the rest of the paper.

	A1	A2	B1	B2	C1	C2
Activités	/	/	4,56	4,70	**4,61**	4,81
Alter Ego	4,37	4,42 (1) 4,48 (2)	4,60 (2) 4,61 (3)	/	/	/
Comp. écrite	/	**4,67**	4,67	/	/	/
Connexions	4,21	/	/	/	/	/
Conn. : prep. DELF	4,30	4,51	/	/	/	/
Delf/Dalf	/	/	/	4,64	4,80	4,88
Festival	4,41	/	4,63	/	/	/
Ici	4,40	4,68	/	/	/	/
Panorama	4,37	4,63 (1) **4,57 (2)**	4,69 (2) 4,68 (3)	**4,53**	/	/
Rond-point	**4,62**	4,61	**4,50**	**4,50**	/	/
Réussir Dalf	/	/	/	/	5	**4,97**
Taxi !	**3,92**	4,41	4,70	/	/	/
Tout va bien !	4,27	**4,25** (1) 4,41 (2)	**4,78 (2)** **4,69** (3)	/	/	/
Total	4,32	4,52	4,64	**4,58**	4,78	4,91

Table 6: Mean number of letters per word for each textbook and per CEFR level. Textbooks with a possible problem of consistency are highlighted in bold. Numbers in parentheses refer to the textbook volume within the series. Some levels indeed have texts extracted from two different textbooks in the same series.

As regards the second hypothesis, it appears valid for **meanNWS** and **NLM** in most cases, although a few textbooks, shown in bold in the tables, diverges from this hypothesis. Some textbooks, such as *Rond Point A1*, *Comp. écrite A2*, and *Tout va bien ! B1 (2)* stand out as particularly complex at the lexical level, while others – such as *Rond Point B1*, *Taxi ! A1*, *Activités C1*, etc. – are remarkable for their weak scores. At the syntactic level, we mainly found work with longer sentences than their level average, among which are *Comp. écrite A2*, *Festival B1* or *Tout va bien ! A2 (1)*. This last textbook is worth noting since it combines a higher-than-average syntactic difficulty with a more simple lexicon than expected. It reveals that, although some of the divergences we observed are probably due to disagreement between textbooks editors, others may be explained because the progression in the various linguistic competences does not

	A1	A2	B1	B2	C1	C2
Activités	/	/	18,2	19,6	**18,3**	21,9
Alter Ego	8,4	11,5 (1) 13,78 (2)	14,9 (2) 16 (3)	/	/	/
Comp. écrite	/	**17,1**	18,1	/	/	/
Connexions	10,1	/	/	/	/	/
Conn. : prep. DELF	12,9	**19,5**	/	/	/	/
Delf/Dalf	/	/	/	17	19,1	20,9
Festival	7,8	/	**19,9**	/	/	/
Ici	10,4	13,5	/	/	/	/
Panorama	8,6	10,6 (1) 12,4 (2)	**13,5** (2) 16,3 (3)	**16,5**	/	/
Rond-point	11,8	15,2	14,8	19,7	/	/
Réussir Dalf	/	/	/	/	21,4	21,7
Taxi !	7,6	15,2	16	/	/	/
Tout va bien !	9,9	**19,4** (1) **13,9** (2)	17,5 (2) 18,3 (3)	/	/	/
Total	9,1	14,54	16,85	18,6	19,36	21,43

Table 7: Mean number of words per sentence for each textbook and per CEFR level. Textbooks with a possible problem of consistency are highlighted in bold.

conform to the average.

Finally, the progression within series may also be also problematic. This is the case for two series: *Comp. écrite* and, especially, *Rond Point*. This observation can be explained by some characteristics of this last series: (1) it is intended for false beginners and therefore quickly progresses in the learning process; (2) the learning process is based on tasks and operates in spiral. The learner is thus quickly brought into contact with more complex forms, which are however not comprehensively studied. As a result, the texts encountered at the initial stages are more difficult than in other textbooks, but the lexical complexity later hardly increase, probably because this is the difficulty of the task to be performed by the learners that rather increases.

To conclude, the qualitative analysis raised strong clues showing that the homogeneity of our corpus is questionable. The nearly "flat" profiles of *Compréhension écrite* and *Rond Point* are particularly of concern. However, globally, most of the series respect the ascending profile requested by hypothesis (1) and presents a coherent progression within the same series i accordance with hypothesis (3). It should also be reminded that our predictors are not perfectly correlated with text difficulty and only approach it from a unique point of view although it is actually a very complex phenomenon. In the next section, we will further investigate hypothesis (2) with quantitative techniques in order to produce a more clear-cut diagnosis on our corpus homogeneity.

4.2.3 Quantitative analysis

The qualitative analysis has provided an accurate picture of the complexity of each textbook as described by lexical and syntactic predictors. As explained above, it is not easy to decide whether or not the corpus must be considered as heterogeneous on this basis alone. To investigate more systematically this issue and determine whether the divergences reported in previous section are significant, we applied ANOVA tests (Howell, 2008, 305-352). ANOVA is a statistical test used to compare two or more means of a quantitative variable across conditions (here, the textbooks within a level). It compares the variation between textbooks and within each

	A1	A2	B1	B2	C1	C2
Activités	/	/	0,464	0,465	0,473	**0,454**
Alter Ego	0,437	**0,476** (1) 0,458 (2)	**0,474** (2) 0,457 (3)	/	/	/
Comp. écrite	/	0,462	0,463	/	/	/
Connexions	0,423	/	/	/	/	/
Conn. : prep. DELF	**0,456**	**0,48**	/	/	/	/
Delf/Dalf	/	/	/	0,471	**0,48**	0,473
Festival	0,42	/	0,461	/	/	/
Ici	0,439	0,46	/	/	/	/
Panorama	0,417	0,447 (1) **0,432** (2)	**0,431** (2) 0,452 (3)	**0,446**	/	/
Rond-point	**0,457**	**0,443**	0,463	**0,452**	/	/
Réussir Dalf	/	/	/	/	0,472	0,479
Taxi !	0,426	0,458	0,466	/	/	/
Tout va bien !	**0,461**	0,45 (1) **0,467** (2)	**0,452** (2) **0,454** (3)	/	/	/
Total	0,43	0,457	0,459	**0,457**	0,475	**0.472**

Table 8: Mean number of ideas per text for each textbook and per CEFR level. Textbooks with a possible problem of consistency are highlighted in bold.

textbook. If this ratio reaches a sufficiently high value (depending on the significance level α, here 0.05), we must conclude that all texts from a level do not come from the same population, which means that they were not annotated by a coherent set of experts.

Before the ANOVA analysis, we checked whether the distributions of **meanNWS** and **NLM** by textbooks are normally distributed and whether their distributions by level have an homoscedastic variance. These are the two main conditions required to apply ANOVA to a dataset. We respectively used the Shapiro-Wilk (Shapiro and Wilk, 1965) test to check the normality and the Levene test (Brown and Forsythe, 1974) for variance homoscedasticity. Normality was rejected by 27 out of 82 tests [7], whereas only 4 levels out of the 12 presented an unequal variance. Since ANOVA can bear to see its conditions violated to a certain extent, we did not deem these results problematic enough to resort to using a non-parametric test such as Kruskal-Wallis.

Results of the ANOVA analysis are reported in Table 9. They clearly show that only a few levels appear to be homogeneously labelled: the texts in C2 for **NLM** and the texts from B2 to C2 for **meanNWS**. The divergences stressed in the qualitative analysis seem large enough to conclude to the heterogeneity of our corpus. However, it should be mentioned that the ANOVA test is an omnibus test, which means that it is enough that a single textbook deviates from the mean to reject the homogeneity hypothesis. As notified previously, textbook series characterized by specific pedagogical orientation are the most problematic and might be the main cause for rejecting the homogeneity hypothesis. We therefore performed the same ANOVA analysis without the two problematic series: *Compréhension écrite* and *Rond Point*. Results of these new tests are also reported in Table 9 as Corpus6Cleaned and show some global improvements: B1 becomes homogeneous and B2 is very close to homogeneity, when we consider **NLM**. For **meanNWS**, the quality of annotations slightly improves for A1, but decreases for B2. In the whole, the situation remains problematic.

[7] Interestingly, **NLM**-based distributions are more normal than those based on **meanNWS**, with only 5 tests rejecting normality.

	A1	A2	B1	B2	C1	C2
NLM						
Corpus6	$***$	$***$	0.02*	0.02*	$***$	0.39
Corpus6Cleaned	$***$	$***$	0.09	0.04*	$***$	0.39
meanNWS						
Corpus6	**	$***$	$***$	0.27	0.11	0.82
Corpus6Cleaned	**	**	$***$	0.01*	0.11	0.82

Table 9: P-value for each ANOVA tests. A value inferior to 0.05 means that the homogeneity hypothesis has been rejected for this level. Significance level are noted as follows: $p < 0.001$: $***$; $p < 0.01$: $**$ et $p < 0.05$: $*$.

The ANOVA tests the homogeneity through a unique predictor, whereas we noticed that some textbooks deviate from their level average for one predictor, but not for the other (e.g. *Tout va bien ! A2*). This limited point of view could have as a result to intensify the seemingly heterogeneity of the corpus. We therefore applied a multivariate version of the ANOVA, the MANOVA (Lewis-Beck, 1993, 340-368). The results are however very similar to those of the ANOVA: the only homogeneous level is C2 ($p = 0.69$); B2 is already considered as heterogeneous, although only slightly ($p = 0.02$); the other four levels are clearly heterogeneous, with p-values lower than 0.001. This is a rather expected finding, as the MANOVA is even stricter than the ANOVA, requiring all textbook means for **NLM** AND **meanNWS** to be similar.

5 Conclusion

This paper focused on a very often overlooked issue in the modern readability literature based on complex machine learning algorithm and trained on texts from educational resources: the coherence of the annotations. Indeed, when one collects a large corpus of texts previously annotated – which means that he/she cannot control the annotation process –, it is very likely that the various experts involved in the educational material creation apply incoherent criteria. This issue was confirmed by the results of van Oosten et al. (2011)'s experiment with real judges. Interestingly, when researchers in readability use real experts, they are more prone to question the reliability of their annotation, applying, for instance, standard inter-annotators agreement metrics. On the contrary, the quality of a corpus largely used in the field such as the Weekly Reader has been hardly questioned. Feng et al. (2010) computed the mean number of words per documents and per sentences and showed a clear progression as the levels increases. However, it is generally agreed in the community that the annotations are coherent, even though not much is known on the text calibrating criteria. Deeming that this question is crucial, we have investigated it, taking advantage of the fact that our corpus is based on textbooks. Each textbook is indeed designed by a well-identified team. It is therefore possible to consider each of them as a kind of "cluster" in the sense of van Oosten et al. (2011). We therefore suggested an alternate methodology to assess the quality of the annotations in a textbook-based readability corpus.

Further contributions of this paper are a discussion about the state-of-the-art of the available criteria for the annotation of text difficulty as well as the description of the collection process of texts from textbooks to the aim of training a readability model. Apart from the heterogeneity issue discussed above, we have stressed other issues that may prove interesting for future similar attempts: (1) the lack of control from the Council of Europe onto the textbook annotations, (2) the lack of texts for advanced levels (C1, and especially C2) that is unfortunate since most of the lower level texts collected could not be used. For future attempts, we suggest starting collecting C2 texts and, afterwards, gather an equivalent number of texts for the lower levels. Finally, we also identified that some types of pedagogical approaches – in our case, the task-oriented approach – are more prone to include heterogeneous materials than textbooks based on a more communicative approach.

Future work regarding the collection and annotation of texts for readability could explore various paths. First, it would be interesting to compare another corpus for FFL, but including only texts intended to a public with a specific L1. This would allow to assess to which extent the L1 impacts the readability of texts for this population. Another interesting experiment would be to compare the textbook annotations with other criteria either classic ones such as those presented at Section 2, or more recent ones, such as eye-tracking or annotations by the crowd (van Oosten and Hoste, 2011). Such comparison would help to be more informed about the validity of the current practice of collecting texts in textbooks or readers.

Acknowledgments

This work has been partially funded by the Belgian Fund for Scientific Research (FNRS). We would like to thank Cédrick Fairon, Jean-Léon Bouraoui and Laurent Hubert for their valuable comments on this work, as well as Bernadette Dehottay for her invaluable help in the collection process of the corpus.

References

Agresti, A. (2002). *Categorical Data Analysis. 2nd edition.* Wiley-Interscience, New York.

Al-Khalifa, S. and Al-Ajlan, A. (2010). Automatic readability measurements of the arabic text: An exploratory study. 35(2C).

Alderson, J. (2007). The cefr and the need for more research. *The Modern Language Journal*, 91(4):659–663.

Antoniadis, G., Echinard, S., Kraif, O., Lebarbé, T., and Ponton, C. (2005). Modélisation de l'intégration de ressources TAL pour l'apprentissage des langues : la plateforme MIRTO. *Apprentissage des langues et systèmes d'information et de communication (ALSIC)*, 8(1):65–79.

Aquino, M., Mosberg, L., and Sharron, M. (1969). Reading comprehension difficulty as a function of content area and linguistic complexity. *The Journal of Experimental Educational*, 37(4):1–4.

Björnsson, C. (1983). Readability of newspapers in 11 languages. *Reading Research Quarterly*, 18(4):480–497.

Bormuth, J. (1969). *Development of Readability Analysis.* Technical report, Projet n°7-0052, U.S. Office of Education, Bureau of Research, Department of Health, Education and Welfare, Washington, DC.

Brown, C., Snodgrass, T., Kemper, S., Herman, R., and Covington, M. (2008). Automatic measurement of propositional idea density from part-of-speech tagging. *Behavior research methods*, 40(2):540–545.

Brown, J. (1952). The Flesch Formula 'Through the Looking Glass'. *College English*, 13(7):393–394.

Brown, J., Frishkoff, G., and Eskenazi, M. (2005). Automatic question generation for vocabulary assessment. In *Proceedings of the conference on Human Language Technology and Empirical Methods in Natural Language Processing*, pages 819–826, Vancouver, Canada.

Brown, M. and Forsythe, A. (1974). Robust tests for the equality of variances. *Journal of the American Statistical Association*, 69(346):364–367.

Carver, R. (1974). *Improving Reading Comprehension: Measuring Readability.* Technical report, Final Report, Contract No. N00014-72-C0240. American Institues for Research in the Behavioral Sciences, Silver Spring, Maryland.

Caylor, J., Sticht, T., Fox, L., and Ford, J. (1973). Methodologies for Determining Reading Requirements of Military Occupational Specialties. Technical report, Projet n°73-5, Human Resources Research Organization, Alexandria, VA.

Chen, C.-Y., Liou, H.-C., and Chang, J. S. (2006). Fast: an automatic generation system for grammar tests. In *Proceedings of the COLING/ACL on Interactive presentation sessions*, pages 1–4.

Collins-Thompson, K. and Callan, J. (2005). Predicting reading difficulty with statistical language models. *Journal of the American Society for Information Science and Technology*, 56(13):1448–1462.

Coniam, D. (1997). A preliminary inquiry into using corpus word frequency data in the automatic generation of English language cloze tests. *Calico Journal*, 14:15–34.

Council of Europe (2001). *Common European Framework of Reference for Languages: Learning, Teaching, Assessment*. Press Syndicate of the University of Cambridge.

Dale, E. and Chall, J. (1948). A formula for predicting readability. *Educational research bulletin*, 27(1):11–28.

Dale, E. and Tyler, R. (1934). A study of the factors influencing the difficulty of reading materials for adults of limited reading ability. *The Library Quarterly*, 4:384–412.

Dascalu, M. (2014). Readerbench (2)-individual assessment through reading strategies and textual complexity. In *Analyzing Discourse and Text Complexity for Learning and Collaborating*, pages 161–188. Springer.

de Landsheere, G. (1978). *Le test de closure : mesure de la lisibilité et de la compréhension*. Nathan, Paris.

Desmet, P. (2006). L'enseignement/apprentissage des langues à l'ère du numérique: tendances récentes et défis. *Revue française de linguistique appliquée*, 11(1):119–138.

Feng, L., Elhadad, N., and Huenerfauth, M. (2009). Cognitively motivated features for readability assessment. In *Proceedings of the 12th Conference of the European Chapter of the Association for Computational Linguistics*, pages 229–237.

Feng, L., Jansche, M., Huenerfauth, M., and Elhadad, N. (2010). A Comparison of Features for Automatic Readability Assessment. In *COLING 2010: Poster Volume*, pages 276–284.

Ferrand, L. (2007). *Psychologie cognitive de la lecture*. De Boeck, Bruxelles.

Flesch, R. (1948). A new readability yardstick. *Journal of Applied Psychology*, 32(3):221–233.

François, T. (2009). Combining a statistical language model with logistic regression to predict the lexical and syntactic difficulty of texts for FFL. In *Proceedings of the 12th Conference of the EACL : Student Research Workshop*, pages 19–27.

François, T. (2011). *Les apports du traitement automatique du langage à la lisibilité du français langue étrangère*. PhD thesis, Université Catholique de Louvain. Thesis Supervisors : Cédrick Fairon and Anne Catherine Simon.

François, T., Brouwers, L., Naets, H., and Fairon, C. (2014). AMesure: une formule de lisibilité pour les textes administratifs. In *Actes de la 21e Conférence sur le Traitement automatique des Langues Naturelles (TALN 2014)*.

François, T. and Fairon, C. (2012). An "AI readability" formula for French as a foreign language. In *Proceedings of the 2012 Conference on Empirical Methods in Natural Language Processing (EMNLP 2012)*, pages 466–477.

Gunning, R. (1952). *The technique of clear writing*. McGraw-Hill, New York.

Heilman, M. (2011). *Automatic factual question generation from text*. PhD thesis, Carnegie Mellon University.

Heilman, M., Collins-Thompson, K., Callan, J., and Eskenazi, M. (2007). Combining lexical and grammatical features to improve readability measures for first and second language texts. In *Proceedings of NAACL HLT*, pages 460–467.

Hosmer, D. and Lemeshow, S. (1989). *Applied Logistic Regression*. Wiley, New York.

Howell, D. (2008). *Méthodes statistiques en sciences humaines, 6ème édition*. De Boeck, Bruxelles.

Jongsma, E. (1969). *The cloze procedure: a survey of the research*. Technical report, Indiana University, Bloomington. School of Education.

Just, M. and Carpenter, P. (1980). A theory of reading: From eye fixations to comprehension. *Psychological review*, 87(4):329–354.

Kincaid, J., Fishburne, R., Rodgers, R., and Chissom, B. (1975). *Derivation of new readability formulas for navy enlisted personnel*. Technical report, n°8-75, Research Branch Report.

Kintsch, W., Kozminsky, E., Streby, W., McKoon, G., and Keenan, J. (1975). Comprehension and recall of text as a function of content variables1. *Journal of Verbal Learning and Verbal Behavior*, 14(2):196–214.

Klenner, M. and Visser, H. (2003). What exactly is wrong and why? tutorial dialogue for intelligent call systems. *Linguistik online*, 17(5/03):57–80.

Lee, H., Gambette, P., Maillé, E., and Thuillier, C. (2010). Densidées: calcul automatique de la densité des idées dans un corpus oral. In *Actes de la douxième Rencontre des Étudiants Chercheurs en Informatique pour le Traitement Automatique des langues (RECITAL)*.

Lewis-Beck, M. (1993). *Experimental Design and Methods*, volume 3 of *International Handbooks of Quantitative Applications in the Social Sciences*. Sage Publications, Singapore.

Little, D. (2006). The common european framework of reference for languages: Content, purpose, origin, reception and impact. *Language Teaching*, 39(3):167–190.

Lively, B. and Pressey, S. (1923). A method for measuring the "vocabulary burden" of textbooks. *Educational Administration and Supervision*, 9:389–398.

Lorge, I. (1944). Predicting readability. *the Teachers College Record*, 45(6):404–419.

Meurers, D., Ziai, R., Amaral, L., Boyd, A., Dimitrov, A., Metcalf, V., and Ott, N. (2010). Enhancing authentic web pages for language learners. In *Proceedings of the NAACL HLT 2010 Fifth Workshop on Innovative Use of NLP for Building Educational Applications*, pages 10–18. Association for Computational Linguistics.

Miller, G. and Coleman, E. (1967). A set of thirty-six prose passages calibrated for complexity. *Journal of Verbal Learning and Verbal Behavior*, 6(6):851–854.

Nerbonne, J. (2003). Computer-assisted language learning and natural language processing. In Mitkov, R., editor, *Handbook of computational linguistics*. Oxford University Press.

Ojemann, R. (1934). The reading ability of parents and factors associated with the reading difficulty of parent education materials. *University of Iowa Studies in Child Welfare*, 8:11–32.

Oller, J. (1972). Assessing competence in ESL: reading. *TESOL Quarterly*, 6(4):313–323.

Pilán, I., Volodina, E., and Johansson, R. (2013). Automatic selection of suitable sentences for language learning exercises. In *20 Years of EUROCALL: Learning from the Past, Looking to the Future: 2013 EUROCALL Conference Proceedings*, pages 218–225.

Pilán, I., Volodina, E., and Johansson, R. (2014). Rule-based and machine learning approaches for second language sentence-level readability. In *Proceedings of the Ninth Workshop on Innovative Use of NLP for Building Educational Applications*, pages 174–184.

Richaudeau, F. (1974). 6 phrases, 200 sujets, 42 lapsus, 1 rêve. *Communication et langages*, 23(1):5–24.

Schwarm, S. and Ostendorf, M. (2005). Reading level assessment using support vector machines and statistical language models. *Proceedings of the 43rd Annual Meeting on Association for Computational Linguistics*, pages 523–530.

Selva, T. (2002). Génération automatique d'exercices contextuels de vocabulaire. In *Actes de TALN 2002*, pages 185–194.

Shanahan, T., Kamil, M., and Tobin, A. (1982). Cloze as a measure of intersentential comprehension. *Reading Research Quarterly*, 17(2):229–255.

Shapiro, S. and Wilk, M. (1965). An analysis of variance test for normality (complete samples). *Biometrika*, 52(3-4):591–611.

Si, L. and Callan, J. (2001). A statistical model for scientific readability. In *Proceedings of the Tenth International Conference on Information and Knowledge Management*, pages 574–576. ACM New York, NY, USA.

Singer, H. (1975). The seer technique: A non-computational procedure for quickly estimating readability level. *Journal of Literacy Research*, 7(3):255–267.

Smith, S., Kilgarriff, A., Sommers, S., Wen-liang, G., and Guang-Zhong, W. (2009). Automatic cloze generation for english proficiency testing. In *Proceedings of LTTC conference*.

Snowdon, D., Kemper, S., Mortimer, J., Greiner, L., Wekstein, D., and Markesbery, W. (1996). Linguistic ability in early life and cognitive function and Alzheimer's disease in late life. *Journal of the American Medical Association*, 275(7):528–532.

Spache, G. (1953). A new readability formula for primary-grade reading materials. *The Elementary School Journal*, 53(7):410–413.

Tanaka-Ishii, K., Tezuka, S., and Terada, H. (2010). Sorting texts by readability. *Computational Linguistics*, 36(2):203–227.

Taylor, W. (1953). Cloze procedure: A new tool for measuring readability. *Journalism quarterly*, 30(4):415–433.

Taylor, W. (1957). "Cloze" readability scores as indices of individual differences in comprehension and aptitude. *Journal of Applied Psychology*, 41(1):19–26.

Todirascu, A., François, T., Gala, N., Fairon, C., Ligozat, A.-L., and Bernhard, D. (2013). Coherence and cohesion for the assessment of text readability. *Natural Language Processing and Cognitive Science*, pages 11–19.

Tufféry, S. (2007). *Data mining et statistique décisionnelle l'intelligence des données*. Éd. Technip, Paris.

Vajjala, S. and Meurers, D. (2012). On improving the accuracy of readability classification using insights from second language acquisition. In *Proceedings of the Seventh Workshop on Building Educational Applications Using NLP*, pages 163–173.

van Oosten, P. and Hoste, V. (2011). Readability Annotation: Replacing the Expert by the Crowd. In *Sixth Workshop on Innovative Use of NLP for Building Educational Applications*.

van Oosten, P., Hoste, V., and Tanghe, D. (2011). A posteriori agreement as a quality measure for readability prediction systems. In Gelbukh, A., editor, *Computational Linguistics and Intelligent Text Processing*, volume 6609 of *Lecture Notes in Computer Science*, pages 424–435. Springer, Berlin / Heidelberg.

Weaver, W. and Kingston, A. (1963). A factor analysis of the cloze procedure and other measures of reading and language ability. *Journal of Communication*, 13(4):252–261.

Towards Automatic Scoring of Cloze Items by Selecting Low-Ambiguity Contexts

Tobias Horsmann, Torsten Zesch

Language Technology Lab
University of Duisburg-Essen
Germany

{tobias.horsmann, torsten.zesch}@uni-due.de

Abstract

In second language learning, cloze tests (also known as fill-in-the-blank tests) are frequently used for assessing the learning progress of students. While preparation effort for these tests is low, scoring needs to be done manually, as there usually is a huge number of correct solutions. In this paper, we examine whether the ambiguity of cloze items can be lowered to a point where automatic scoring becomes possible. We utilize the local context of a word to collect evidence of low-ambiguity. We do that by seeking for collocated word sequences, but also taking structural information on sentence level into account. We evaluate the effectiveness of our method in a user study on cloze items ranked by our method. For the top-ranked items (lowest ambiguity) the subjects provide the target word significantly more often than for the bottom-ranked items (59.9% vs. 36.5%). While this shows the potential of our method, we did not succeed in fully eliminating ambiguity. Thus, further research is necessary before fully automatic scoring becomes possible.

Keywords: cloze tests, language proficiency tests, automatic scoring.

Tobias Horsmann and Torsten Zesch 2014. Towards automatic scoring of cloze items by selecting low-ambiguity contexts. *Proceedings of the third workshop on NLP for computer-assisted language learning.* NEALT Proceedings Series 22 / Linköping Electronic Conference Proceedings 107: 33–42.

1 Introduction

Cloze items (Taylor, 1953, 1956; O'Toole and King, 2011) are frequently used to test language proficiency. A cloze item consists of a sentence with usually one word being blanked. The learner's task is to find the correct word for the blank:

(1) He sold his ____ yesterday below price.

As we can see from example (1), blanks can be quite ambiguous, i.e. a very high number of correct solutions exists. In this example, a wide range of nouns are acceptable solutions including *books*, *house*, or *bike*, but also *daughter* or *kidney* cannot be ruled out in this (quite limited) context. Such ambiguity is not only a problem for language learners, but even native speakers frequently fail when facing such a task (Klein-Braley and Raatz, 1982).

If cloze items should be automatically generated and scored, ambiguous items pose a serious problem, as we only know for sure one correct answer namely the one that was used in the original sentence. Students might get frustrated if they provide a valid solution that is not recognized by the system. The same problem affects an alternative solution to the problem: providing a list of alternative answer options - called distractors (Sumita et al., 2005). Determining whether a distractor is actually another valid solution is equivalent to the problem described above. Thus, finding good distractors is still an unsolved problem that attracts a lot of research (Lee and Seneff, 2007; Smith and Avinesh, 2010; Sakaguchi et al., 2013; Zesch and Melamud, 2014). Furthermore, providing distractors for cloze items also considerably changes the nature of the task, as distractors are recognition stimuli, i.e. the student recognizes the correct answer rather than having to actively produce it (Gonzáles, 1996).

Now consider example sentence (2):

(2) I went to the ____ today and now I have sand in my shoes.

Most people would come up with *beach* or maybe *desert*, while other solutions are highly unlikely, which means that the blank is less ambiguous than example (1). This leads to our research question, whether it is possible to find contexts that are specific enough to only allow one correct solution. Such a setup would dramatically simplify automatic scoring.

We limit the scope of this work to determine low-ambiguity contexts for single-word nouns and leave other parts of speech for future work. In the next section, we describe how such contexts can be detected.

2 Detecting Low-Ambiguity Contexts

In order to determine low-ambiguity contexts, we introduce several detectors that collect evidence of low ambiguity. Figure 1 shows the process chain: First, a target word is chosen for which a context of low ambiguity shall be found. If a sentence contains the target word, we run all detectors in parallel and combine their scores to form the final score. We manually determined the perceived reliability of the detectors and assigned them to three classes *strong*, *medium*, and *weak*. Each of the classes correspond to a certain weight of the detector in the final score: a medium detector is 5 times as important as a weak one, and a strong detector is 20 times more important than a weak one. Table 1 provides an overview of the class assignments for detectors. As this is basically a linear

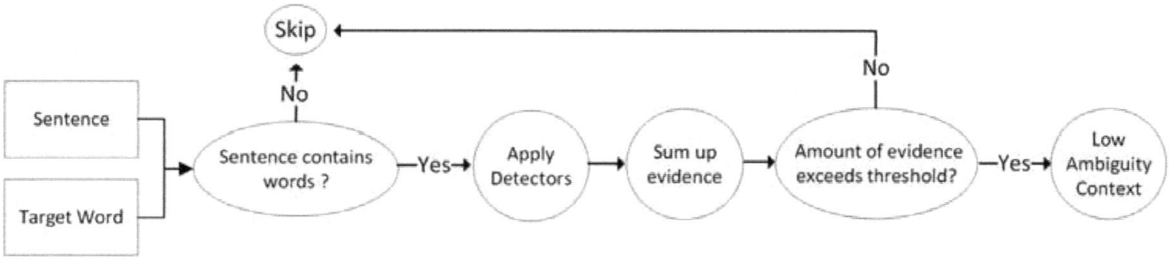

Figure 1: Low Ambiguity Context Determination Process Chain

Detector	Reliability	Weigth
Distributional Thesaurus	*weak*	1
POS Pattern Sliding Window	*weak*	1
Bigram Sliding Window	*medium*	5
Skip-Bigrams	*medium*	5
Hearst-Patterns	*medium*	5
3-5 Gram Sliding Window	*strong*	20
Word Repetition	*strong*	20

Table 1: List of detectors with their reliability and assigned weigth

regression with hand-assigned weights, the weights can (and should) be learned if labeled training data is available.

In the remainder of this section, we describe our detectors in more detail. The detectors are not mutually exclusive and a word might be detected by several detectors.

2.1 Collocation-based Detectors

Subsequently, we will introduce three detectors that are variations of testing a word for being collocated with one or more nearby words. These detectors are motivated by the research field of word prediction where an algorithm tries to determine the next word a user might want to type on a keyboard based on the already entered word sequence (Li and Hirst, 2005; Trnka, 2008; Aliprandi et al., 2007). We hypothesize that if a word is easy to predict it should also be less ambiguous in that context. We further expect that longer collocated sequences are easier to predict than shorter ones.

Another way to look at this problem is its relation to language model perplexity (Chen et al., 1998). Classically, perplexity makes a statement about how well a model predicts test data. In our task, we try to do the exact opposite. We want to determine a test set on which we would achieve a low perplexity on our (static) language model.

3-5 Gram Sliding Window This detector tests if the target word and its neighboring words are collocated, taking into account three, four, and five grams.

We start by moving a 5-gram context-window over the sentence and signal a match if the association strength of the ngram exceeds the threshold. Otherwise, we move the window one position to the right and repeat until either a match occurs or the target word became the most left-hand word in the window. If no match occurs, the window size is decreased and the procedure repeated.

An example sentence that demonstrates the detection of a three word collocation is depicted in

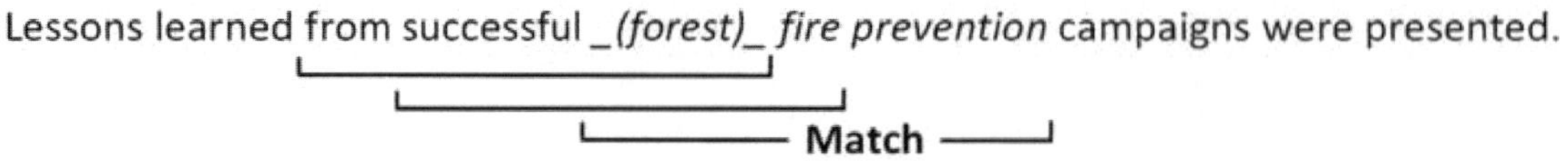

Figure 2: Sliding Window: Collocation detection with window size of three

Figure 2. The target word is *forest*. The window has to be shifted two times until it is over the phrase *forest fire prevention* in order to match.

In order to quantify word association strength, we use pointwise mutual information (PMI) (Church and Hanks, 1990) and obtain the required word frequencies from the Google Web1T corpus (Brants and Franz, 2006). As PMI is only defined for bigrams, sequences of length $n \geq 3$ have to be split into two units that are pseudo-bigrams.[1] For example, calculating the PMI for *forest fire prevention*, would either lead to a split such as [*forest fire*] [*prevention*] or [*forest*] [*fire prevention*].

Following Korkontzelos et al. (2008), we use the so called "pessimistic split" to compute PMI by using the split with the highest likelihood of all possible splits:

$$\mathrm{PMI}_{pess}(w_1, \ldots, w_n) = log \frac{P(w_1,\ldots,w_n)}{P(w_1,\ldots,w_i)P(w_{i+1},\ldots,w_n)}$$

Using the highest likelihood split decreases the number of false alarms by the detector. This is a pessimistic, conservative way of calculating PMI (Hartmann et al., 2012) because the best-split of many actually collocated words will not have co-occurrences high enough to exceed the threshold.[2] Hence, we increase the precision in detection of true collocations, but lower the recall. In combination with the high threshold, we limit the detected word-sequences to those which are extremely frequent to occur in daily life. We expect that the frequency and commonness of such a word sequence will provide the most ideal circumstance to restore a deleted word.

Bigram Sliding Window We also use a bigram sliding window detector, but found that it does not work as reliable as the 3-5 gram detector. Thus, we assign a *medium* reliability. Also, PMI values are usually lower so that we need to set a different threshold (5 instead of 10) in order to ever trigger the detector.

Skip Bigrams Words that occur frequently together do not need to be directly adjacent, but can be separated by other words. To detect such cases, this detector calculates the PMI value between the target word and adjectives or verbs occurring in an n-word window around it. We consider the four words to the left and to the right of the target word. The words directly adjacent to the target word are omitted as this case is already handled by the *Bigram Sliding Window* detector.

For example, we want to detect cases such as:

*It aims to be both, **empirical**, but novel ____. , → research.*

The word *empirical* is clearly referencing to *research* in this case.

We assign a *medium* reliability to this detector and used the same PMI threshold of 5 as for the other bigram detector.

[1] "pseudo-bigram" because such a bigram does not necessarily contain two words, it might only be one, but also three or more depending on the length of the word sequence.

[2] We use a threshold of 10

2.2 POS Pattern Sliding Window

This detector works like the other sliding window detectors, but relies on part-of-speech (POS) ngrams instead of token ngrams. We use a list of POS pattern from Arranz et al. (2005) that were originally used for detecting multiword expressions. We found that the approach did not work well, as contexts with low and high ambiguity can have the same POS patterns. For example, "balance of international payment" (NN-IN-JJ-NN) has the same POS pattern as "car with expensive tires" but is less ambiguous depending on the position of the cloze item. We thus assign a *low* reliability, but still think that the detector can provide supporting evidence for other more important detectors.

2.3 Word Repetition

If the deleted word is repeated later in the sentence, it proposes itself as possible candidate for solving the blank. The detector matches if the target word occurs a second time in the sentence in any inflection form.

Go through the ____ and mark each affected slice., → *slices*

We found that this is a *strong* indicator.

2.4 Distributional Thesaurus

A sentence may contain many words that are semantically related to the target word, but that do not appear in a collocation:

The ***compressor*** *is necessitated by ____ which injects fuel into the* ***cylinder*** → air

In the example, we show semantically related words in bold-face. They help to guide the reader towards the right choice for the blank.

We detect semantically related words using the distributional thesaurus from Biemann and Riedl (2013) that was computed over the top 1 million words of the English Google Books Corpus (Goldberg and Orwant, 2013). We retrieve the fifty highest ranked words that are associated with our target word in the thesaurus. These words are compared with all words occurring in the sentence. If two or more associated words are found in the sentence the detector matches.

Unfortunately, the detector fires quite often, even in cases of a rather weak relationship between two words. We thus assign a *low* reliability.

2.5 Hearst Patterns

Hearst patterns (Hearst, 1992) are lexico-syntactic pattern like "X such as Y, and Z" that are frequently used to detect hierarchical relationships between words. We argue that wherever such a pattern can be found in a sentence, the ambiguity should be reduced as the reader can be guided by the explicitly stated relationships.

Already small amounts of ____
such as ***beer*** *or* ***wine*** *can affect your ability to drive.* → alcohol

This structure allows the reader to abstract to the more general, deleted word. In the case of *beer* and *wine*, the reader may conclude that the deleted word is *alcohol*. Thus, if the more general word is deleted, the list of more specific words allows determining the deleted word. Note that the other direction is usually more difficult, e.g. 'fruit → orange' is harder than 'orange → fruit' as there are many different fruit, but only one more general concept.

We found that the detector works quite well, but produces some false alarms. We thus assign a *medium* reliability.

3 Experimental Setup

In order to evaluate our methods, we have to determine how often human subjects are able to complete the cloze items with the target word. If subjects consistently only give the correct answer, our method would work perfectly. However, as this might be too optimistic, we will measure how often the correct word (the originally deleted word) is provided and how many different alternatives human subjects provide.

In order to create the evaluation dataset, we randomly select sentences from the UkWaC corpus (Baroni et al., 2009) which contains general-purpose text obtained from uk-domain websites. The sentences are filtered by their reading-difficulty using the Flesch–Kincaid test (Kincaid et al., 1975): we remove all sentences requiring more than 10 years of school-education. We then only keep sentences that contain a noun from a randomly chosen subset of common nouns. We then apply our method to the remaining sentences obtaining weight scores from 0 to 52, where a higher number means more evidence (less ambiguity). From this ranking, we select the 25 top-ranked sentences and the 25 bottom-ranked sentences. The bottom-ranked sentences have a score-range of 11 to 16, thus, none of the *strong* detectors contributed to their score. We compiled a cloze test from both collections (replacing the common noun with a blank) and asked volunteer participants to solve the items.

Overall, 30 native speakers of English completed the study, which was conducted online. Before the actual study, participants were shown a detailed manual describing the study. Participants were asked not to cheat and not to use any search engines or ask other people for second opinions. If they could not come up with an answer, participants were instructed to move to the next sentence. The fifty sentences were offered over 4 web pages; each page briefly repeated the manual.

4 Results & Discussion

Figure 3 shows the result of the study in terms of how often participants provided the target word. For the top-ranked items, participants provided the target word on average in 59.9% of the cases, while the average was only 36.5% in the bottom-ranked group. This clearly shows that our method is effective in reducing the ambiguity of cloze items. However, we did not succeed in fully eliminating ambiguity.

The achieved ambiguity reduction can also be measured by considering how many different answers were provided for solving a cloze item. The top-ranked cloze items had an average of 4.5 different answers per item including the target word. Thus, three to four alternative answers were always provided although the frequency for choosing the target word clearly outweighs those of the alternatives. For the bottom-ranked cloze items, participants provided on average almost twice as much different answers (8.4).

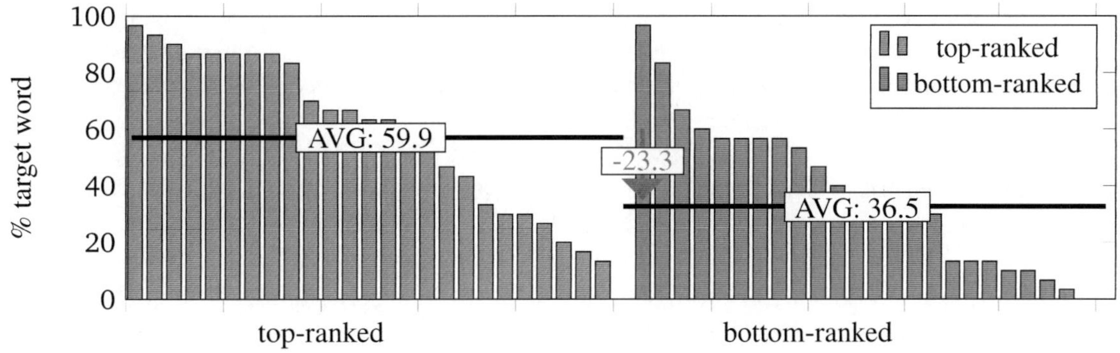

Figure 3: Ratio of participants providing correct answer for top-ranked and bottom-ranked items

4.1 Error Analysis

Our methods worked well in some cases but also yielded poorly performing cases. We discuss subsequently examples for both.

Top-ranked (correct) The following sentences are examples where the user study confirmed a low-ambiguity context with at least 80% of all human subjects providing the target word.

> (A) It is important that you spend some ____ over the next few weeks to help your kitten adjust to its new family so please take the time to read our information before you get your new kitten . → *time* (96%)
>
> (B) Effects : A trip can take from 20 minutes to an ____ to start and usually lasts about 12 hours . → *hour* (93%)
>
> (C) In 1974 the former girls' premises were occupied by Orange Hill junior high ____ and the boys ' by Orange Hill senior high school . → *school* (86%)

The cloze items in sentence (A-C) is placed within very common phrases. In (A) and (C) the local word context alone was sufficiently specific to fill the item with its original word. In sentence (B) we have even more hints: (i) the target word is repeated within the sentence, and (ii) the determiner "an" right in front of the blank further limits the possible candidate answers.

Top-ranked (wrong) For the following sentences only 20% or less of the participants provided the target word:

> (E) They have various difficulties including learning difficulties, physical difficulties, emotional and behavioural ____ as well as mental health problems. → *problems* (20%)
>
> (F) All stores offer a wide and varied ____ of hot tubs and spas, please call us to arrange a dip at anytime on 0800 085 8880 or go to the showroom locator to find your nearest branch. → *range* (16%)
>
> (G) The ground floor has a well equipped living room, dining ____ and kitchen and the private seating area is only a few steps away, in the garden. → *area* (13%)

The sentences in the top-ranked group are mainly from matches of collocation-based detectors and word redundancy. In sentence (E) *difficulties* (30%) is provided most frequently, but was not used in the original sentence probably due to stylistic considerations. In (G) *room* (80%) is selected due to a similar pattern. In sentence (F) the most frequent answer is *selection* (63%) instead of *range*. *Selection* is a synonym of *range* in this context. In order to correctly rank cases like this we need to take competing candidates into account in the ranking process.

Bottom-ranked (wrong) Two items stand out in the bottom-ranked group, because participants provided the target word in over 80% of cases so they should actually be in the top-ranked group.

> (H) I managed to ride the bike to work with the handlebars pointing in a different ____ to the wheel and almost in tears. → *direction* (96%)
>
> (I) The disease usually starts in the wrists, hands or feet, and can spread to other joints and other ____ of the body. → *parts* (83%)

In case of sentence (H) *pointing in a different direction* missed the threshold, but is actually a quite strong collocation. In sentence (I), the enumeration of body parts provided the needed context to determine the deleted word. Our *Hearst* detector matched, but its weight was not enough to put the item in the top-ranked group.

Bottom-ranked (correct) The following two sentences were not answered by a single participants with the target word. Although they belong in the bottom-ranked group, the especially low score deserves some discussion.

> (J) This new edition contains many more illustrations and anecdotes, and two new chapters on ____'s surviving Bristol Channel pilot cutters and their restoration and model making of these craft. → today (0%)
>
> (K) Anta Scotland Ltd Specialise in fabrics and ceramics and have various contemporary versions of traditional ____ such as tartans. → designs (0%)

In case of (J), the possessive case of the deleted word confused almost all participants. This blank remained unanswered quite often (40%). If an answer was provided it was rather a proper noun. Sentence (K) was most frequently answered with *fabrics* (40%). The *Hearst* detector matched, but we assume that our participants were unfamiliar with the word *tartans*, and thus could not take advantage of this structural hint. This illustrates why we only put medium weights on the *Hearst* detector. The conditions under which a detector is useful remains difficult to predict.

5 Conclusion & Future Work

In this paper, we discussed methods for determining cloze items with reduced ambiguity. We introduced seven detectors in order to find such items. We found that our methods are able to significantly reduce the ambiguity of blanks, but that we could not reach our goal of a single valid answer per item.

In future work, we want to improve the detectors in order to further reduce ambiguity of selected sentences. We also need to address the problem that cloze items might become to easy, as e.g. word repetition is a strong detector, but obviously not very useful when generating a language proficiency test.

References

Aliprandi, C., Carmignani, N., and Mancarella, P. (2007). In *International Journal of Computing and Information Sciences*, volume 5, pages 79–85.

Arranz, V., Atserias, J., and Castillo, M. (2005). Multiwords and word sense disambiguation. In Gelbukh, A., editor, *Computational Linguistics and Intelligent Text Processing*, volume 3406 of *Lecture Notes in Computer Science*, pages 250–262. Springer Berlin Heidelberg.

Baroni, M., Bernardini, S., Ferraresi, A., and Zanchetta, E. (2009). The wacky wide web: A collection of very large linguistically processed web-crawled corpora. *Language Resources and Evaluation*, 3:209–226.

Biemann, C. and Riedl, M. (2013). Text: now in 2d! a framework for lexical expansion with contextual similarity. *Journal of Language Modelling*, 1:55–95.

Brants, T. and Franz, A. (2006). Web 1t 5-gram corpus version 1.1. *Linguistic Data Consortium.*

Chen, S., Beeferman, D., and Rosenfeld, R. (1998). Evaluation Metrics for Language Models. In *DARPA Broadcast News Transcription and Understanding Workshop (BNTUW)*, Lansdowne, Virginia, USA.

Church, K. W. and Hanks, P. (1990). Word association norms, mutual information, and lexicography. *Comput. Linguist.*, 16(1):22–29.

Goldberg, Y. and Orwant, J. (2013). A dataset of syntactic-ngrams over time from a very large corpus of english books.

Gonzáles, A. B. (1996). Testing english as a foreign language: an overview and some methodological considerations. *Revista española de lingüística aplicada*, 11:71–94.

Hartmann, S., Szarvas, G., and Gurevych, I. (2012). Mining multiword terms from wikipedia. In Pazienza, M. T. and Stellato, A., editors, *Semi-Automatic Ontology Development: Processes and Resources*, pages 226–258. IGI Global, Hershey, PA, USA.

Hearst, M. A. (1992). Automatic acquisition of hyponyms from large text corpora. In *In Proceedings of the 14th International Conference on Computational Linguistics*, pages 539–545.

Kincaid, P. J., Fishburne, R. P. J., Rogers, R. L., and Chissom, B. S. (1975). Derivation of new readability formulas (automated readability index, fog cound and flesch reading ease formula) for navy enlisted personnel. *Naval Technical Training Command: Research Branch Report 8-75.*

Klein-Braley, C. and Raatz, U. (1982). Der c-test: ein neuer ansatz zur messung von allgemeiner sprachbeherrschung. *AKS-Rundbrief*, pages 23–37.

Korkontzelos, I., Klapaftis, I., and Manandhar, S. (2008). Reviewing and evaluating automatic term recognition techniques. In Nordström, B. and Ranta, A., editors, *Advances in Natural Language Processing*, volume 5221 of *Lecture Notes in Computer Science*, pages 248–259. Springer Berlin Heidelberg.

Lee, J. and Seneff, S. (2007). Automatic generation of cloze items for prepositions. *Interspeech.*

Li, J. and Hirst, G. (2005). Semantic knowledge in word completion. In *Proceedings of the 7th international ACM SIGACCESS conference on Computers and accessibility*, Assets '05, pages 121–128, New York, NY, USA. ACM.

O'Toole, J. M. and King, R. A. R. (2011). The deceptive mean: Conceptual scoring of cloze entries differentially advantages more able readers. *Language Testing*.

Sakaguchi, K., Arase, Y., and Komachi, M. (2013). Discriminative approach to fill-in-the-blank quiz generation for language learners. In *Proceedings of the 51st Annual Meeting of the Association for Computational Linguistics*, pages 238–242.

Smith, S. and Avinesh, P. (2010). Gap-fill tests for language learners: Corpus-driven item generation. In *Proceedings of ICON-2010: 8th International Conference on Natural Language Processing*.

Sumita, E., Sugaya, F., and Yamamoto, S. (2005). Measuring non-native speakers' proficiency of english by using a test with automatically-generated fill-in-the-blank questions. In *Proceedings of the second workshop on Building Educational Applications Using NLP*, EdAppsNLP 05, pages 61–68, Stroudsburg, PA, USA. Association for Computational Linguistics.

Taylor, W. (1953). Cloze procedure: A new tool for measuring readability. *Journalism Quarterly*, 30:415–433.

Taylor, W. (1956). Recent developments in the use of cloze procedure. *Journalism Quarterly*, 33:42.

Trnka, K. (2008). Adaptive language modeling for word prediction. In *Proceedings of the ACL-08: HLT Student Research Workshop*, pages 61–66, Columbus, Ohio. Association for Computational Linguistics.

Zesch, T. and Melamud, O. (2014). Automatic Generation of Challenging Distractors Using Context-Sensitive Inference Rules. In *Proceedings of the 9th Workshop on Innovative Use of NLP for Building Educational Applications at ACL*, Baltimore, USA.

Leveraging Known Semantics for Spelling Correction

Levi King and *Markus Dickinson*
Indiana University
Bloomington, IN USA

leviking@indiana.edu, md7@indiana.edu

ABSTRACT
Focusing on applications for analyzing learner language which evaluate semantic appropriateness and accuracy, we build from previous work which modeled some aspects of interaction, namely a picture description task (PDT), with the goal of integrating a spelling correction component in this context. After parsing a sentence and extracting semantic relations, a surprising number of analysis failures stem from misspellings, deviating from expected input in ways that can be modeled when the content of the interaction is known. We thus explore the use of spelling correction tools and language modeling to correct misspellings that often lead to errors in obtaining semantic forms, and we show that such tools can significantly reduce the number of unanalyzable cases. The work is useful for any context where image descriptions or some expected content is available, but not necessarily expected linguistic forms.

KEYWORDS: picture description task, semantic analysis, spelling correction, language modeling.

Levi King and Markus Dickinson 2014. Leveraging known semantics for spelling correction. *Proceedings of the third workshop on NLP for computer-assisted language learning.* NEALT Proceedings Series 22 / Linköping Electronic Conference Proceedings 107: 43–58.

1 Motivation

Much current work on analyzing learner language focuses on grammatical error detection and correction (e.g., Dale et al., 2012) and less on semantic analysis; many Intelligent Computer-Assisted Language Learning (ICALL) and Intelligent Language Tutoring (ILT) systems (e.g., Heift and Schulze, 2007; Meurers, 2012) also focus more on grammatical feedback. An exception to this rule is *Herr Komissar*, an ILT for German learners that includes rather robust content analysis and sentence generation (DeSmedt, 1995), but this involves a great deal of hand-built tools and does not connect to modern NLP. Some work addresses content assessment for short answer tasks (Meurers et al., 2011), but there is still a need to move towards naturalistic, more conversational interactions (see Petersen, 2010). Such interactions are both more and less difficult to process: to provide feedback requires keeping track of the content of the interaction, but such content can also be used to disambiguate new learner productions. We exploit this tension in the context of spelling correction, as semantic information severely restricts the learner's expected content, and thus also their word forms.

Since our overarching goal is to move towards the facilitation of ILTs and language assessment tools that maximize free interaction, we have to deal with removing impediments to interaction. Given the preponderance of spelling errors in learner data, and specifically interactive data (King and Dickinson, 2013), our specific goal is to use basic NLP (pre)processing—namely, language modeling for spelling correction—to make the meaning of a learner's sentence clearer. We examine methods for automatically correcting misspellings, showing that preprocessing with spelling correction tools, when information about the interactive context is known (i.e., the picture's description), can greatly reduce downstream errors.

This may seem like a niche problem, but: 1) spelling errors are generally a major problem in analyzing learner data (Leacock et al., 2010; Flor et al., 2013); 2) the specific focus we have right now, on picture description tasks (PDTs), connects not only with a desire for more interactive tools, but also for language assessment (Somasundaran and Chodorow, 2014); and 3) our work seeks to unpack the connection between relatively "shallow" errors, namely spelling errors, with "deeper" errors, namely semantic ones. Unlike, for example, linguistic abstractions such as part-of-speech, both are intimately rooted in the particular lexical items used. This then raises the question of whether we are modeling what the learner said (modulo some spelling variation), what the learner intended, or what the learner should have intended, an issue we take up in section 4, after covering the background in section 3. The methods are covered in section 5 and the evaluation in section 6.

2 Related Work

Research into the patterns of spelling errors particular to native speakers (NSs) and non-native speakers (NNSs) highlights the challenge of applying spelling correction techniques to non-native text. Flor et al. (2013) examined spelling errors found in the ETS Spelling Corpus (3000 GRE and TOEFL essays) and found that NNS spelling errors were more severe (i.e., had a greater edit distance from the intended word) than NS errors. Moreover, NNSs made more spelling errors than NSs for words of 3-7 letters, but this trend reversed for words of 8 letters or more. These effects were shown to disappear among the most proficient NNSs in the sample, however. Similarly, Hovermale (2010) compared the spelling errors in corpora of Japanese learners of English to previous studies of NS spelling errors and found that the learner errors have a greater average edit distance and are nearly twice as likely to involve the first letter of the word. Given such variability in form, correcting spelling errors for NNSs strictly via edit distance operations would thus seem to have its limits.

Using the ETS Spelling Corpus and the ConSpell spelling correction tool, Flor (2012) demonstrates significant gains in automatic spelling correction when modules using contextual information are added. Four types of context, each of which benefitted spelling correction, were explored: 1) word n-grams (length 1–5) and a web-scale language model (LM); 2) word n-grams and the positive normalized pointwise mutual information (PNPMI) of the words within them (based on a web-scale distributional model); 3) the entire essay (and the recurrence or lack of a given candidate spelling correction in the essay); and 4) the text of the essay prompt. Notably, a 3.8% improvement comes through the use of "global mutual optimization", i.e., at each given spelling correction decision, the module is biased not only toward other words in the text, but also the candidate spelling lists of these other words. The work presents a strong case for the use of n-grams with both LMs and PNPMI, as the best results come from this setting, boosting performance 11.48% above the non-contextual spelling correction baseline.

Flor and Futagi (2012) further examine the use of context for correcting learner misspellings and claim that three major issues contribute to the task's difficulty: "local error density" (a misspelled word near other misspellings) weakens n-gram approaches; poor grammar can lead to the selection of an incorrect spelling candidate based on its agreement with nearby incorrect words; and competition among closely related spelling candidates can lead to the selection of an incorrect inflectional variant. These challenges indicate that for potentially error-rich learner sentences, sentence or n-gram level contexts may be more effective when combined with higher-level contextual information, such as task prompts and discourse-level information about verb inflections. We explore including information about picture content.

3 Background

3.1 Data

In previous work (King and Dickinson, 2013), we collected responses to a picture description (PDT) task to approximate interactive behavior. The current study relies on the same set of responses. We use a PDT because it helps constrain both form and content, without providing textual prompts that may influence a learner. Moreover, PDTs are a well-established tool in areas of study ranging from SLA to Alzheimer's disease (Ellis, 2000; Forbes-McKay and Venneri, 2005). The use of visual stimuli also helps model the visual nature of online games. The stimuli are chosen to elicit relatively unambiguous transitive sentences.

The PDT consisted of 10 items (8 line drawings and 2 photographs) intended to elicit a single sentence each; an example is given in Figure 1. Participants were asked to view the image and describe the action in a complete

Response (L1)
The man killing the beard. (Arabic)
A man is shutting a bird. (Chinese)
A man is shooting a bird. (English)
The man shouted the bird. (Spanish)

Figure 1: Example item and responses

sentence, with any tense or aspect appropriate. 25 of the 39 non-native speaker (NNS) participants performed the task in a setting where automatic spell checking was disabled; the remaining 14 performed the task online on their own computers, and although they were instructed to disable spell checking, we have no way of knowing if they did so.

The NNSs were intermediate and upper-level adult English learners in an intensive English as a Second Language program at Indiana University. This data set contains responses from 53 informants, including native speakers (NSs) (14 NSs, 39 NNSs), for a total of 530 sentences. The distribution of first languages (L1s) is: 16 Arabic, 7 Chinese, 14 English, 2 Japanese, 4 Korean, 1 Kurdish, 1 Polish, 2 Portuguese, and 6 Spanish.

3.2 Method

As in King and Dickinson (2013), our method to obtain a semantic form from a NNS production takes two steps: 1) obtain a syntactic dependency representation from the off-the-shelf Stanford parser (de Marneffe et al., 2006; Klein and Manning, 2003), and 2) obtain a semantic form from the parse, via a small set of hand-written rules. To illustrate this process, consider (1). This sentence is passed through the parser to obtain the dependency parse shown in Figure 2. Based on the presence of the `nsubjpass` (noun subject, passive) node, the extraction script takes the logical subject from under the `agent` label, the verb from `root`, and the logical object from `nsubjpass`. This results in the semantic triple *shot(man,bird)*, lemmatized to *shoot(man,bird)*, using the Stanford CoreNLP lemmatizer (Manning et al., 2014). Very little effort is needed: the parser is pre-built; the decision tree is small; and the extraction rules are minimal. Note, too, that certain relations (e.g., `det`) are completely ignored in the extraction.

(1) A bird is shot by a man.

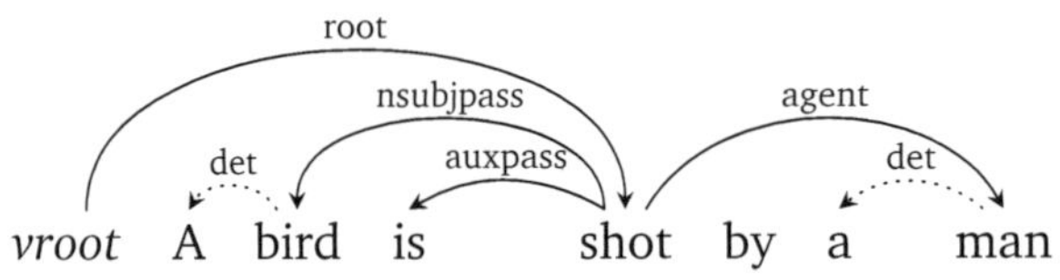

Figure 2: The dependency parse of (1)

One is able to use little effort in part due to the constraints in the pictures. For figure 1, for example, *the artist*, *the man in the beret*, and *the man* are all acceptable subjects, whereas if there were multiple men in the picture, *the man* would not be specific enough.

Evaluation in King and Dickinson (2013) addresses two major questions. First, how accurate is the extraction of semantic information from potentially innovative sentences? Secondly, how much coverage does one have in a gold standard of semantic forms (triples), to capture the variability in meaning in learner sentences? We focus more on the first question and again use native speaker semantic forms as a proxy for a gold standard—albeit, limited by mismatches between native and (correct) non-native ways of saying the same thing. To mitigate this and better see the effect of spelling correction, much of our evaluation relies on hand-analysis which determines whether a "reasonable gold standard" could contain the information (see section 4).

Semantic extraction For the purpose of evaluating an extraction system, King and Dickinson (2013) define two major classes of errors. The first are *triple errors*, responses for which the system fails to extract one or more of the desired subject, verb, or object, based on the sentence at hand and without regard to the target content. Second are *content errors*, responses for which the system extracts the desired subject, verb and object, but the resulting triple does not accurately describe the image (i.e., is an error of the participant's). In this paper, we focus on reducing the triple errors, i.e., system errors. For example, the spelling error in (2) leads to a completely incorrect triple. We will unpack our error types in section 4.

(2) A man swipped leaves. ⇒ leave(swipped,man)

Focusing on triple (system) errors, we have obtained 92.3% accuracy on extraction for NNS data and roughly the same for NS data, 92.9% (King and Dickinson, 2013). Furthermore, more than half of the errors for NNSs involve misspellings (4.1% of the total 7.7% of errors). For a system interacting with learners, spelling errors are thus a high priority (cf. Hovermale, 2008).

Content errors are subcategorized as *spelling* or *meaning* errors, depending on whether the resulting triple has spelling errors that do not result in real words—as in (3)—or that do result in real but unintended words and thus convey an inappropriate meaning (e.g., *shout(man,bird)* instead of *shoot(man,bird)*). We will see this distinction play out in the spelling correction techniques in section 5.

(3) The artiest is drawing a portret. ⇒ drawing(artiest,portret)

Approximately 15% of NNS triples are content errors (King and Dickinson, 2013). These cases are ones for which the learner needs feedback, but there are two barriers in providing feedback: 1) without fixing the triple errors, they will be automatically grouped into the content error cases, since they do not match the gold standard; and 2) even if one knows something is an error, to obtain feedback one would ideally know the target the learner was (or should have been) aiming for. Our approach to spelling correction addresses both of these concerns by cleaning up the misspelled cases—including many of the "content" errors rooted in misspellings.

Semantic coverage In King and Dickinson (2013), we take a set of native speaker (NS) responses for the same PDTs as the gold standard, garnering coverage numbers around 25% for types and 50% for tokens—i.e., about half of *correct* NNS responses are not in the gold standard. Since our focus is on improving accuracy, we use the same gold standard, but augment the analysis with hand-evaluation of whether a response should have been in the gold standard (section 4). Still, with spelling modifications being made to make a NNS response more native-like, we may be able to increase coverage, i.e., to find a (gold) NS triple that matches.

4 Error Types

As alluded to above, our goal is to model a close intended meaning of every NNS sentence, in order to provide a platform for providing feedback. By *close intended meaning*, we mean, *a meaning that matches some correct answer and whose corresponding form is a reasonable distance to what the NNS wrote.* Since we have not interviewed participants with follow-up questions about the intention of their responses and cannot assume a follow-up in the general case, we take the close intended meaning as the meaning they should have intended, given their production.

For evaluation, then, we want to measure the extent to which we are able to take a NNS form and produce a plausible target meaning for their "intention," i.e., a viable semantic triple. The evaluation should answer: 1) Is there a valid meaning? and, if not, 2) what step in the process prevented a valid meaning from being derived?

The entire system is outlined in section 5.2 (see Figure 3), but essentially we have this pipeline:

0. Sentence produced by NNS
1. (optional) Spelling corrector to generate close intended form
2. Syntactic parser to obtain word-word relations
3. Semantic extractor to obtain semantic forms
4. Comparison to gold standard

Starting with the gold standard comparison and working backwards, we evaluate at every step:

1. Is the triple covered by the gold standard? **Yes:** Not an error. **No:** Continue to next step.
2. Should the triple be covered by a reasonable gold standard? **Yes:** *Gold* miss ("error"). **No:** Continue to next step.
   - Given the limited coverage of the NS gold standard, we add this manual step, so as not to focus too much on one particular gold standard.
3. Is the form (either the NNS sentence or the close intended meaning chosen by the correction module) well-formed and appropriate for the item but the extracted triple is not covered by a reasonable gold standard? **Yes:** *Triple* error. (These could be subcategorized as parser, lemmatizer, or extractor errors.) **No:** *Form* error.

Note that for our purposes here, a "good" triple should indicate an appropriate subject, verb and object, whether directly or indirectly. In most cases, this is a complete *V(S,O)* triple. For some concepts, however, a verb may imply its object, or vice versa. Item 3 of the PDT, for example, shows a woman riding a bicycle. This could be represented as a transitive action, resulting in a triple like *ride(woman,bicycle)*. However, this could also be construed as an intransitive, such as *cycle(woman,NONE)*. Both of these triples should be considered appropriate. A form like *A woman is on a bicycle* should also be considered appropriate, because the obvious action involving a person on a bicycle is *ride* (or *pedal*, *travel*, etc.), even though the extracted triple (*be(woman,bicycle)*) is less descriptive. An intransitive resulting in a triple like *ride(woman,NONE)* is inadequate, however, because *ride* does not sufficiently imply the object.

Similar cases occur among the responses to item 9, which shows two boys rowing a boat. We might consider *row(boy,boat)* to be an ideal triple for this item, but we also accept *be(boy,boat)* here, as in *Two boys are on a boat*. Note that this is only acceptable because in the absence of more detail, a reasonable person given the information that some human is performing some action on or involving a boat would likely assume that the action involves using the boat for its intended purpose—to travel on water, and that could be represented with a more specific verb. We should also accept *row(boy,NONE)* here, because (unlike *ride*) the verb *row* sufficiently implies its object (a boat). Similarly, *boat(boy,NONE)* is adequate, because as a verb, *boat* indicates both the presence of a boat and the action of riding the boat.

5 Spelling Correction Modifications

5.1 Motivation for spelling correction via language modeling

The initial approach to this task in King and Dickinson (2013) revealed that the ability of the system to recognize NNS responses as correct was often hindered by minor errors in spelling. Misspellings are especially problematic here because they can derail the semantic evaluation of a response by leading to errors in the syntactic interpretation of the sentence. Whereas human listeners or readers can use the context and their knowledge of the language to infer the intended pronunciation or spelling of a mispronounced or misspelled word, the initial approach lacked any such compensatory strategies. To improve the system's ability to handle NNS data, we implement a spelling correction module, which we see as an attempt to endow the system with some of the general language knowledge that a human would use upon encountering a misspelling. Importantly, we incorporate contextual information about the picture by giving this module access to NS responses (i.e., picture descriptions), allowing it to prefer corrected spellings that may be relevant to the context.

We begin with a context-independent spelling corrector, Aspell (Atkinson, 1998), but on finding mixed results with only this basic spelling correction module—due to its lack of incorporation of context—we expand the process to include a statistical language model (LM) based on word trigrams (section 5.2). The n-gram LM essentially takes a large body of English text, counts the occurrences of each sequence of n words, converts these counts to relative frequencies, and uses these relative frequencies to calculate the probability of new texts. The LM has the effect of evaluating the likelihood of multiple possible spellings for a misspelled word (as provided by a context-independent spelling correction module) in the context of surrounding words. In this way, we further attempt to use contextual information and general knowledge of the language to model the close intended meaning while overlooking minor errors in orthography.

The implementation of these tools raises some questions about about how fair or appropriate it is to try to estimate a learner's intended utterance, and just exactly what spelling correction is and is not (or should and should not be). Any automatic or manual approach at correcting malformed learner language or interpreting its meaning encounters ambiguous and challenging cases. This is why we defined our goal in section 4 as that of deriving a close intended form, essentially sidestepping the question of what the ultimate correction *means* and instead focusing on what the correction can tell us about the linguistic utterance's relation to the picture.

This goal, it should be pointed out, is in keeping with a prioritization on encouraging learners to produce more language and on interaction with learners, as opposed to prioritizing grammatical or orthographic perfection. Deriving a close intended form should be able to inform a system towards an appropriate piece of feedback. This can also be seen as "giving the benefit of the doubt" to learners, finding the gold item that looks close; giving the benefit of the doubt is particularly true in the joint evaluation described in Section 6.2, where we consider each original response as well as its corrected version.

5.2 Spelling correction process

Aspell In our first attempt at spelling correction, we added a preprocessing step using Aspell, a spelling correction tool (Atkinson, 1998). For each PDT item, the NNS sentences were passed through Aspell. Words recognized by Aspell were not changed. For words that Aspell considered misspelled, the ranked list of Aspell suggestions was compared with a list of words used in the

NS sentences. The highest ranked suggestion that was also in the NS word list was accepted as the corrected spelling. If no match was found, the first suggested word was accepted, and the sentences were then passed to the rest of the pipeline. A major limitation of this correction was the fact that misspellings resulting in real words were not addressed. For example, several participants responded to one item with the real word *shout* but clearly intended *shoot* (cf. *A man shoots a bird*). Indeed, evaluation of this simple Aspell approach revealed that it introduced significantly more errors than it corrected. Thus, we omit this method from further discussion and focus on a more contextually informed approach incorporating language modeling.

LM pipeline In the approach discussed hereafter (the *LM pipeline*), Aspell (via the Enchant python package (Lachowicz, 2003)) is used to obtain a list of spelling suggestions for all words, including those that appear to be properly spelled. These candidate spellings are combined to form a list of candidate sentences for each response. Each candidate sentence is then compared with an *n*-gram language model to obtain a perplexity score—i.e., a measure of how likely the sentence is, given the LM. The candidate sentence with the lowest perplexity is chosen automatically as the best correction. A diagram of the entire semantic extraction process incorporating the spelling correction and language modeling tools is given in Figure 3.

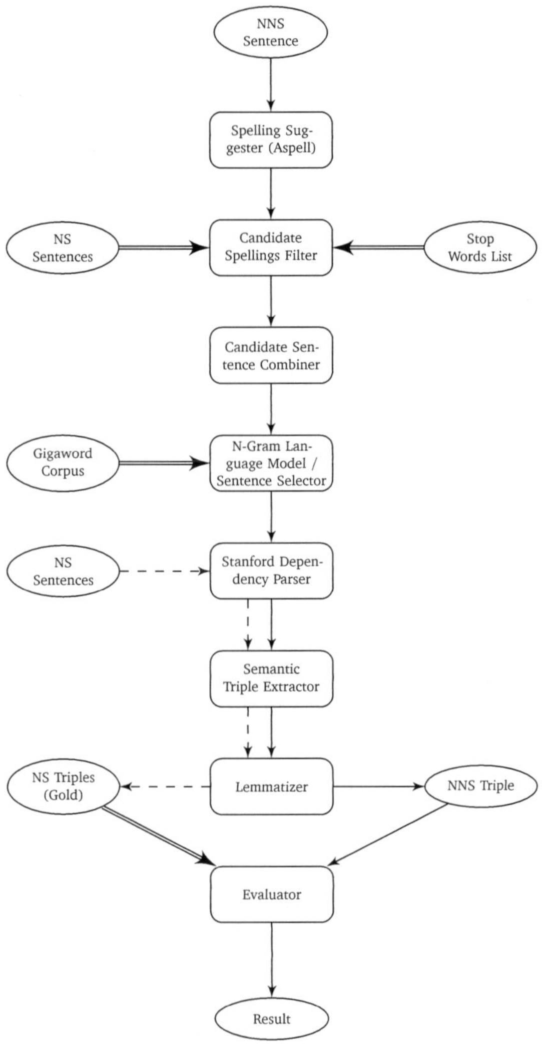

Figure 3: Semantic triple evaluation pipeline. Boxes are system components, circles are data; double arrows indicate training, dashed arrows show the obtaining of gold standard triples.

The computational costs of this approach have the potential to be very great. The number of spelling suggestions for a given word range between zero—for egregious misspellings of long words, unlike anything in the dictionary—and up to 50, for words within a short edit distance of known words (e.g., *pet*). The average number of suggestions for the words in the NNS responses is roughly 31. The average sentence length among the entire data set of NNS responses is 7.2 words. This would result in approximately $31^{7.2}$ (nearly 55 billion) candidate sentences for a single NNS response. We took several steps to prune the number of candidate words and sentences in order to make this process more manageable.

For this pruning, we draw on the NS responses; this decision is based on the assumptions that NS responses are correct and that the PDT constrains the content of responses. We create a NS word list by taking every word form found in the NS responses. We also use a list of stop words consisting of the 200 most common English words, to filter out short function words that would create too many candidates.

This process of forming candidate sentences for a NNS response assumes that while there may be misspellings, the number of words in the sentence is fixed. That is, a word may be replaced by another word, but no word may be removed and no additional words may be inserted. (Rare exceptions may occur when the spelling correction tool suggests that an unrecognized word be split into two words.) This is a limitation of the current implementation and should be addressed in the future, perhaps incorporating techniques for word normalization over word lattices from the speech recognition literature, such as those in Sproat et al. (2001).

For a given NNS response in this pipeline, each token is given a status of `fixed` or `unfixed`. Each word enters the pipeline as `unfixed`; it is then compared with the stop words list, and if a match is found, the status is changed to `fixed`. The remaining `unfixed` words are then compared with the NS word list and again, matches are `fixed`. For any token with a `fixed` status, no candidate spelling corrections will be considered. Thus we assume that a NNS word that matches a stop word is correct, as English learners at this level are unlikely to misspell common function words. We also assume, given the constraints of the PDT, that a NNS word that matches a NS word is correct.

Next, we handle misspellings where no sentential context is needed, given the contents of the picture. Each `unfixed` word is passed to Enchant and a list of candidate spellings is obtained. Note that a ranked list of spelling suggestions is generated even for words that appear to be properly spelled. This list is compared with the NS list; if one or more matches are found, the highest ranked candidate word is selected, and the status is `fixed`. If no match is found, the status remains `unfixed`, and the entire list of candidate words is added to that word position.

After that pruning, a list of candidate sentences can now be generated by iterating through candidate words for `unfixed` positions to generate every possible combination with all the `fixed` words. As mentioned above, NNS responses in the data set contain an average of 7.2 words, and at this stage, 6.5 words are `fixed` and 0.7 words are `unfixed`, resulting in an average of $31^{0.7}$ (roughly 11) candidate sentences per NNS response, drastically reducing the computational costs of the remaining steps in the pipeline. Many well-formed responses result in no candidate sentences beyond the original form, while the largest number of candidates seen among the entire set was 57,300, for a 10-word sentence.

For each NNS sentence, the original sentence and its list of candidates are passed to the language model for evaluation. Here we use the CMU Statistical Language Modeling Toolkit (Clarkson and Rosenfeld, 1997) in a trigram setting trained on a sample of the English Gigaword Corpus (Graff et al., 2007) containing roughly 250 million words in 10 million sentences of newspaper text. The candidate sentences are ranked according to their perplexity with regard to the language model. The sentence with lowest perplexity is selected as the most likely sentence and passed through the remaining steps of the pipeline, as shown in the lower half of Figure 3.

The source of PDT descriptions We use the NS responses here as our proxy for a description of the picture content. This is distinct from using the NS responses as a gold standard to compare the final triples against, as in King and Dickinson (2013); indeed, this is why we manually check triples in this work, assuring that we truly know whether a triple is valid or not. In either case, we will see the limitations of using NS responses for these purposes.

6 Spelling Correction Evaluation

Here we present the results of the modifications detailed above. At this stage, we are primarily interested in our system's ability to robustly extract evaluable triples, potentially in the face of minor errors. While we present coverage scores in the following sections—calculating coverage with respect to the particular (and limited) gold standard set of triples—we focus mainly on the effect the modifications have on (Form) error counts.

	NNS	LM	Joint(NNS)	Joint(LM)	Joint(Oracle)
Coverage	134	149	152	152	152
Gold Misses	125	110	125	109	141
Triple Errors	13	13	13	14	15
Form Errors	118	118	100	115	82
Total Form/Triple Errors	131	131	113	129	97

Table 1: Errors types and coverage for the full set of responses (390 sentences). *Joint* indicates a joint analysis of both sources (NNS & LM); the default source in parentheses was chosen in cases where neither triple was found (see Section 6.2).

6.1 LM pipeline errors

With no attempt at spelling correction, the 390 NNS responses result in a total of 131 true errors, with an additional 125 misses due to an incomplete gold standard and coverage of 134 non-errors, as seen in Table 1. For our evaluation, we are most concerned with reducing the Form errors—which may result in more Gold misses, depending upon whether a valid triple is in the gold standard or not.

Evaluating the LM output results in reducing the number of Gold misses by 8.3%, from 125 to 110, with the Triple and Form error counts unchanged. But this does not tell the full story of changes. If we look closer, as in the first column of Table 2, we see that in comparing the LM triples to the NNS triples, a total of 73 responses change from one error type to another. This includes the conversion of 18 Form errors to non-errors (∅) and three non-errors to Form errors. An example of a "recovered" Form error can be seen in (4). In this case, *shoots* and *bird* are both present in the NS gold standard responses, which helps the LM obtain an acceptable triple.

Change		LM	J(NNS)	J(O)
∅ ↦ ∅	⟷	131	149	152
∅ ↦ Gold	↓	0	0	0
∅ ↦ Trip.	↓	0	0	0
∅ ↦ Form	↓	3	0	0
Gold ↦ ∅	↑	0	0	0
Gold ↦ Gold	⟷	93	94	125
Gold ↦ Trip.	↓	1	0	0
Gold ↦ Form	↓	31	15	0
Trip. ↦ ∅	↑	0	0	0
Trip. ↦ Gold	↑	0	1	0
Trip. ↦ Trip.	⟷	11	11	13
Trip. ↦ Form	↓	2	2	0
Form ↦ ∅	↑	18	3	0
Form ↦ Gold	↑	16	30	16
Form ↦ Trip.	↑	2	2	2
Form ↦ Form	⟷	82	83	82
Changed		73	53	18
Unchanged		317	337	372
Total	⟷	317	337	372
Total	↑	36	36	18
Total	↓	37	17	0

Table 2: The number of changes between error types, moving from NNS to LM, from LM to J(NNS), and from J(NNS) to J(Oracle).

(4) a. NNS: the old man shouts to beird. ⇒ NONE(shout,NONE)
b. LM: the old man shoots to bird. ⇒ shoot(man,bird)

An example of a Form error introduced by the LM pipeline is seen in (5). Here we see that given the NNS sentence, the lemmatizer was robust enough to properly arrive at *shoot* from the misspelled *shooted*. While both *shoot* and *shot* were among the 12 words suggested by Aspell to replace *shooted*, the LM preferred *shouted*.

(5) a. NNS: a man shooted a bird. ⇒ shoot(man,bird)
b. LM: a man shouted a bird. ⇒ shout(man,bird)

Additionally, the LM pipeline changes 31 Gold "errors" to Form errors. While this does not affect coverage or the total error counts when evaluated under the current gold standard, these cases are clearly problematic. One example is shown in (6b), modified by the LM pipeline from (6a).

(6) a. NNS: a person was cutting fruit. ⇒ cut(person,fruit)
b. LM: a person was cutting fraud. ⇒ cut(person,fraud)

The issue stems from the fact that the LM was trained on newspaper text, leading it to prefer words and phrases prevalent in the news, (*cutting fraud*), while giving higher perplexity to those less common in news stories (*cutting fruit*). Other examples of this domain-based over-correction include the changing of *biking* to *backing*, *cleaning* to *learning*, and *chopping* to *shipping*. Besides choosing better LM training data, future work could use other methods of analysis to avoid these problems. For example, using WordNet (Fellbaum, 1998) to discover that "fruit" is a hypernym of "apple" (the object described by all NSs), and thus (possibly) acceptable, would eliminate the need to process some spelling candidates via the LM.

Due to the design of the LM pipeline, these problems are compounded by the sparseness of the gold standard. The NS responses are used to derive the gold standard, but also to derive a list of context-appropriate words for each item. As described above, this word list is used to select appropriate spelling candidates from the correction tool before the recombined sentences are evaluated by the LM. The over-correction problem is exacerbated when the PDT item depicts an action for which NSs know a specific word but NNSs may not, like *raking* or *rowing*. These items highlight the disadvantages of relying on NS responses. For such prompts, we observe: a) relatively high numbers of candidate sentences, because fewer candidate spellings are decided by the NS word list, as well as: b) higher numbers of Form errors, because we shift the burden of deciding contextually appropriate words to the LM.

6.2 Joint Evaluation

So far, each sentence form and triple output by the LM pipeline is evaluated alone, without regard to the NNS form or the output of the the original process. In this section we present a joint analysis, wherein we take both the LM triple and its NNS counterpart; in cases where one of the two triples is found in the set of NS responses, we keep that triple and ignore the other; in cases where neither triple is found, we default to the NNS triple; we refer to this as *Joint(NNS)*. (A joint analysis defaulting to the LM (*Joint(LM)*) was also performed, but this resulted in weaker performance, as shown in Table 1, and is omitted from the discussion). The idea behind this joint analysis is simply to give the system the choice between two triples for a single response, using information about the picture's contents (NS responses) to pick one, effectively allowing us to undo any errors introduced by Aspell or the LM.

We again focus primarily on the changes in error counts. Unlike the analyses above, however, under this joint evaluation there is an unavoidable possibility for the set of NS responses to affect error counts. This is because a triple's presence or absence in this set determines which of the two triple versions is considered. Consider the following constructed example to illustrate this concern. Under our joint analysis, given an original triple of *shout(hunter,bird)*, which is an error (and of course absent from the list) and an LM triple of *shoot(hunter,bird)*, which is correct but absent from the NS list, we default to the original triple, thus including an error that would have been avoided if the NS list had covered the LM triple.

Such cases illustrate the fact that the error types are not equally (un)desirable. A Gold miss is better than a Form or Triple error for us, because the Gold miss is not a system error at all and could be covered by an improved gold standard. Likewise, a (NNS) Form error changed to a (LM) Triple error is a partial success, because this means the spelling correction module was successful, while the parser or semantic extractor needs improvement. To address these issues, we perform a *Joint(Oracle)* experiment (section 6.2.2), in which errors were ranked by preference, from non-error, to Gold miss, to Triple error, to Form error. In cases where neither the NNS nor the LM triple was found and the error types were different, the oracle chooses the preferred error type, minimizing Form errors and maximizing Gold misses. The results of this experiment give a better approximation of the potential of the current system given an ideal set of triples covering the content of the picture (which the NS responses serve as a proxy for).

6.2.1 Joint(NNS) errors

The Joint(NNS) experiment gives coverage to 152 triples, and compared with the LM pipeline, it results in a net reduction of 18 Form/Triple errors, from 131 to 113. While the error type was changed for 53 responses, this improvement is partly the result of three Form errors converting to non-errors (Table 2). An example of such a gain is seen in the NNS response (5a) and the LM version (5b); this time, as the LM triple is not found, we default to the correct NNS triple, undoing the error introduced by the LM pipeline. Another example of an LM error avoided under the joint analysis is shown in (7b), as it defaults to the NNS response seen in (7a).

(7) a. NNS: a boy is playing a soccer alone. ⇒ play(boy,soccer)
    b. LM: a boy is playing a soccer one. ⇒ play(boy,one)

Importantly, we also see 30 Form errors from the LM model become Gold misses (Table 2), leading to an overall reduction of Form errors from 118 to 100 (Table 1). This Joint(NNS) model, then, is doing exactly what it is designed to do: removing Form errors by changing the spelling into something with a valid semantics.

6.2.2 Joint(Oracle) errors

As mentioned in section 6.2, many positive changes introduced by the LM pipeline are not fully realized under the LM or Joint(NNS) experiments. We investigate that here by using an oracle to choose the preferred error type in cases where neither triple is found. As a result, 18 correct changes introduced by the LM—but ignored by defaulting to the NNS under the Joint(NNS) setting—are retained under the Joint(Oracle) setting. These include two Form errors converted to Triple errors and 16 Form errors converted to Gold misses (Table 2). Note that coverage remains at 152 (Table 1).

An example of a Form error converted to a Triple error can be seen in (8b), the form and triple derived from the NNS response in (8a). We consider (8a) to be a Form error, because *cycle* does not fully describe a bicycle. In (8b), despite the fact that the LM pipeline made an appropriate correction and returned a perfectly acceptable form, the derived triple is incorrect. This is the result of an inappropriate parse, with *rides* given a plural noun (NNS) part of speech tag and *the woman rides* labeled as a noun phrase.

(8) a. NNS: the woman rides on her cycle. ⇒ NONE(ride,cycle)
    b. LM: the woman rides on her bicycle. ⇒ NONE(ride,bicycle)

This kind of error is representative of a pattern among the Triple errors found across the dataset: third person present tense verbs are regularly analyzed (via the parser's built-in part-of-speech tagger) as plural nouns, leading to the extraction of an incorrect triple. This is seen for *rides, boats, rows,* and *paints*. A game setting would likely alleviate this problem by constraining responses to the past tense, but NNSs may also need to be reminded that the simple present is usually reserved for describing general truths.

An example from the 16 Gold misses corrected from Form errors is shown in (9b), derived from the NNS response in (9a). Here, while (9b) is an appropriate form and triple, the triple is not found in the gold standard, because every NS respondent described the PDT item as a *raking* action, not a sweeping action.

(9) a. NNS: a men is swapping the leaves. ⇒ swap(man,leaf)
    b. LM: a man is sweeping the leaves. ⇒ sweep(man,leaf)

Another example of a NNS Form error changed to an LM Gold miss under the Joint(NNS) experiment is the correction of *draw(artiest,portrait)* (seen above in (3)) to *draw(artist,portrait)*.

7 Summary and Outlook

We have implemented a system for automatically correcting NNS responses for visual stimuli by relying on a small set of known appropriate responses to influence the correction process. Even with a very limited gold standard, these corrections boosted coverage by 13.4% and decreased the total rate of Form and Triple errors by 13.7% (with potential for a decrease of 25.9%, as in the oracle experiments). These results can help guide the development of systems that aim to process the meaning of NNS statements, which contain a significantly higher rate of spelling errors compared to NS statements. There is much to be gained with a small amount of computational effort; as demonstrated here, more work needs to go into delineating a proper set of appropriate responses.

Indeed, we see the construction of a robust set of appropriate responses as the most immediate means of improving system performance. As NSs were shown to converge on a limited vocabulary for some items, while NNSs do not, simply collecting more NS responses would result in diminishing returns. Future work will need to uncover the best means of obtaining a sufficient set of responses to describe a picture, whether it involves a more sophisticated and in-depth elicitation of NS responses or a deliberate attempt by the researchers at exhaustively describing the images. Moreover, as this work will ideally lead toward a game or ILT, it may be preferable to allow for "partial credit" (and the presentation of feedback) in the case of triples that do not constitute a complete match but may match one or two of the subject, verb, and object.

Similarly, as the correction module relies on the words used by NSs to influence corrections, expanding the list of "influential" words is likely to be beneficial. While in the current study this consisted of a simple list derived from the same responses in the gold standard, this is simply in keeping with (King and Dickinson, 2013) and may not be optimal. A more sophisticated approach could allow this influence to be probabilistic rather than binary, and could rely on methods like TF-IDF to determine which words in NS responses are particularly relevant to the item, and which words are incidental.

Another obvious source of improvement for future work is in the choice of training texts for the LM, which was shown to have serious biases against the contents of the PDT responses, which tend to describe physical actions or scenarios not common in newspaper text. Finding training texts that contain the necessary kinds of sentences but also the sheer volume needed to cover the variability of NNS responses is a challenge for future experiments in this area.

Given that this study primarily investigated transitive verbs, research on this problem will need to examine interactions with other types of constructions, including the definition of more elaborate semantic forms (Hahn and Meurers, 2012). Moving to a wider range of sentence types may require the use of a semantic role labeler or similar tools and has the potential to increase the complexity of spelling correction, due to, e.g., longer sentences.

Acknowledgments

We would like to thank the task participants, David Stringer for assistance in developing the task, and Kathleen Bardovi-Harlig, Marlin Howard and Jayson Deese for help in recruiting participants. We also thank Abigail Elston and Alex Rudnick for their helpful advice during the system development. Finally, for their insightful feedback, we would like to thank the two anonymous reviewers and the attendees of the computational linguistics colloquium series at Indiana University.

References

Atkinson, K. (1998). GNU Aspell. `http://aspell.net`.

Clarkson, P. and Rosenfeld, R. (1997). Statistical language modeling using the CMU-Cambridge Toolkit. In *Eurospeech*, volume 97, pages 2707–2710.

Dale, R., Anisimoff, I., and Narroway, G. (2012). HOO 2012: A report on the preposition and determiner error correction shared task. In *Proceedings of the Seventh Workshop on Building Educational Applications Using NLP*, pages 54–62, Montréal.

de Marneffe, M.-C., MacCartney, B., and Manning, C. D. (2006). Generating typed dependency parses from phrase structure parses. In *Proceedings of LREC 2006*, Genoa, Italy.

DeSmedt, W. (1995). Herr Kommissar: An ICALL conversation simulator for intermediate German. In Holland, V. M., Kaplan, J., and Sams, M., editors, *Intelligent Language Tutors: Theory Shaping Technology*, pages 153–174. Lawrence Erlbaum, Mahwah, NJ.

Ellis, R. (2000). Task-based research and language pedagogy. *Language Teaching Research*, 4(3):193–220.

Fellbaum, C., editor (1998). *WordNet: An Electronic Lexical Database*. The MIT Press, Cambridge, MA.

Flor, M. (2012). Four types of context for automatic spelling correction. *TAL*, 53(2):61–99.

Flor, M. and Futagi, Y. (2012). On using context for automatic correction of non-word misspellings in student essays. In *Proceedings of the Seventh Workshop on Building Educational Applications Using NLP*, pages 105–115. Association for Computational Linguistics.

Flor, M., Futagi, Y., Lopez, M., and Mulholland, M. (2013). Patterns of misspellings in L2 and L1 English: A view from the ETS Spelling Corpus. In *Proceedings of the Second Learner Corpus Research Conference (LCR 2013)*.

Forbes-McKay, K. and Venneri, A. (2005). Detecting subtle spontaneous language decline in early Alzheimer's disease with a picture description task. *Neurological Sciences*, 26(4):243–254.

Graff, D., Kong, J., Chen, K., and Maeda, K. (2007). English Gigaword, Third Edition.

Hahn, M. and Meurers, D. (2012). Evaluating the meaning of answers to reading comprehension questions: A semantics-based approach. In *Proceedings of the 7th Workshop on Innovative Use of NLP for Building Educational Applications (BEA7)*, pages 326–336, Montreal, Canada. Association for Computational Linguistics.

Heift, T. and Schulze, M. (2007). *Errors and Intelligence in Computer-Assisted Language Learning: Parsers and Pedagogues*. Routledge.

Hovermale, D. (2008). SCALE: Spelling Correction Adapted for Learners of English. Pre-CALICO Workshop on "Automatic Analysis of Learner Language: Bridging Foreign Language Teaching Needs and NLP Possibilities". March 18-19, 2008. San Francisco, CA.

Hovermale, D. (2010). An analysis of the spelling errors of L2 English learners. In *CALICO 2010 Conference, Amherst, MA, USA*.

King, L. and Dickinson, M. (2013). Shallow semantic analysis of interactive learner sentences. In *Proceedings of the Eighth Workshop on Innovative Use of NLP for Building Educational Applications*, pages 11–21, Atlanta, Georgia.

Klein, D. and Manning, C. D. (2003). Accurate unlexicalized parsing. In *Proceedings of ACL-03*, Sapporo, Japan.

Lachowicz, D. (2003). Enchant. `http://abisource.com/projects/enchant`.

Leacock, C., Chodorow, M., Gamon, M., and Tetreault, J. (2010). *Automated Grammatical Error Detection for Language Learners*. Synthesis Lectures on Human Language Technologies. Morgan Claypool.

Manning, C. D., Surdeanu, M., Bauer, J., Finkel, J., Bethard, S. J., and McClosky, D. (2014). The Stanford CoreNLP natural language processing toolkit. In *Proceedings of 52nd Annual Meeting of the Association for Computational Linguistics: System Demonstrations*, pages 55–60, Baltimore, Maryland. Association for Computational Linguistics.

Meurers, D. (2012). Natural language processing and language learning. In Chapelle, C. A., editor, *Encyclopedia of Applied Linguistics*. Blackwell.

Meurers, D., Ziai, R., Ott, N., and Bailey, S. (2011). Integrating parallel analysis modules to evaluate the meaning of answers to reading comprehension questions. *Special Issue on Free-text Automatic Evaluation. International Journal of Continuing Engineering Education and Life-Long Learning (IJCEELL)*, 21(4):355–369.

Petersen, K. A. (2010). *Implicit Corrective Feedback in Computer-Guided Interaction: Does Mode Matter?* PhD thesis, Georgetown University, Washington, DC.

Somasundaran, S. and Chodorow, M. (2014). Automated measures of specific vocabulary knowledge from constructed responses ('Use these words to write a sentence based on this picture'). In *Proceedings of the Ninth Workshop on Innovative Use of NLP for Building Educational Applications*, pages 1–11, Baltimore, Maryland.

Sproat, R., Black, A. W., Chen, S., Kumar, S., Ostendorf, M., and Richards, C. (2001). Normalization of non-standard words. *Computer Speech & Language*, 15(3):287–333.

Paraphrase Detection for Short Answer Scoring

Nikolina Koleva, Andrea Horbach, Alexis Palmer, Simon Ostermann, Manfred Pinkal

Saarland University, Saarbrücken, Germany

(nikkol|andrea|apalmer|simono|pinkal)@coli.uni-saarland.de,

ABSTRACT

We describe a system that grades learner answers in reading comprehension tests in the context of foreign language learning. This task, also known as short answer scoring, essentially requires determining whether a semantic entailment relationship holds between an individual learner answer and a target answer; thus semantic information is a necessary part of any automatic short answer scoring system. At the same time the method must be robust to the particularities of learner language. We propose using paraphrase detection, a method that meets both requirements. The basis for our specific paraphrasing method is word alignment learned from parallel corpora which we create from the available data in the CREG corpus (Corpus for Reading Comprehension Exercises for German). We show the usefulness of this kind of information for the task of short answer scoring. Combining our results with existing approaches we obtain an improvement tendency.

KEYWORDS: paraphrase fragments, short answer scoring, reading comprehension.

Nikolina Koleva, Andrea Horbach, Alexis Palmer, Simon Ostermann and Manfred Pinkal 2014. Paraphrase detection for short answer scoring. *Proceedings of the third workshop on NLP for computer-assisted language learning.* NEALT Proceedings Series 22 / Linköping Electronic Conference Proceedings 107: 59–73.

1 Introduction

Reading comprehension exercises are a common means of assessment for language teaching: students read a text in the language they are learning and are then asked to answer questions about the text. Answers to such questions typically consist of one sentence, sometimes two or three. They are graded taking the semantic content into consideration, ignoring spelling or grammatical errors. Developing methods for the automatic scoring of answers (in short: **short answer scoring**) is a task of considerable practical relevance, in particular with regard to the increasing availability of online language courses. At the same time, it is an interesting challenge for computational semantics, and it calls for the use of methods from semantics-focused natural language processing. The short answer scoring (SAS) task stands in a close relationship to the task of recognizing textual entailment (RTE): A correct student answer should entail (ideally, be identical in content with) one of the *target answers*, i.e., the sample solutions created by a teacher. Moreover, the student answer should be entailed by the text.

Figure 1 shows an example of a passage of a reading text, a question about the text, the target answer and both a correct and incorrect learner answer. Note that the first learner answer is graded as correct because it is a paraphrase of the target answer, despite the errors it contains.

<table>
<tr><td rowspan="4">TEXT:

(...)
Sent$_i$: The Hessian government wants to prevent this reform, because "when it comes to apple wine all Hessians agree."
Sent$_{i+1}$: It's easier for other apple wine nations like France or Spain.
Sent$_{i+2}$: There, the beverage is called "Cidre" or "Sidra" and may keep that name, because the term "wine" is not part of the name.
(...)</td><td>QUESTION:
Do other European countries experience similar problems as Hesse. Why?</td></tr>
<tr><td>TARGET ANSWER:
No, [in other apple wine nations like France or Spain the beverage is called "Cidre"] or "Sidra" and may keep that name, because the term "wine" is not part of the name.</td></tr>
<tr><td>LEARNER ANSWER (CORRECT):
No. other countries, like [France or Spain, have other name for apple drinking, like "Cidre".]</td></tr>
<tr><td>LEARNER ANSWER (INCORRECT):
Against - the Hessian government should this reform.</td></tr>
</table>

Figure 1: Example reading text, question, and answers (from CREG, translation by authors). The extracted paraphrase fragments between the target answer and the correct learner answer are in bold-print and square brackets.

In the standard RTE setting, the task is, given a text and a hypothesis sentence, to determine automatically whether the hypothesis is entailed by the text. Of course, there are substantial differences between SAS and the standard RTE setting. Most importantly, the linguistic quality of student answers may be very poor. Answers may be ungrammatical or contain many spelling errors, which makes deep entailment modeling difficult or even completely impossible, as can be seen in the learner answer of figure 1. Also, both the target answers and, in particular, the student answers, have a tendency to keep close to the text surface. Therefore, shallow approaches considering only surface information form a strong baseline. Existing approaches to automatic short answer scoring typically rely on alignments between learner and target answer, mostly using lexical and shallow syntactic information, plus possibly lexical-semantic resources such as WordNet (Fellbaum, 1998), in part with impressively good results (for an overview, see Ziai et al. (2012)).

In the present paper, we describe an approach to short answer scoring that uses semantic information which is easily obtained and robust to learner language and other requirements of the SAS setting. Central to our approach is a method that provides information about paraphrase relations between (parts of) student answer and target answer. We adopt the approach of Wang and Callison-Burch (2011) and Regneri and Wang (2012), who extract sub-sentential paraphrase candidates ("paraphrase fragments") from monolingual parallel corpora, making essential use of GIZA++, a word alignment algorithm originally developed for aligning bilingual parallel texts in Machine Translation (Och and Ney, 2003). The alignment algorithm learns semantic information from the corpus in an unsupervised way, without any labeled training material. Once this semantic information is given, paraphrase fragments are predicted in a robust manner, using no or (in the chunk-based version of the algorithm) only very shallow additional linguistic information. An example for the fragments that are extracted from a learner answer and the corresponding target answer are the bold-print parts of the example in figure 1.

We create a parallel corpus using the Corpus of Reading Comprehension Exercises in German (CREG) (Ott et al., 2012) in a rather straightforward way by providing sentence pairs that consist of e.g. a learner answer and the corresponding target answer. We train a paraphrase fragment recognition system on this corpus following the approach by (Wang and Callison-Burch, 2011). The detected paraphrases are then used to assess the correctness of the learner answers in the CREG corpus. We do so by extracting features from the paraphrase fragments detected between a learner answer and the target answer and use these features as input to a linear regression learner. We consider features that are indicators for the strength of the semantic connection. The rationale is that a learner answer that shares no paraphrase fragment with the target answer is likely to be false, whereas a learner answer – target answer pair whose fragments are strongly linked is likely to involve a correct learner answer.

To our knowledge, we are the first to use automatic paraphrase fragment detection (and associated methods from machine translation) for the short answer scoring task. This method enables access to semantic knowledge in a robust and (almost) unsupervised way which is transferrable to other languages or domains with minimal additional effort. Evaluation on the CREG Corpus shows that information provided by paraphrase detection alone leads to quite good scoring results. More importantly, combining the system with shallow and deep semantic state of the art systems leads to consistent performance gains. A combination of all three systems results in an accuracy of 88.9 %, which surpasses the state of the art and seems to be appropriate for practical application.

The remainder of this paper is structured as follows: we discuss related approaches in section 2, and describe and evaluate paraphrase fragment detection on the CREG corpus in section 3. Section 4 describes and evaluates our use of paraphrases for short answer scoring, after which we conclude.

2 Related Work

Approaches to automatic short answer scoring usually target the grading task by comparing the learner answer to a target answer specified by a teacher. While early systems used handcrafted patterns (Pulman and Sukkarieh, 2005), most systems rely on alignments between learner and target answer, mostly using lexical and syntactic information (Leacock and Chodorow, 2003; Mohler et al., 2011; Meurers et al., 2011a,b), and sometimes explicitly using lexical paraphrase resources such as WordNet (Fellbaum, 1998).

Horbach et al. (2013) include the text as an additional source of information in grading learner answers, by comparing whether learner answer and target answer can be linked to the same text sentence. The restriction to sentence-sized units is one limitation addressed by our approach.

We compare our work to our reimplementation of the alignment-based approach by Meurers et al. (2011b). This model uses alignments on different linguistic levels (like words, lemmas, chunks and dependency triples) to align elements in the learner answer to elements in the target answer. Features (e.g. percentage of aligned tokens/chunks/triples in the learner answer and target answer, percentage of aligned words that are string-identical, lemma-identical, or synonyms, etc.) are then extracted for a machine learner that classifies an answer as correct or incorrect. They report an accuracy of 84.6% on the CREG corpus. Our reimplementation reaches an accuracy of 86.8% using a linear regression classifier.

The only deep semantic approach to short answer scoring known to us is described in Hahn and Meurers (2012). They provide an interesting solution to the robustness problem: as a semantic formalism they use Lexical Resource Semantics (LRS), which is a formalism enabling arbitrary degrees of underspecification, and a syntax-semantic interface using atomic dependency information. In effect, this guarantees that some kind of semantic representation is computed for any (grammatical or ungrammatical) input expression. The LRS representations for target and learner answer are aligned, and alignment features are extracted and used by a classifier. They reach state of the art accuracy of 86.3% on the CREG corpus, with a system that requires hand-coded language-specific semantic knowledge.

A widely used method for paraphrase detection is the extraction of equivalent sentences from either parallel or comparable monolingual corpora (Barzilay and McKeown, 2001; Barzilay and Elhadad, 2003; Quirk et al., 2004). However, for many NLP applications, sentences may turn out to be an impractical unit for paraphrasing, as the situation that two sentences convey exactly the same meaning is rather rare.

Recently, the research focus for paraphrase extraction has therefore been expanded to also consider sub-sentential paraphrase fragments as units of analysis that are not restricted to a particular category. This is done to account for partial semantic overlap between sentences that can be expressed using various types of categories, as e.g. *her preference* vs. *what she prefers*.

Recent approaches to paraphrase fragment extraction include Bannard and Callison-Burch (2005), Zhao et al. (2008) and Wang and Callison-Burch (2011). As pure word matching is not enough to achieve good results, most systems include syntactic information in the form of constituent or dependency structures (Callison-Burch, 2008; Regneri and Wang, 2012).

Gleize and Grau (2013) apply sentential paraphrase identification for scoring student answers. Their method is based on substitution by Basic English variants. They project the actual form of the answers onto a simple language and argue that in this way it is easier to draw inferences. However, by the mapping to the simplified representation not the entire semantic content is transferred. In addition, this method relies on available resources like dictionary and some hand-crafted rules, which is problematic when dealing with low resource languages.

3 Paraphrase Fragment Detection

This section describes our work on detecting paraphrase fragments in the context of reading comprehension exercises for learners of German as a foreign language. After describing the corpus (section 3.1) and method (section 3.2), we present an evaluation and analysis of the paraphrase fragments we detect (section 3.3 and section 3.4).

3.1 Data

We use the Corpus of Reading Comprehension Exercises in German (CREG) (Ott et al., 2012), first for paraphrase fragment detection and later (see section 4) as a testbed for using the extracted fragments in a short answer grading scenario. The corpus consists of *reading texts*, *questions* about the texts, *target answers* provided by teachers and *learner answers* given by German as a Foreign Language learners from two universities in the US; an example appears in figure 1. Each (paper-based) hand-written learner answer has been transcribed by two teachers, resulting in two potentially slightly different transcripts for each learner answer. The learner answers in CREG have also been scored as correct or incorrect by teachers. Following previous work, we use the balanced subset of 1032 learner answers, half correct and half incorrect.

Horbach et al. (2013) extend CREG with a set of annotations linking each target and learner answer to the sentence in the associated reading text that best matches the meaning of an answer and thus is its expected source. These are human annotations, providing a set of *gold text sentences* that we also use in our experiments. In the example in figure 1, both the target answer and the correct learner answer can be linked to sentence $i+1$, while the incorrect learner answer has a link to sentence i.

3.2 Method

Wang and Callison-Burch (2011) and Regneri and Wang (2012) describe a procedure for extracting paraphrase fragments which consists of the following steps: constructing a parallel/comparable corpus, estimating word alignments over this corpus, computing positive and negative lexical associations, refining the alignment and, finally, detecting paraphrases. We follow this general method, customizing some steps to suit the needs of our application context.

For paraphrase fragment detection, we present two versions of our system: *basic*, which uses only word alignments for the detection step, and *chunk-based*, which also makes use of shallow syntactic analysis.

Building a comparable corpus. The aim in building a comparable corpus is to collect pairs of sentences which are likely to contain paraphrase fragments. To build our collection of sentence pairs, we exploit properties of the short answer grading scenario (via the CREG corpus).

Target answers (TA) and (correct) learner answers (LA) are the first, most obvious candidate pairs, as they convey the same meaning. We also include TAs paired with incorrect LAs. Such pairs are sometimes completely unrelated, thus introducing noise to the data, but sometimes they overlap enough to share one or more paraphrase fragments. Our aim is specifically pairs of sentences. In cases where an answer consists of more than one sentence, we include all possible combinations of TA sentence and LA sentence. This expands the number of sentence pairs, but also introduces additional noise.

In order to provide a richer source of lexical variation, we extend the input with pairs consisting of a TA or LA and its corresponding sentence from the reading text: Horbach et al. (2013) describe both human annotations of the best fitting sentence from the reading text for an answer and a procedure for automatically identifying the most closely-linked text sentence. We use both in the experiments described below: the *goldlink condition* uses human annotations, and the *autolink condition* takes the sentence which has the highest alignment weight to the answer when the two sentences are aligned using the method described in (Meurers et al., 2011c).

We thus arrive at an input corpus, consisting of five sub-corpora: TA – *correct* LA, TA – *incorrect* LA, TA – *text sentence*, *correct* LA – *text sentence*, *incorrect* LA – *text sentence*.

We increase the training material available by boosting the corpus in several ways. First, to emphasize the importance of lexical identity for learning word alignments, we add trivially-identical pairs: each reading text sentence paired with itself, and each word in the CREG corpus vocabulary, also paired with itself. Additionally, we repeat non-identical sentence pairs, with the number of repetitions linked to the nature of the sub-corpus in which the pair appears. We have also begun experiments adding word pairs from GermaNet (Hamp and Feldweg, 1997), in order to learn lexical paraphrases, but the results reported here do not include GermaNet-based boosting.

For intrinsic evaluation of the detected paraphrase fragments (Section 3.3), we aim to reduce noise in the data and emphasize reliable sentence pairs. Accordingly, each pair involving correct LAs, as well as those with TAs and text sentences, is copied 10 times. Pairs involving incorrect LAs appear just one time. The trivially-identical pairs are entered 10 times for sentences and 20 times for word pairs.

Preprocessing. To prepare the data for word alignment, we apply a standard linguistic preprocessing toolchain, consisting of sentence segmentation using `OpenNLP`,[1] tokenization with the `Stanford Tokenizer`,[2] lemmatization and part-of-speech (POS) tagging, both using the `TreeTagger` (Schmid, 1995). We use the `Stanford Named Entity Recognizer`[3] to identify persons, organizations, locations and dates. For robustness against grammatical errors and to reduce vocabulary size, all tokens are replaced with their lemmatized forms. We replace all occurrences of NEs with the corresponding NE-tag (e.g. *PERSON*).

Learner answers frequently contain spelling errors. We treat them in the following way: we run all the learner answers through the German version of the spellchecker `aspell`[4] and check for non-words. For those non-words we first look up whether the word is nevertheless a correct word (like a proper name) from the connected material (target answer, question, text) that is for some reason not known to `aspell`. If that is not the case we look for a spelling alternative in the connected material, i.e. we check whether a token with a levenshtein distance up to a certain threshold occurs (in that order) either in the target answer, the question, or the text. If so, we replace the non-word learner answer token by this word.

Detecting paraphrase fragments. Following previous work (Wang and Callison-Burch, 2011; Regneri and Wang, 2012), we pass our input corpus to GIZA++ (Och and Ney, 2003) in order to: (a) estimate word alignments for input sentence pairs, and (b) obtain a lexical correspondence table with scores for individual word pairs.

Links between aligned words in the sentence pairs are then classified as positive or negative based on their scores, a technique which has previously been applied to extract paraphrase fragments from non-parallel bilingual corpora and has been shown to improve a state of the art machine translation system (Munteanu and Marcu, 2006). Word pairs containing punctuation or stop words are excluded from the alignment prior to scoring.[5]

Afterwards, the alignment is refined by removing all negatively-scored word pairs, such that only very strong alignments survive. We then smooth the alignment by recomputing scores for each word, averaging over a window of five words. In this way we often capture context words

[1] http://opennlp.apache.org/
[2] http://nlp.stanford.edu/software/tokenizer.shtml
[3] http://nlp.stanford.edu/software/CRF-NER.shtml
[4] http://aspell.net/
[5] http://www.ranks.nl/stopwords/german.html

that are left out of the alignment process (e.g. determiners, prepositions, or particles) but are nonetheless necessary for producing linguistically well-formed fragments.

For the *basic* version, a source-side fragment is detected by extracting sequences of adjacent words with positive scores after smoothing. The corresponding target-side fragment is induced using one of two methods: The *unidirectional* approach finds the target fragment by using the lexical scores for the source side plus alignment links to the target side. In the *bidirectional* approach, we also compute lexical scores for the target side and extract target-side fragments in that manner.

Despite the use of smoothing for producing more grammatical fragments, the basic approach often produces output of questionable readability, e.g. "hm, so" is a fragment that lacks context in order to understand the intended semantic content. Especially if these fragments might be used to give feedback to learners, it is important to produce readable output. This is the motivation for the second version of the system.

In the *chunk-based* version we reset the boundaries of the basic fragments in a post-processing step by taking syntactic chunk information into consideration. If a fragment has some overlap with a chunk, then the remainder of that chunk is also included in the fragment. We also apply some heuristics to account for aspects of the German language: e.g. prefixes of separable verbs and past participles often appear in sentence-final position and should be covered by the fragment.

The fragment extracted from the source sentence is the same for all configurations but the target fragment differs. Example (1) illustrates the difference of fragments extracted by the unidirectional vs. bidirectional method and example (2) the one of basic vs. chunk based.

(1) **source fragment**: in front of the PC or the TV
target fragments:
`uni`: with the PC or the TV
`bi`: all time with the the PC or the TV

(2) **source fragment**: in vegetable garden one has to chop and water
target fragments:
`basic`: in vegetable garden chop and waterz
`chunk`: one can chop and water in vegetable garden

An interesting observation is that the bidirectional method tends to be too greedy. Target fragments returned with it contain additional information that has no corresponding part on the source side. The chunk-based system is useful because it augments a fragment but also slightly modifies its semantic content.

3.3 Intrinsic Evaluation of Detected Paraphrases

To evaluate precision of the extracted paraphrases, we again follow Wang and Callison-Burch (2011) and Regneri and Wang (2012). For each of the two systems, 300 fragment pairs are randomly extracted, half with the unidirectional version and half with the bidirectional. These are evenly distributed across LA-TA pairs and answer-text sentence pairs. Each fragment is labeled by two annotators with one of four categories: paraphrase, related, unrelated, or invalid. The label *related* is assigned when there is overlap between the two fragments, but they are not

	unidirectional	bidirectional
basic	0.78	0.74
chunk-based	0.69	0.71

Table 2: Precision of paraphrase fragment detection

paraphrases, and *invalid* is assigned if one or both fragments are completely ungrammatical or not readable. Annotators were not told the type of the sentence pair, and they were instructed to ignore spelling and grammatical errors in evaluating paraphrases.
Table 1 shows the inter-annotator agreement in 2 conditions: if we consider all 4 labels separately, and if we instead merge *paraphrase* and *related* as well as *unrelated* and *invalid*. Results are along the lines of (Regneri and Wang, 2012) who report Kappa values of 0.55 for four-label annotation and 0.71 for a two-label condition. Our basic system shows worse agreement than the chunk-based. This is due to the fact that basic fragments are often linguistically not well-formed and are therefore harder to annotate. For the final gold-standard, all conflicts have been resolved by a third annotator.

	4 categories	2 categories
basic	0.22 (fair)	0.69 (good)
chunk-based	0.52 (moderate)	0.84 (very good)

Table 1: Inter-annotator-agreement

This gold-standard annotation is then used for evaluating the quality of the fragments. For measuring the precision of the extracted paraphrases, i.e. for measuring what percentage of the fragment pairs identified should be considered as paraphrases or related, we use the two-label condition. Results are presented in table 2. Precision on our dataset is in the same range as that reported by Wang and Callison-Burch (2011) (62 to 67%) on a monolingual comparable corpus. Note however that this evaluation covers only a very small dataset as compared to the overall parallel corpus. Overall the performance of the basic system is better than the chunk-based. This is an unexpected result because the chunk-based system was developed specifically to improve the quality of the basic fragments. However, missing tokens like prepositions that are added to a fragment by the chunk system can change its meaning and as a consequence the fragments are no longer related.

Between the unidirectional and bidirectional approaches there is no stastically significant difference, according to a chi-squared test (Pearson, 1900).

For the application of the extracted paraphrase fragments to short answer scoring, the unidirectional approach is used, because it gave us the best results for the generally better *basic* version of the system.

We expect variability across correct and incorrect answers, because in scoring a learner answer, strict paraphrases are not always necessary. For example a question in the corpus asking "*Wer war an der Tür*" (*Who was by the door?*) with the target answer "*Drei Soldaten (three soldiers) waren an der Tür*" the learner answer "*Drei Männer (three men) waren an der Tür*", although less specific, was also graded as correct by the teachers. To investigate this variability, we look at the distribution of the four categories across the various subcorpora.

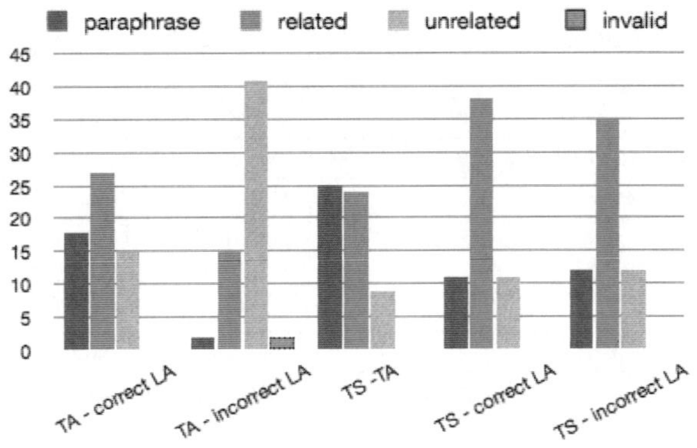

Figure 2: Distribution of annotation labels for the five subcorpora. TA stands for target answer, LA for learner answer and TS for the corresponding text sentence.

sub-corpus	productivity in %
`ta-corr la`	95
`ta-incorr la`	**78**
`textSent-ta`	95
`textSent-corr la`	94
`textSent-incorr la`	92
total	91

Table 3: Productivity by subcorpus

Figure 2 depicts the distribution of the labels – exemplarily for the chunk-based version – showing how often each annotation label occured within the five subcorpora TA – *correct* LA, TA – *incorrect* LA, TA – *text sentence*, *correct* LA – *text sentence*, *incorrect* LA – *text sentence*. We can see that correct learner answers lead to more paraphrases of the target answer (18) than do incorrect learner answers (2). Incorrect learner answers, however, have a much higher degree of unrelated fragments with the target answer (41 vs 15). Correctness has not much influence on the validity. In the subcorpora involving text sentences, both correct and incorrect learner answers have a similarly high degree of paraphrase and related cases. That is the case because both correct and incorrect learner answers are often paraphrases of some part of the text. In the case of an correct answer, the target answer is often a paraphrase of the same text sentences as the text sentence for the learner answer, in the case of an incorrect learner answer, the student often erroneously paraphrased a text sentence that has nothing to do with the correct answer.

3.4 Analysis of the Detected Fragments

This section presents continued analysis of the detected fragments from various subcorpora, covering productivity and variability of lexical material.

Productivity of the Detected Fragments

Table 3 shows productivity by subcorpus, measured by how often at least one fragment pair is detected per input sentence pair. As expected, productivity is lowest for incorrect LAs paired with TAs. Incorrect LAs paired with text sentences, however, show productivity similar to other

	source	target
1	Die Stadtverwaltung sagt nein	Die Stadtverwaltung ist dagegen
2	kein glücklisches Ende	ein schlechte Ende
3	die Broadway-Version erhielt sechs Tonys	Es hat sechs Tonys gewonnen
4	Damit lachen die anderen Kinder sie ja aus	die anderen Kinder lachen Julchen aus
5	darf nicht mehr verwendet werden	dann nicht mehr erlaubt
6	Die Leute wissen *nicht* ihre genauen monatlichen Ausgaben	die meisten Leute wissen wie eine Budgetplan zu machen
7	in einem *Neu*bau	in einem *Alt*bau
8	würde mit *Computer* arbeiten	würde mit *Wissenschaftlerin* arbeiten
9	[Nicht, sagten die Augen] der Frau, nicht lachen	[Er sollte nicht] lachen, weil das Kind [schlief]

Table 4: Fragments output with the `unidirectional` method for the *chunk-based* system

subcorpora. This is not surprising, as incorrect learner answers often stem from some part of the text (Horbach et al., 2013), although not necessarily the same as the target answer.

Lexical Variety of the Detected Paraphrases

In many cases, there are only minor differences between learner answers and target answers. Inspection of the data shows that our approach detects real paraphrase fragments, beyond the trivial case of identical spans of text in paired sentences.

To evaluate lexical variety, we measure the degree of lemma overlap between sentence pairs and fragment pairs. Figure 3 shows that there is a significantly higher overlap between paraphrase pairs than between sentences, but on the other hand, the overlap is not so extensive that it makes the paraphrase detection task trivial.

Table 4 shows example fragments detected by the chunk-based, unidirectional method. The qualitative analysis shows that non-identical material contained in the fragments often captures alternative expressions of the same semantic content. However, we can see that the method would benefit from handling of phenomena such as negation, antonymy, or relatedness between nouns or other content words.

Fragment pair 7 illustrates the difficulty faced in cases where antonymy is present. The compound words "Altbau" and "Neubau" both carry the main meaning of a building (*der Bau*) and are therefore related, but the modifying words "alt" and "neu" (*old* and *new*) are antonyms.

Fragment pair 8 highlights the problem that word alignments like *Computer-Wissenschaftlerin (scientist)* are learned, even though they are not valid paraphrases and the word *Wissenschaftlerin* only occurs in incorrect answers. This happens in cases when an input sentence pair shares many identical words, and one or more non-identical words that occur very infrequently (or even nowhere else) in the corpus. In such a case, GIZA++ learns strong alignments between the identical words and also between the two unrelated words, as there are no other options for linking those words.

The last fragment pair 9 shows an example of unrelated fragments, which are probably (mistakenly) classified as paraphrases because of the high token overlap.

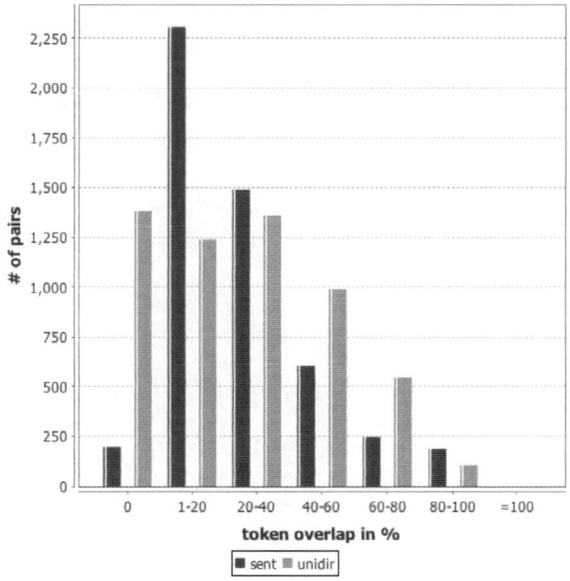

Figure 3: Percentage of identical tokens in sentence pairs (sent) and fragment pairs (unidir)

4 Short Answer Scoring

We use the results of the paraphrase fragment detection (section 3) as the basis for automatic short answer scoring. In this section we describe our method (section 4.1) and evaluate it on the CREG corpus (section 4.2).

4.1 Method

We base the assessment of the correctness of the learner answer on the paraphrase relation between learner answer and target answer. We take the case when no paraphrase is found to be strong evidence against correctness. If a paraphrase pair is detected, we want to make the scoring decision dependent on properties of the single paraphrases and their interrelation. Technically, we use a binary classifier, which bases its prediction on features extracted from the paraphrase fragments. Concretely, we employ the linear regression classifier from the Weka Toolkit (Witten and Frank, 2005).

As outlined in the introduction, we employ different modes to identify pairs of LA and TA paraphrases: In the direct mode, we directly determine a TA-LA paraphrase pair based on the alignment between LA and TA. In the indirect mode, we pair each of LA and TA with a text sentence (these may be identical or different sentences), independently derive paraphrase pairs for LA with text sentence and TA with text sentence, respectively, which in the success case gives us a TA-LA paraphrase pair obtained in an indirect way. We assume that the indirect mode provides additional information through the relatedness between LA, TA, and the text.

For each of the two comparison modes a set of features is extracted, which provide information about the relation between the paraphrase fragments f_1 and f_2, which are extracted from a sentence pair s_1 and s_2 or about single fragments.

The following features are considered:

1. token overlap: jaccard coefficient $J(tokens(f_1), tokens(f_2)) = \frac{|tokens(f_1) \cap tokens(f_2)|}{|tokens(f_1) \cup tokens(f_2)|}$, 0 if there are no fragments
2. difference in fragment length $|f_1 - f_2|$, -1 if there are no fragments
3. percentage of tokens in the s_1 covered by f_1
4. percentage of tokens in the s_2 covered by the f_2
5. average of lexical scores for the target answer (resulting from word alignment)

Because we use the unidirectional alignment version and take the text sentence to be the source sentence, only lexical scores for the text sentences are computed in the indirect case. Therefore the fifth feature is not available in the indirect mode.

4.2 Evaluation

We compare our approach to both the alignment model (as in (Meurers et al., 2011b; Horbach et al., 2013)) and the deep semantic model by (Hahn and Meurers, 2012). We re-implement the alignment model using features for token and chunk alignment reaching an accuracy of 86.8% on the CREG corpus (compared to 84.6% in the (Meurers et al., 2011b) model). The deep semantic model reaches an accuracy of 86.3%, also on the CREG data. We make direct comparison against these two scores; a random baseline for this balanced data set is 50%.

We evaluate using tenfold cross-validation, running the complete paraphrase fragment detection method (Section 3) on nine folds for training. For the test corpus, of course, we don't know ahead of time whether answers are correct or not. Thus we build our input corpus without taking advantage of this information. In this setting, each pair involving a LA or TA is included 10 times, regardless of the answer's correctness.

We evaluate our model alone and using additional features from the other two models, as is shown in table 5: In order to see the contribution of the direct and indirect feature sets, we evaluate those sets individually (*paraphrases direct* and *paraphrases indirect*) and together (*paraphrases combined*). For combining with the other models, we always use the combined set of paraphrase features.

To evaluate our model in combination with the alignment model (*paraphrases + aligment system*), we add the features from our reimplementation. We also combine our model with both of the other two models (*paraphrases + aligment model + deep semantics*), using the semantic scores obtained by Hahn and Meurers (2012) as an additional feature.

Evaluation Corpus	paraphrases direct	paraphrases indirect	paraphrases combined	paraphrases + alignment	paraphrases + deepSemScore	paraphrases + deepSemScore + Alignment	alignment + deepSemScore
autolink - basic	76.9	70.6	78.3	86.5	86.9	87.7	87.5
autolink - chunk	76.8	70.1	77.1	86.4	86.7	88.1	87.5
goldlink - basic	77.5	72.8	77.6	86.5	87.0	88.1	87.5
goldlink - chunk	76.6	72.1	77.4	86.7	87.1	**88.9**	87.5

Table 5: Accuracy on CREG balanced corpus with various model combinations

Table 5 summarizes our results: We can see that our system alone, while being far from reaching the state of the art, can reasonably differentiate between correct and incorrect answers. The direct comparison of learner answer and target answer (*paraphrases direct*) works better than just the indirect comparison via fragments obtained from alignment with the text. In combination, the indirect features still contribute to the performance *paraphrases combined*, although not in a statistically significant way.

When combining the paraphrase features with the features from the alignment system, we don't get an improvement over the alignment system (86.8%). When additionally adding the semantic score to both feature sets, we reach our best result with an accuracy of 88.9% which is not significantly better (α=0.25 according to a McNemar test) than the comparison figure of 86.8%.

When comparing the *goldlink* to the *autolink* condition, we see an advantage of having the optimal information about the best matching sentence in the indirect feature set.

There is no clear trend as to whether the *basic* or the *chunk-based* system performs better. The paraphrase fragments model on its own is not good enough to beat the other methods. However, combining the three systems gives an improvement of 2.1%, which is an indication of complementary information provided by the different feature sets.

5 Conclusion

In this paper we have presented the first approach which uses paraphrase information for automatically scoring short answers. We successfully adapt a paraphrase fragment extraction method to the new domain of reading comprehension data for learning German as a foreign language. In this way we frame the short answer scoring task with respect to semantic information that is robust to noise in the input. Because of this robustness, and because of its (nearly) unsupervised nature, the approach is readily adaptable for other languages or domains. We obtain good scoring results using detected paraphrases, and when we combine our method with shallow and deep semantic systems, we surpass the state of the art on the CREG corpus.

We see three obvious extensions for future research. First, paraphrase fragments detected between target and learner answers, or between learner answers and the reading text, could be very useful in practical applications, such as providing direct feedback to language learners. This could be done by highlighting for a learner the paraphrased regions of his answer and, more importantly, those which do not stand in such a semantic relationship to the target answer or the text. Second, we are interested in investigating the influence of information structure on scoring; fragments which cover information from the question should receive less weight than fragments which offer new information, and our fragment detection method is one way of making such distinctions. Finally, our method can be adapted to handle online input, computing alignments based on previously-existing lexical correspondence tables and in this way providing immediate output for new learner answers.

References

Bannard, C. and Callison-Burch, C. (2005). Paraphrasing with bilingual parallel corpora. In *Proceedings of the 43rd Annual Meeting of the ACL'05*, pages 597–604.

Barzilay, R. and Elhadad, N. (2003). Sentence alignment for monolingual comparable corpora. In Collins, M. and Steedman, M., editors, *Proceedings of the 2003 Conference on Empirical Methods in Natural Language Processing*, pages 25–32.

Barzilay, R. and McKeown, K. R. (2001). Extracting paraphrases from a parallel corpus. In *Proceedings of 39th Annual Meeting of the Association for Computational Linguistics*, pages 50–57, Toulouse, France. Association for Computational Linguistics.

Callison-Burch, C. (2008). Syntactic constraints on paraphrases extracted from parallel corpora. In *Proceedings of the 2008 Conference on Empirical Methods in Natural Language Processing*, pages 196–205, Honolulu, Hawaii. Association for Computational Linguistics.

Fellbaum, C. (1998). *WordNet: An Electronic Lexical Database*. Bradford Books.

Gleize, M. and Grau, B. (2013). Limsiiles: Basic english substitution for student answer assessment at semeval 2013. In **SEM, Volume 2: Proceedings of SemEval 2013*, pages 598–602, Atlanta, Georgia, USA. Association for Computational Linguistics.

Hahn, M. and Meurers, D. (2012). Evaluating the meaning of answers to reading comprehension questions: A semantics-based approach. In *Proceedings of the 7th Workshop on Innovative Use of NLP for Building Educational Applications (BEA7)*, pages 326–336, Montreal, Canada. Association for Computational Linguistics.

Hamp, B. and Feldweg, H. (1997). Germanet - a lexical-semantic net for German. In *In Proceedings of ACL workshop Automatic Information Extraction and Building of Lexical Semantic Resources for NLP Applications*, pages 9–15.

Horbach, A., Palmer, A., and Pinkal, M. (2013). Using the text to evaluate short answers for reading comprehension exercises. In **SEM, Volume 1: Proceedings of the Main Conference and the Shared Task: Semantic Textual Similarity*, pages 286–295, Atlanta, Georgia, USA. Association for Computational Linguistics.

Leacock, C. and Chodorow, M. (2003). C-rater: Automated scoring of short-answer questions. *Computers and the Humanities*, 37(4):389–405.

Meurers, D., Ziai, R., Ott, N., and Bailey, S. (2011a). Integrating parallel analysis modules to evaluate the meaning of answers to reading comprehension questions. *Special Issue on Free-text Automatic Evaluation. International Journal of Continuing Engineering Education and Life-Long Learning (IJCEELL)*, 21(4):355–369.

Meurers, D., Ziai, R., Ott, N., and Kopp, J. (2011b). Evaluating answers to reading comprehension questions in context: Results for German and the role of information structure. In *Proceedings of the TextInfer 2011 Workshop on Textual Entailment*, pages 1–9, Edinburgh, Scotland, UK.

Meurers, D., Ziai, R., Ott, N., and Kopp, J. (2011c). Evaluating answers to reading comprehension questions in context: Results for German and the role of information structure. In *Proceedings of the TextInfer 2011 Workshop on Textual Entailment*, pages 1–9, Edinburgh, Scotland, UK. Association for Computational Linguistics.

Mohler, M., Bunescu, R. C., and Mihalcea, R. (2011). Learning to grade short answer questions using semantic similarity measures and dependency graph alignments. In Lin, D., Matsumoto, Y., and Mihalcea, R., editors, *ACL*, pages 752–762.

Munteanu, D. S. and Marcu, D. (2006). Extracting parallel sub-sentential fragments from non-parallel corpora. In *Proceedings of the 21st International Conference on Computational Linguistics and the 44th annual meeting of the ACL*, pages 81–88, Stroudsburg, PA, USA. ACL.

Och, F. J. and Ney, H. (2003). A systematic comparison of various statistical alignment models. *Comput. Linguist.*, 29(1):19–51.

Ott, N., Ziai, R., and Meurers, D. (2012). Creation and analysis of a reading comprehension exercise corpus: Towards evaluating meaning in context. In Schmidt, T. and Wörner, K., editors, *Multilingual Corpora and Multilingual Corpus Analysis*, Hamburg Studies in Multilingualism (HSM), pages 47–69. Benjamins, Amsterdam.

Pearson, K. (1900). On the criterion that a given system of deviations from the probable in the case of a correlated system of variables is such that can be reasonably supposed to have arisen from random sampling. *Philosophical Magazine*, 50:157–175.

Pulman, S. G. and Sukkarieh, J. Z. (2005). Automatic short answer marking. In *Proceedings of the second workshop on Building Educational Applications Using NLP*, EdAppsNLP 05, pages 9–16.

Quirk, C., Brockett, C., and Dolan, W. (2004). Monolingual machine translation for paraphrase generation. In Lin, D. and Wu, D., editors, *Proceedings of EMNLP 2004*, pages 142–149, Barcelona, Spain. Association for Computational Linguistics.

Regneri, M. and Wang, R. (2012). Using discourse information for paraphrase extraction. In *Proceedings of EMNLP-CoNNL 2012*, Jeju, Korea.

Schmid, H. (1995). Improvements in part-of-speech tagging with an application to German. In *In Proceedings of the ACL SIGDAT-Workshop*, pages 47–50.

Wang, R. and Callison-Burch, C. (2011). Paraphrase fragment extraction from monolingual comparable corpora. In *Proceedings of the 4th Workshop on Building and Comparable Corpora: Comparable Corpora and the Web*, pages 52–60, Portland, Oregon. ACL.

Witten, I. H. and Frank, E. (2005). *Data Mining: Practical Machine Learning Tools and Techniques*. Morgan Kaufmann, San Francisco, 2nd edition.

Zhao, S., Wang, H., Liu, T., and Li, S. (2008). Pivot approach for extracting paraphrase patterns from bilingual corpora. In *Proceedings of ACL-08: HLT*, pages 780–788, Columbus, Ohio. Association for Computational Linguistics.

Ziai, R., Ott, N., and Meurers, D. (2012). Short answer assessment: Establishing links between research strands. In *Proceedings of the 7th Workshop on Innovative Use of NLP for Building Educational Applications (BEA7)*, Montreal, Canada.

An approach to measure pronunciation similarity in second language learning using radial basis function kernel

Christos Koniaris

University of Gothenburg, Centre for Language Technology
Department of Philosophy, Linguistics and Theory of Science
Dialogue Technology Lab, Gothenburg, Sweden

christos.koniaris@gu.se

ABSTRACT

This paper shows a method to diagnose potential mispronunciations in second language learning by studying the characteristics of the speech produced by a group of native speakers and the speech produced by various non-native groups of speakers from diverse language backgrounds. The method compares the native auditory perception and the non-native spectral representation on the phoneme level using similarity measures that are based on the radial basis function kernel. A list of ordered problematic phonemes is found for each non-native group of speakers and the results are analyzed based on a relevant linguistic survey found in the literature. The experimental results indicate an agreement with linguistic findings of up to 80.8% for vowels and 80.3% for consonants.

KEYWORDS: pronunciation error detection, similarity measure, radial basis function kernel, phoneme, second language learning.

Christos Koniaris 2014. An approach to measure pronunciation similarity in second language learning using radial basis function kernel. *Proceedings of the third workshop on NLP for computer-assisted language learning.* NEALT Proceedings Series 22 / Linköping Electronic Conference Proceedings 107: 74–86.

1 Introduction

Second language (L2) speakers are generally having trouble with certain phonemes of the target language that do not exist in the sound system of their native language (Flege, 1995; Guion et al., 2000). It is therefore common practice to include speech sounds from their first language (L1) or ignore unfamiliar ones (Piske et al., 2001) while practicing a new language. Within a computer-assisted language learning (CALL) program, the task of automatic *pronunciation error detection* (PED) is to find effective techniques to diagnose and detect mispronunciations in order to assist L2 learners to improve their oral capabilities.

In (Neumeyer et al., 1996; Franco et al., 1997; Neumeyer et al., 2000) a system used for performing automatic speech recognition (ASR) is turned into an automatic pronunciation scoring system, in which several different scores, e.g., hidden Markov models (HMM) phone log-likelihood, are compared to human listeners' evaluation. The experiments show that certain scores, such as the log-posterior and the normalized duration correlate well with human ratings. Scoring is also the main characteristic of the goodness of pronunciation (GOP) proposed in (Witt and Young, 2000), which measures the quality of pronunciations of non-native speakers. The idea is to score each phone of an utterance depending on how close the pronunciation of the non-native speaker is to that of native speakers. A method that combines knowledge from acoustic-phonetic, linguistic, and from expert listeners is presented in (Park and Rhee, 2004), in which the analysis of the results is done by finding the correlation of human listeners and machine-based rating. In (Truong et al., 2005), a set of classification approaches based on linear discriminant analysis (LDA) and decision trees is presented. These classifiers are used to analyze the mispronunciations of second language learners of Dutch. In (Tepperman and Narayanan, 2008), the research is oriented in introducing articulatory information in PED by reformulating the hidden-articulator Markov models (HAMM) (Tepperman and Narayanan, 2005) and deriving new articulatory-based features for classification. In (Strik et al., 2009), four different classification systems are examined: a GOP-based, one combining cepstral coefficients and LDA, a method based on the work described in (Weigelt et al., 1990), which is an algorithm that discriminates voiceless fricatives from voiceless plosives, and an LDA-acoustic-phonetic feature classifier. It is found that the two LDA-based classification systems perform better in mispronunciation detection. In (Wei et al., 2009), the authors use support vector machines (SVM) to model phones with several parallel acoustic models that represent the variation in pronunciation at various proficiency levels. This approach seems to achieve better results in comparison to more traditional posterior probability based methods.

Since the pronunciation of a phone is not only related to its acoustics, aspects, such as fluency, syllable structure, word stress, intonation, prosody or segmental quality may also be considered for investigation of pronunciation errors. For example, the work that is presented in (Delmonte, 2000) concerns a prosodic module of a CALL system called SLIM. This module deals with phonetic and prosodic problems both at the word but also at the segmental level. Prosodic measures based on F0, power and duration of L2 and L1 speech are used in (Yamashita et al., 2005) within a multiple regression framework to predict the prosodic proficiency of L2 learners. In (Raux and Kawahara, 2002), a probabilistic algorithm is applied to derive intelligibility from error rates and also define a function of error priority to indicate which errors are most critical to intelligibility. Finally, in (Xu et al., 2009), linguistic knowledge obtained from the non-native speakers' most common mistakes, and pronunciation space constructed using revised log-posterior probability vectors is considered along with an SVM classifier.

In this paper, a PED method based on psychoacoustic knowledge from a spectral auditory model (van de Par et al., 2002) is presented that models the native perception to evaluate non-native pronunciations based on acoustic and auditory processing of the speech sounds. The fundamental assumption is based on the ability of the human auditory system to distinguish speech sounds of various type. The method compares the acoustic and auditory-perceptual characteristics of uttered phones on a frame-by-frame basis. In doing so, it utilizes a similarity measure based on radial basis function kernel or RBF kernel, which is compared with a Euclidean distance measure that was used in (Koniaris and Engwall, 2011; Koniaris et al., 2013). The motivation for this arrives from the fact that the data become sparse in a high dimensional space and hence choosing RBF kernel seems a more suitable solution since it is considered more appropriate for such conditions (Braun et al., 2008). Roughly speaking, the method performs a comparison between speech sounds generated by a group of native speakers with the corresponding speech sounds generated by different L2 groups of speakers. This is done separately for each phoneme category and the uttered phones are transformed into their auditory representations for the native speech, and into their spectrum representations for the non-native speech. In each domain, a distortion measure based on the RBF kernel is computed for each speech frame and then the two distortion measures are explored – considering all the frames – to investigate, quantitatively, the similarities between the native and the non-native phones.

The paper is organized as follows. Section 2 presents the method and implementation issues, Section 3 discusses the experiments and the findings and finally Section 4 provides conclusions.

2 Method

The underlying idea behind the pronunciation error detection method that is described here is based on the auditory ability of a native speaker to discriminate the mispronounced phonemes produced by L2 speakers while hearing them speaking. The diagnostic evaluation of the pronunciation errors is done on the speech signal level by comparing the similarities between the auditory perceptual domain of the native speech and the power spectrum domain of the non-native speech. It is assumed that a non-native acoustic representation will have very similar characteristics to native provided that the non-native speech is produced without significant mispronunciation. On the other hand, if the non-native speech suffers from severe pronunciation errors then the two representations, of the L2 and L1 speakers, will differ a lot and thus the measured similarities will become minimal (Koniaris et al., 2013).

In short, the approach tries to measure the distortion in a set of phones that belong to a specific phoneme, produced by a group of native speakers n and compare it to that of non-native speakers of some specific language background ℓ. For this, it is assumed that some form of acoustic representation $\mathbf{x}$ is extracted from the speech signal $\mathbf{s}$ of a phone $\mathbf{p}$ to evaluate the distortion measure ϕ in the corresponding transformed domain, where $\phi : \mathbb{R}^N \times \mathbb{R}^N \rightarrow \mathbb{R}^+$, with $\mathbb{R}^+$ denoting the non-negative real numbers and N indicating the dimensionality of the vector $\mathbf{x}$. Then, the RBF kernel-based similarity measure is,

$$\phi(\mathbf{s}_i, \hat{\mathbf{s}}_{i,j}) = e^{\gamma \|\mathbf{x}(\mathbf{s}_i) - \mathbf{x}(\hat{\mathbf{s}}_{i,j})\|^2}, \tag{1}$$

where $i \in \mathbb{Z}$ is the index of the considered speech frame, $\hat{\mathbf{s}}_{i,j}$ is the j'th perturbation of $\mathbf{s}_i$ that is used to compute distortion and $\gamma = -\frac{1}{2\sigma^2}$. It is noted that σ will determine the size of the considered area around $\mathbf{s}_i$. An analogous measure is defined for the auditory perception domain where the speech signal is transformed into the auditory model output representation $\mathbf{y}$. Again, a RBF kernel-based distortion measure is computed in the auditory domain $\upsilon : \mathbb{R}^M \times \mathbb{R}^M \rightarrow \mathbb{R}^+$, where M is the dimensionality of the internal representation $\mathbf{y}$, as

$$\upsilon(\mathbf{s}_i, \hat{\mathbf{s}}_{i,j}) = e^{\gamma \|\mathbf{y}(\mathbf{s}_i) - \mathbf{y}(\hat{\mathbf{s}}_{i,j})\|^2}. \tag{2}$$

The above distortion measures of Eqs. (1) and (2) are then compared using the following similarity measure

$$\mathscr{A} = \frac{1}{\mathscr{I}} \sum_{i \in \mathscr{I}} \frac{1}{\mathscr{J}_i} \sum_{j \in \mathscr{J}_i} \left[\upsilon(\mathbf{s}_i, \hat{\mathbf{s}}_{i,j}) - \phi(\mathbf{s}_i, \hat{\mathbf{s}}_{i,j})\right]^2, \tag{3}$$

where $i \in \mathscr{I}$ and $j \in \mathscr{J}_i$ represent a finite frame sequence and a finite set of acoustic perturbations, respectively. This measure is used to find mispronunciations as described in (Koniaris et al., 2013), i.e., by computing the distortion measure $\upsilon(\mathbf{s}_i, \hat{\mathbf{s}}_{i,j})$ using only native speech and the spectral distortion measure $\phi(\mathbf{s}_i, \hat{\mathbf{s}}_{i,j})$, calculated separately for non-native (and thus computing $\mathscr{A}_\ell$) and native speech (and thus computing $\mathscr{A}_n$). Finally, the *native-perceptual assessment degree (nPAD)* is computed for every phoneme and L1 background as

$$nPAD = \frac{\mathscr{A}_\ell}{\mathscr{A}_n}, \tag{4}$$

which is a normalized ratio that shows the degree of the similarity between the native perceptual outcome and the non-native speech signal representation, as compared to the native-only case. The higher the nPAD value is, the more problematic the L2 phoneme is.

2.1 Practical implementation

Considering $\mathbf{p}$ to be a phone that a speaker has produced, the speech power spectrum $\mathbf{x}(\mathbf{p})$ can be seen simply as a function of $\mathbf{p}$ that maps this phone onto the spectral domain. If additionally is considered a small area around $\mathbf{p}$, a local approximation is possible using the Taylor series expansion, thus

$$\mathbf{x}(\hat{\mathbf{p}}) \approx \mathbf{x}(\mathbf{p}) + \mathbf{J}_\mathbf{x}[\hat{\mathbf{p}} - \mathbf{p}], \tag{5}$$

where $\mathbf{J}_\mathbf{x} = \left.\frac{\partial \mathbf{x}(\mathbf{p})}{\partial \hat{\mathbf{p}}}\right|_{\hat{\mathbf{p}}=\mathbf{p}}$ and $\hat{\mathbf{p}}$ is the perturbed phone. Assuming that the small distortion $[\hat{\mathbf{p}} - \mathbf{p}]$ remains the same independently of the language background of the speaker, Eq. (5) can be used either for native speech $\mathbf{x}_n$ or non-native speech $\mathbf{x}_\ell$ of a language background ℓ. This means that is possible to find a linearized relation between these two and compute the speech power spectrum distortion in a non-native subspace into the native speech power spectrum domain. Thus,

$$\mathbf{x}_\ell(\hat{\mathbf{p}}) \approx \mathbf{x}_\ell(\mathbf{p}) + \mathbf{W}_\ell\,[\mathbf{x}_n(\hat{\mathbf{p}}) - \mathbf{x}_n(\mathbf{p})], \tag{6}$$

where $\mathbf{W}_\ell = \mathbf{J}_{\mathbf{x}\ell}\,[\mathbf{J}_{\mathbf{x}n}]^{-1}$. Eq. (6) implies that a different $\mathbf{W}_\ell$ should be calculated for each frame. However, the duration of phones or silence mismatches between the native and non-native speech signal prevent such computation. In addition, the matrices are non-invertible. Therefore the estimation of $\mathbf{W}_\ell$ is done by considering a common matrix for all frames i of a specific L2 group of speakers ℓ. In speech processing is often assumed that a speech signal follows a Gaussian distribution. Thus, Eq. (6) can be expressed as $\mathscr{N}(\boldsymbol{\mu}_\ell,\ \boldsymbol{\Sigma}_\ell) \sim \mathscr{N}(\mathbf{W}_\ell\,\boldsymbol{\mu}_n,\ \mathbf{W}_\ell\,\boldsymbol{\Sigma}_n\,[\mathbf{W}_\ell]^T)$, where $\boldsymbol{\mu}_\ell$, $\boldsymbol{\mu}_n$ are the mean vectors of the distortion in non-native and native speech signals, respectively and $\boldsymbol{\Sigma}_\ell$, $\boldsymbol{\Sigma}_n$ their covariance matrices.

Considering a matrix decomposition (e.g., eigendecomposition), the two covariance matrices can be expressed as

$$\mathbf{\Sigma}_\zeta = \mathbf{V}_\zeta \, \mathbf{S}_\zeta \, [\mathbf{V}_\zeta]^T, \tag{7}$$

where $\zeta = n$ for the native language group, and $\zeta = \ell$ for the non-native language group. Next, assuming the following distributions

$$\begin{aligned} Z &\sim \mathscr{N}([\mathbf{V}_n]^T \boldsymbol{\mu}_n, \; [\mathbf{V}_n]^T \mathbf{\Sigma}_n \mathbf{V}_n) \\ Q &\sim \mathscr{N}([\mathbf{S}_n]^{-\frac{1}{2}} \boldsymbol{\mu}_Z, \; [\mathbf{S}_n]^{-\frac{1}{2}} \mathbf{\Sigma}_Z \, [\mathbf{S}_n]^{-\frac{T}{2}}), \\ K &\sim \mathscr{N}([\mathbf{S}_L]^{\frac{1}{2}} \boldsymbol{\mu}_Q, \; [\mathbf{S}_L]^{\frac{1}{2}} \mathbf{\Sigma}_Q \, [\mathbf{S}_L]^{\frac{T}{2}}), \\ \Psi &\sim \mathscr{N}(\mathbf{V}_L \, \boldsymbol{\mu}_K, \; \mathbf{V}_L \, \mathbf{\Sigma}_K \, [\mathbf{V}_L]^T), \end{aligned} \tag{8}$$

and performing a decomposition in each of them, it can be proved that matrix $\mathbf{W}_\ell$ is given by

$$\mathbf{W}_\ell = \mathbf{V}_\ell \, [\mathbf{S}_\ell]^{\frac{1}{2}} \, [\mathbf{S}_n]^{-\frac{1}{2}} \, [\mathbf{V}_n]^T. \tag{9}$$

Then, the power spectrum distortion measure for the non-native speech signal is calculated as

$$\phi_\ell(\mathbf{x}_{\ell_i}, \hat{\mathbf{x}}_{\ell_{i,j}}) \cong \phi_\ell(\mathbf{x}_{n_i}, \hat{\mathbf{x}}_{n_{i,j}}; \mathbf{x}_{\ell_i}, \hat{\mathbf{x}}_{\ell_{i,j}}) \approx [\mathbf{x}_{n_i} - \hat{\mathbf{x}}_{n_{i,j}}]^T \, [\mathbf{W}_\ell]^T \, \mathbf{W}_\ell \, [\mathbf{x}_{n_i} - \hat{\mathbf{x}}_{n_{i,j}}], \tag{10}$$

where $i \in \mathscr{I}$, $j \in \mathscr{J}_i$.

As mentioned above, a small area is considered around each phone. In practice, this is done by allowing small perturbations, i.e., adding 30 dB SNR independent and identically distributed (i.i.d.) Gaussian noise to each $\mathbf{x}_i$ and generate a set of 100 vectors $\hat{\mathbf{x}}_{i,j}$ for the native speech data n as well as for non-native speech data of all language backgrounds ℓ. All data from native speech are used to calculate the perceptual distortion measure Eq. (2) on a frame by frame basis by exploiting auditory information from the psychoacoustic model presented in (van de Par et al., 2002). Analogously, all data from non-native speech of each language group ℓ are used to compute Eq. (1) and, separately, all data from native speech, too. Next, the similarity measure $\mathscr{A}_\ell$ is calculated using the native perceptual distortion and the non-native spectral distortion measures and also the corresponding similarity measure for the native speakers $\mathscr{A}_n$ using the native perceptual and spectral measures. Then for each phoneme class, the RBF kernel-based *nPAD* Θ_ℓ^{rbf} is computed for every L2 background using Eq. (4). Finally, a Euclidean-based *nPAD* Θ_ℓ, described in (Koniaris and Engwall, 2011; Koniaris et al., 2013), is calculated by considering Euclidean distances in Eqs. (1) and (2), i.e., $\phi(\mathbf{s}_i, \hat{\mathbf{s}}_{i,j}) = \| \mathbf{x}(\mathbf{s}_i) - \mathbf{x}(\hat{\mathbf{s}}_{i,j}) \|^2$ and $\upsilon(\mathbf{s}_i, \hat{\mathbf{s}}_{i,j}) = \| \mathbf{x}(\mathbf{s}_i) - \mathbf{x}(\hat{\mathbf{s}}_{i,j}) \|^2$, respectively.

3 Experiments

This section describes the experiments and discusses the findings of the RBF kernel-based approach in relation to the Euclidean-based approach and the theoretical linguistic survey presented in (Bannert, 1984).

3.1 Speech data

The speech data were recorded with a sampling frequency of 16 kHz consisting of 23 phonetically rich single words and 55 sentences of varying complexity and length. The utterances were specifically designed for L2 learners of Swedish that were using a CALL program (Wik and Hjalmarsson, 2009). The collection of the data was done through a desktop microphone while

L1 bkgr.	male/female	utt.	L1 bkgr.	male/female	utt.	L1 bkgr.	male/female	utt.
Eng.(US)	1/1	318	*Russian*	1/3	583	*Arabic*	0/1	164
German	2/0	249	*Greek*	3/0	393	*Chinese*	2/3	832
French	3/0	347	*Spanish*	4/1	882	*Persian*	3/3	987
Polish	0/2	317	*Turkish*	4/0	604	*Swedish*	9/2	888

Table 1: Distribution of the total number of male and female speakers and the number of utterances (utt.) for each language background (L1 bkgr.).

students repeated a word or sentence after the virtual language tutor, the main character of the program. The procedure was simple; first, the animated agent produced an utterance – a pre-recorded natural speech produced by a native speaker – accompanied by a subtitle text and the student repeated afterwards.

The total number of participants was 37 of which 23 were male students and 14 female, from 11 different language backgrounds as it is shown in Table 1. The data recordings took place twice within one month's time, before and after practicing at home. The duration of each recording session was approximately 30 minutes. In addition, 9 male and 2 female Swedish speakers without regional accent varieties were also recorded once each. Non-linguistic information, such as coughs, long pauses, repetitions or fillers was excluded from the final corpus used for experiments. Each speech file was accompanied by a text file, the content of which was adjusted to the actual utterance, thus any deletion or insertion that may have occurred was not considered into the text file. A phone-level transcription was then automatically generated from the speech signal and the text file, using an HMM-based aligner (Sjölander, 2003). These phone-level transcription files were used to separate the speech data into phoneme categories. The material contained all Swedish phonemes, but the two short and more open pre-r allophones /æ/, /œ/ and the retroflexes /ɳ/, /ɖ/, and /ɭ/ were not considered in the experiments because the number of occurrences in the database was not sufficiently large.

For each language background, the speech data were divided into different phoneme categories according to the phone-level transcription files. The speech signal was first pre-emphasized and then windowed every 25 ms with an overlap of 10 ms using a Hamming window. A discrete Fourier transform of 512 points was applied to the windowed frame to compute the signal's power spectrum.

3.2 Results

This section deals with the experiments and results of the described method. The goal is to identify a list of the most problematic phonemes for a given group of L2 speakers using previously recorded data. Hence, the experiments are done offline and the error detection was not made on an utterance basis but on the whole data for each phoneme category. The method is focusing on repeated mispronunciations made by the L2 speakers that deviate from the L1 speakers. Only the speech signal is considered without further linguistic or paralinguistic information. The list of problematic phonemes for each language group is then compared to a linguistic study (Bannert, 1984).

Table 2 lists the vowels identified by the PED algorithms as being problematic for the different groups of non-native speakers. For each L2 speaker group, the first line shows, in decreasing order, the most deviating vowels according to the Euclidean-based nPAD Θ_ℓ. Correspondingly,

L1 bkgr.	nPAD ver.	detected phonemes	missed phonemes accord. to Bannert (1984)
English (US)	Θ_ℓ	æ:, ɛ, y:, u:, ʊ, œ:, ɛ:, ø, ɵ, ø:, (i:), ɑ:, (ə), e:, e, ɔ, a, ʉ:	ʏ, o:
	Θ_ℓ^{rbf250}	e:, ɛ:, æ:, ɑ:, ʏ, ø:, ɛ, a, ʉ:, (i), y:, (ə), (i:), ɔ, ɵ, ʊ, o:, e	u:, œ:, ø
	Θ_ℓ^{rbf500}	æ:, ɛ:, e:, ɑ:, ɛ, ø:, ʏ, a, ʉ:, (i), y:, (ə), (i:), e, œ:, ɔ, ɵ, ʊ	u:, o:, ø
	$\Theta_\ell^{rbf1000}$	æ:, ɛ:, e:, ɛ, ɑ:, ø:, ʏ, a, ʉ:, œ:, e, (i), ø, (ə), y:, (i:), ɔ, ɵ	u:, o:, ʊ
German	Θ_ℓ	æ:, (ɛ), y:, u:, (ʊ), ɛ:, (ø), œ:, ø:, i:, ə, ɑ:	ʉ:, ɵ, ʏ
	Θ_ℓ^{rbf250}	æ:, (e:), ʏ, ø:, ɑ:, ʉ:, ɛ:, (i), y:, (a), ə, i:	u:, ɵ, œ:
	Θ_ℓ^{rbf500}	æ:, (e:), ʏ, ø:, ɑ:, ɛ:, ʉ:, (a), (i), y:, ə, i:	u:, ɵ, œ:
	$\Theta_\ell^{rbf1000}$	æ:, ø:, ʏ, (e:), ɑ:, ɛ:, (a), ʉ:, (i), œ:, y:, ə	u:, ɵ, i:
French	Θ_ℓ	æ:, ɛ, y:, u:, œ:, (ʊ), ɛ:, (ø), ɵ, ø:, i:, ə, ɑ:, e:, e, ɔ, (a)	ʉ:, o:, ʏ
	Θ_ℓ^{rbf250}	e:, ɛ:, æ:, ʏ, ø:, ɑ:, ʉ:, (a), (i), y:, i:, ə, ɛ, ɔ, o:, (ʊ), ɵ	u:, œ:, e
	Θ_ℓ^{rbf500}	æ:, e:, ɛ:, ʏ, ø:, ɑ:, (a), ʉ:, ɛ, (i), y:, ə, i:, œ:, ɔ, e, o:	u:, ɵ
	$\Theta_\ell^{rbf1000}$	æ:, ɛ:, e:, ø:, ʏ, ɑ:, ɛ, (a), œ:, ʉ:, (i), (ø), e, y:, ə, i:, ɔ	u:, ɵ, o:
Polish	Θ_ℓ	æ:, (ɛ), y:, u:, œ:, (ʊ), ɛ:, ø, ɵ, ø:, i:, ɑ:, ə, e:, (e), (ɔ)	ʉ:, ʏ, o:, a
	Θ_ℓ^{rbf250}	e:, ɛ:, æ:, ɑ:, ʏ, ø:, (ɛ), a, ʉ:, (i), y:, i:, ə, (ɔ), o:, ɵ	u:, ø, œ:
	Θ_ℓ^{rbf500}	æ:, ɛ:, e:, ɑ:, (ɛ), ø:, ʏ, a, ʉ:, (i), y:, ə, (e), i:, œ:, (ɔ)	u:, ɵ, o:, ø
	$\Theta_\ell^{rbf1000}$	æ:, ɛ:, (ɛ), e:, ɑ:, ø:, ʏ, a, œ:, ʉ:, (e), (i), ø, ə, y:, i:	u:, o:, ɵ
Russian	Θ_ℓ	ɛ, y:, ɛ:, ø, ø:, i:, ɑ:, ɵ, e:, e, ʉ:, a, (ɔ), ʏ, (ə), (i), œ:	u:, æ:, o:
	Θ_ℓ^{rbf250}	ʏ, ɛ:, ʉ:, ø:, y:, e:, ɑ:, i:, a, ɵ, (ɔ), æ:, (i), (ə), œ:, e, u:	ø, o:, ɛ
	Θ_ℓ^{rbf500}	ʏ, ɛ:, ʉ:, ø:, y:, e:, ɑ:, a, œ:, i:, æ:, ø, ɵ, e, (ɔ), (i), (ə)	u:, o:, ɛ
	$\Theta_\ell^{rbf1000}$	ʏ, ɛ:, ø:, ʉ:, œ:, ø, ɑ:, e:, y:, a, i:, e, æ:, ɛ, ɵ, (ɔ), (i)	u:, o:
Greek	Θ_ℓ	æ:, (ɛ), y:, u:, œ:, (ʊ), ɛ:, ø, ɵ, ø:, i:, ɑ:, ə, e:, e, (ɔ)	ʉ:, ʏ, o:
	Θ_ℓ^{rbf250}	ɛ:, e:, æ:, ɑ:, ʏ, ø:, (ɛ), (a), ʉ:, (i), y:, i:, ə, (ɔ), ɵ, o:	u:, ø, œ:, e
	Θ_ℓ^{rbf500}	æ:, ɛ:, e:, ɑ:, (ɛ), ʏ, ø:, (a), ʉ:, (i), y:, ə, e, i:, œ:, (ɔ)	u:, ɵ, o:, ø
	$\Theta_\ell^{rbf1000}$	æ:, ɛ:, (ɛ), e:, ɑ:, ø:, ʏ, (a), œ:, e, ʉ:, (i), ø, ə, y:, i:	u:, ɵ, o:
Spanish	Θ_ℓ	u:, æ:, ɛ, ø, i:, ɵ, e:, e, ø:, (a), ʉ:, ɑ:, (i), ə, ʏ, (ɔ), o:	y:, ɛ:, œ:
	Θ_ℓ^{rbf250}	ʉ:, æ:, e:, (a), ɛ:, i:, ʏ, (i), ɵ, ɑ:, ø:, ə, (ɔ), e, œ:, o:, (ʊ)	u:, y:, ɛ, ø
	Θ_ℓ^{rbf500}	ʉ:, (a), e:, ʏ, i:, (i), ɛ:, ɑ:, ɵ, œ:, æ:, ø:, e, ə, (ɔ), ɛ, ø	u:, y:, o:
	$\Theta_\ell^{rbf1000}$	ʉ:, (a), e:, ʏ, (i), i:, œ:, e, ø, ø:, ɛ, ɵ, ɑ:, ə, æ:, ɛ:, (ɔ)	u:, y:, o:
Turkish	Θ_ℓ	æ:, (ɛ), y:, (ɛ:), (ø), u:, ɵ, ʊ, ø:, i:, ɑ:, e:, (ə)	e, ʉ:, o:, œ:
	Θ_ℓ^{rbf250}	e:, (ɛ:), (ʏ), ø:, æ:, (a), ʉ:, (i), ɑ:, i:, y:, (ɔ), (ə)	e, u:, ʊ, ɵ, o:, œ:
	Θ_ℓ^{rbf500}	e:, (ʏ), æ:, (ɛ:), ø:, (a), ɑ:, (i), ʉ:, (ɛ), i:, y:, (ɔ)	e, u:, ʊ, ɵ, o:, œ:
	$\Theta_\ell^{rbf1000}$	e:, æ:, (ʏ), (ɛ:), ø:, (a), (ɛ), ɑ:, (i), ʉ:, (o), œ:, e	u:, ʊ, ɵ, o:, y:, i:
Arabic	Θ_ℓ	æ:, ɛ, y:, u:, œ:, (ʊ), ɛ:, ø, ɵ, ø:, i:, ɑ:, ə, e:, e, (ɔ), a, ʉ:	ʏ, o:
	Θ_ℓ^{rbf250}	e:, ɛ:, æ:, ɑ:, ʏ, ø:, ɛ, a, ʉ:, (i), y:, i:, ə, (ɔ), o:, (ʊ), ɵ, e	u:, ø, œ:
	Θ_ℓ^{rbf500}	æ:, e:, ɛ:, ɑ:, ɛ, ø:, ʏ, a, ʉ:, (i), y:, ə, e, i:, œ:, (ɔ), (ʊ), ɵ	u:, o:, ø
	$\Theta_\ell^{rbf1000}$	æ:, ɛ:, e:, ɛ, ɑ:, ø:, ʏ, a, œ:, ʉ:, e, (i), ø, ə, y:, i:, (ɔ), ɵ	u:, o:
Chinese	Θ_ℓ	ɵ, æ:, ɛ, y:, u:, ɛ:, ø, ø:, i:, ɑ:, e:, e, ɔ, (ə), a, ʉ:, (i), o:	ʏ, œ:
	Θ_ℓ^{rbf250}	ɵ, ɑ:, ʉ:, e:, (i), ɛ:, ø:, æ:, i:, ɔ, a, y:, o:, (ə), u:, e, (ʊ), œ:	ʏ, ø, ɛ
	Θ_ℓ^{rbf500}	ɵ, ɑ:, æ:, ʉ:, ɛ:, e:, ø:, (i), a, ɔ, i:, y:, o:, œ:, e, (ə), u:, ɛ	ʏ, ø
	$\Theta_\ell^{rbf1000}$	ɑ:, æ:, ɛ:, ø:, ʉ:, e:, (i), a, œ:, ɔ, e, i:, ɛ, o:, y:, ø, (ə), u:	ʏ, ɵ
Persian	Θ_ℓ	ɵ, æ:, y:, (ɛ), ø, ø:, ʏ, (i), ʉ:, e:, a, (e), (ɑ:), o:, (ɔ)	i:, u:, ɛ:, œ:, ə
	Θ_ℓ^{rbf250}	ɵ, æ:, (e), (ɛ), ə, ɛ:, a, ø:, e:, ʏ, (i), ʉ:, (ɑ:), u:, œ:	i:, y:, o:, ø
	Θ_ℓ^{rbf500}	æ:, ɵ, (e), (ɛ), ø:, ə, ɛ:, œ:, ʉ:, ø, ʏ, e:, a, (i), (ɑ:)	i:, u:, y:, o:
	$\Theta_\ell^{rbf1000}$	æ:, ø:, ø, œ:, ɛ:, (e), (ɛ), ɵ, ʏ, ʉ:, (i), ə, e:, (ɑ:), a	i:, y:, o:, u:

Table 2: Problematic vowels per language background. To the left, the vowels are shown in decreasing order, starting from the one with the highest nPAD. Phonemes that differ from the linguistic study findings are in parentheses, and the seriously problematic according to Bannert (1984) are underscored. To the right, the missed vowels.

	Θ_ℓ	Θ_ℓ^{rbf250}	Θ_ℓ^{rbf500}	$\Theta_\ell^{rbf1000}$
Better performance in no. of language groups	3	2	3	***4***
Mismatches with theory (total)	***19.2%***	22.0%	20.9%	***19.2%***
Seriously problematic phonemes missed (total)	***21.3%***	22.0%	26.0%	25.2%
Mismatches in top 5 phonemes	8	***7***	8	***7***
Seriously problematic captured in top 5 phonemes	34	***35***	34	34

Table 3: Summary of findings for vowels.

the second, third and fourth lines show the results of the RBF kernel-based nPAD Θ_ℓ^{rbf} for $\sigma^2 = 0.002$, 0.001 and 0.0005, respectively. These are shown in table as Θ_ℓ^{rbf250}, Θ_ℓ^{rbf500} and $\Theta_\ell^{rbf1000}$, respectively because γ in Eqs. (1) and (2) becomes 250, 500 and 1000, respectively. As ground truth is considered the linguistic survey described in (Bannert, 1984). False rejections according to (Bannert, 1984) are indicated in parentheses and false accepts according to (Bannert, 1984) are listed in the right-most column. Some phonemes are shown underscored. These are the seriously problematic phonemes according to (Bannert, 1984), i.e., they are totally mispronounced by the non-native speakers. Generally, the nPAD methods capture most of the common errors made by each language group when its members are trying to learn Swedish. The Euclidean-based nPAD Θ_ℓ is better for American English, Spanish and Turkish speakers. The RBF kernel-based nPAD Θ_ℓ^{rbf250} is better for Polish, Θ_ℓ^{rbf500} is better for French and Chinese and $\Theta_\ell^{rbf1000}$ is better for Russian, Greek, Arabic and Persian speakers. For the German speaking group both Θ_ℓ^{rbf250} and Θ_ℓ^{rbf500} perform equally well.

Table 3 summarizes the findings of the approaches for vowels. The Euclidean-based measure achieves a lower percentage of mismatches with the theoretical linguistic findings and also misses less seriously mispronounced vowels compared to the RBF kernel-based measures. On the other hand, Θ_ℓ^{rbf250} captures the most seriously problematic vowels of all methods when looking only at the top 5 vowels of the list of problematic ones and also has the least mismatches with Bannert, again when only the five most problematic phonemes according to the method are considered. Θ_ℓ^{rbf500} seems not achieving better performance compared to the rest of the methods according to the table list and finally, $\Theta_\ell^{rbf1000}$ is generally performing better in more groups of L2 speakers, has the least mismatches with theory (as Θ_ℓ does, too) and also has less mismatches when only the top 5 most problematic vowels are considered (the same as Θ_ℓ^{rbf250}).

The reported findings show clearly that for many groups of L2 speakers the open pre-r allophone /æː/ is very problematic as it appears most of times at the top of the problematic vowels. Another vowel that appears problematic is /ɛː/, which is often not pronounced with a long duration as it is supposed but rather short, often being replaced by /ɛ/. Generally, it is revealed that most of the foreign speakers face difficulties when trying to produce the Swedish long vowels. Hence, /ʉː/, /ɑː/ and /eː/ are vowels that both the tested methods and Bannert's linguistic survey diagnose as seriously problematic for most of the L2 groups.

Table 4 lists the consonants that are diagnosed as being mispronounced by the L2 groups. As in Table 2, the first row shows, in decreasing order, the most deviating consonants according to the Euclidean-based nPAD Θ_ℓ and the following rows the three RBF kernel-based nPADs Θ_ℓ^{rbf250}, Θ_ℓ^{rbf500} and $\Theta_\ell^{rbf1000}$, respectively. Θ_ℓ is better for French, Greek, Spanish and Turkish speakers. $\Theta_\ell^{rbf1000}$ is better for Persian speakers while all three RBF kernel-based nPADs are

L1 bkgr.	nPAD ver.	detected phonemes	missed phonemes accord. to Bannert (1984)
English (US)	Θ_ℓ	ɧ̲, ŋ̲, (v), m, n, (b), r̲, (d), l̲, k, ʂ, t	s̲, ɕ̲, ʈ
	Θ_ℓ^{rbf250}	ʂ, ɕ̲, s̲, (j), ɧ̲, r̲, l̲, (g), (d), ŋ̲, k, t	m, n, ʈ
	Θ_ℓ^{rbf500}	ʂ, ɕ̲, s̲, (j), r̲, l̲, ɧ̲, (g), ŋ̲, k, (d), t	m, n, ʈ
	$\Theta_\ell^{rbf1000}$	ʂ, ɕ̲, s̲, (j), r̲, l̲, (g), k, ŋ̲, ɧ̲, t, (d)	m, n, ʈ
German	Θ_ℓ	ɧ̲, ŋ̲, v̲, n, (m), b̲, r̲, d̲, (l), k, ʂ̲, t, p, (h), f, ɕ, s̲	g̲, ʈ̲, j
	Θ_ℓ^{rbf250}	ʂ̲, ɕ, s̲, r̲, (l), ɧ̲, g̲, ŋ̲, d̲, k, t, b̲, (h), f, v̲, n, p	ʈ̲, j
	Θ_ℓ^{rbf500}	ɕ, ʂ̲, s̲, r̲, (l), g̲, ŋ̲, d̲, k, ɧ̲, t, b̲, (h), f, v̲, n, p	ʈ̲, j
	$\Theta_\ell^{rbf1000}$	ɕ, ʂ̲, s̲, r̲, (l), g̲, ŋ̲, k, d̲, t, (h), b̲, f, v̲, n, ɧ̲, j	ʈ̲, p
French	Θ_ℓ	ŋ̲, ɧ, (v), m, n, b̲, r̲, (l), d̲, ʂ, k̲, t̲, p̲, h, ɕ̲, g̲	s, ʈ
	Θ_ℓ^{rbf250}	ʂ, ɕ̲, (j), r̲, (l), g̲, ŋ̲, s, d̲, ɧ, b̲, k̲, h, t̲, m, (v)	p̲, ʈ, n
	Θ_ℓ^{rbf500}	ʂ, ɕ̲, (j), r̲, (l), g̲, ŋ̲, s, d̲, b̲, k̲, h, t̲, m, ɧ, n	p̲, ʈ
	$\Theta_\ell^{rbf1000}$	ʂ, ɕ̲, (j), r̲, (l), ŋ̲, s, g̲, k̲, d̲, b̲, h, t̲, m, n, (v)	p̲, ʈ, ɧ
Polish	Θ_ℓ	ɧ̲, ŋ̲, v̲, (m), n, b̲, (r), d̲, (l), k̲, ʂ̲, t̲, p̲, s̲, (f)	g̲, h̲, ɕ, ʈ
	Θ_ℓ^{rbf250}	ʂ̲, s̲, ɕ, (j), ɧ̲, (l), (r), g̲, ŋ̲, d̲, t̲, k̲, b̲, (f), v̲	h̲, p̲, n, ʈ
	Θ_ℓ^{rbf500}	ʂ̲, s̲, ɕ, (j), (r), (l), ɧ̲, g̲, ŋ̲, k̲, t̲, b̲, d̲, (f), v̲	h̲, p̲, n, ʈ
	$\Theta_\ell^{rbf1000}$	ʂ̲, s̲, ɕ, (j), (r), (l), g̲, ŋ̲, k̲, t̲, ɧ̲, b̲, d̲, (f), v̲	h̲, p̲, n, ʈ
Russian	Θ_ℓ	v̲, ŋ̲, (m), (n), (r), d̲, (l), h, b̲, k̲, t̲, g̲, (s), f, j	p̲, ɧ̲, ʂ̲, ɕ, ʈ
	Θ_ℓ^{rbf250}	j, (l), (s), (r), ŋ̲, g̲, v̲, k̲, f, (m), (n), t̲, b̲, d̲, p̲	ɧ̲, ʂ̲, ɕ, h, ʈ
	Θ_ℓ^{rbf500}	j, (s), (l), (r), ŋ̲, g̲, v̲, k̲, (m), f, (n), t̲, b̲, d̲, p̲	ɧ̲, ʂ̲, ɕ, h, ʈ
	$\Theta_\ell^{rbf1000}$	j, (s), (l), (r), ŋ̲, g̲, v̲, k̲, (m), (n), f, t̲, b̲, d̲, p̲	ɧ̲, ʂ̲, ɕ, h, ʈ
Greek	Θ_ℓ	ɧ̲, ŋ̲, (v), m, n̲, b̲, (r), d̲, l, ʂ̲, k̲, t̲, p̲, ɕ̲, (f), s̲	g̲, h̲, t̲
	Θ_ℓ^{rbf250}	ʂ̲, ɕ̲, (j), s̲, ɧ̲, (r), l, g̲, ŋ̲, d̲, t̲, b̲, k̲, (f), (v), m	h̲, n̲, p̲, ʈ
	Θ_ℓ^{rbf500}	ʂ̲, ɕ̲, (j), s̲, (r), l, g̲, ɧ̲, ŋ̲, t̲, d̲, k̲, b̲, (f), (v), m	h̲, n̲, p̲, ʈ
	$\Theta_\ell^{rbf1000}$	ʂ̲, ɕ̲, (j), s̲, (r), l, g̲, ŋ̲, t̲, k̲, d̲, b̲, ɧ̲, (f), (v), m	h̲, n̲, p̲, ʈ
Spanish	Θ_ℓ	ŋ̲, v̲, (r), n, (l), b̲, t̲, ʂ̲, (f), k̲, g̲, d̲, j, p̲, ɕ̲, s̲, h̲	ɧ̲, m, ʈ
	Θ_ℓ^{rbf250}	(l), (r), ʂ̲, ŋ̲, (f), v̲, n, t̲, k̲, g̲, p̲, d̲, b̲, m, h̲, j, ʈ	s̲, ɧ̲, ɕ̲
	Θ_ℓ^{rbf500}	(l), ʂ̲, (r), ŋ̲, (f), v̲, n, t̲, k̲, p̲, g̲, d̲, m, b̲, j, h̲, ʈ	s̲, ɧ̲, ɕ̲
	$\Theta_\ell^{rbf1000}$	(l), ʂ̲, (r), ŋ̲, (f), v̲, n, t̲, k̲, g̲, p̲, d̲, m, b̲, j, h̲, ʈ	s̲, ɧ̲, ɕ̲
Turkish	Θ_ℓ	ŋ̲, v̲, (m), n̲, b̲, r, l, d̲, k̲, (ʂ), t̲, p̲, f, h, g̲, ʈ̲, j, s	ɧ̲, ɕ̲
	Θ_ℓ^{rbf250}	(ʂ), j, l, r, ŋ̲, g̲, k̲, t̲, b̲, s, v̲, f, d̲, (m), p̲, n̲, h, ʈ̲	ɧ̲, ɕ̲
	Θ_ℓ^{rbf500}	(ʂ), j, l, r, ŋ̲, g̲, k̲, t̲, s, b̲, v̲, f, (m), d̲, n̲, p̲, h, ʈ̲	ɧ̲, ɕ̲
	$\Theta_\ell^{rbf1000}$	(ʂ), j, l, r, ŋ̲, k̲, g̲, t̲, s, b̲, v̲, (m), d̲, f, n̲, p̲, h, ʈ̲	ɧ̲, ɕ̲
Arabic	Θ_ℓ	ɧ̲, ŋ̲, v̲, (m), (n), (b), r̲, d, (l), k̲, ʂ̲, t̲, p̲	f̲, s̲, ɕ̲, ʈ
	Θ_ℓ^{rbf250}	ʂ̲, ɕ̲, s̲, (j), ɧ̲, r̲, (l), (g), d, ŋ̲, k̲, t̲, (b)	f̲, p̲, v̲, ʈ
	Θ_ℓ^{rbf500}	ɕ̲, ʂ̲, s̲, (j), r̲, (l), ɧ̲, (g), k̲, d, ŋ̲, t̲, (b)	f̲, p̲, v̲, ʈ
	$\Theta_\ell^{rbf1000}$	ɕ̲, ʂ̲, s̲, (j), r̲, (l), k̲, (g), ŋ̲, t̲, d, ɧ̲, (b)	f̲, p̲, v̲, ʈ
Chinese	Θ_ℓ	ɧ̲, ŋ̲, v̲, m, n̲, b, r̲, l̲, d, k̲, t̲, f, g, ʈ, p̲, j̲, (h), (s)	ʂ̲, ɕ̲
	Θ_ℓ^{rbf250}	ɧ̲, l̲, r̲, ŋ̲, j̲, g, f, k̲, b, v̲, m, n̲, t̲, ʈ, p̲, d, (h), (s)	ʂ̲, ɕ̲
	Θ_ℓ^{rbf500}	l̲, r̲, ɧ̲, ŋ̲, j̲, g, k̲, f, b, v̲, m, n̲, t̲, ʈ, p̲, d, (h), (s)	ʂ̲, ɕ̲
	$\Theta_\ell^{rbf1000}$	l̲, r̲, ŋ̲, j̲, g, k̲, ɧ̲, b, f, m, v̲, n̲, t̲, ʈ, p̲, d, (h), (s)	ʂ̲, ɕ̲
Persian	Θ_ℓ	b, d, (ɧ), v̲, (f), g, (h), t̲, s̲, (j), ɕ̲, p̲, ʈ̲, k̲, l, r	n̲, ŋ̲, ʂ̲, m
	Θ_ℓ^{rbf250}	b, (f), (ɧ), v̲, g, t̲, (h), p̲, n̲, l, ʈ̲, r, d, ŋ̲, k̲, m	s̲, ʂ̲, ɕ̲
	Θ_ℓ^{rbf500}	b, (f), (ɧ), v̲, g, t̲, (h), p̲, n̲, l, k̲, ʈ̲, r, ŋ̲, d, m	s̲, ʂ̲, ɕ̲
	$\Theta_\ell^{rbf1000}$	(f), v̲, (ɧ), g, t̲, p̲, (h), n̲, k̲, b, l, ʈ̲, ŋ̲, r, d, m	s̲, ʂ̲, ɕ̲

Table 4: Problematic consonants per language background. To the left, the consonants are shown in decreasing order, starting from the one with the highest nPAD. Phonemes that differ from the linguistic study findings are in parentheses, and the seriously problematic according to Bannert (1984) are underscored. To the right, the missed consonants.

	Θ_ℓ	Θ_ℓ^{rbf250}	Θ_ℓ^{rbf500}	$\Theta_\ell^{rbf1000}$
Better performance in no. of language groups	5	***6***	5	5
Mismatches with theory (total)	20.2%	20.2%	***19.7%***	20.2%
Seriously problematic phonemes missed (total)	19.5%	***18.6%***	***18.6%***	***18.6%***
Mismatches in top 5 phonemes	***15***	16	18	18
Seriously problematic captured in top 5 phonemes	28	***29***	27	27

Table 5: Summary of findings for consonants.

equally better for American English, German, Russian and Arabic speakers in comparison to the Euclidean-based measure. Finally, Θ_ℓ and Θ_ℓ^{rbf250} are better for the Polish group and Θ_ℓ^{rbf250} and Θ_ℓ^{rbf500} for the Chinese speakers.

Table 5 summarizes the findings of the Table 4. The Euclidean-based measure has less mismatches with Bannert in the top five most problematic consonants as compared to the RBF kernel-based approaches. Θ_ℓ^{rbf250} is better in most language groups and can better capture the seriously problematic consonants both when the focus is on the five most problematic ones, but also in terms of the total number of the seriously problematic consonants (although in the latter case, all three RBF kernel-based approaches perform equally good). In addition, Θ_ℓ^{rbf500} has the least mismatches with the linguistic study.

The Swedish retroflex /ʂ/ is very problematic according to the reported results and likewise the unique "sje-sound" /ɧ/, a rounded velar fricative that does not exist in other languages. Moreover, many L2 speakers seem to have problems producing the velar nasal /ŋ/, which is commonly mispronounced as /ŋg/. Another difficult consonant is the fricative /ɕ/ that is also one of the most problematic sounds for second language speakers of Swedish.

In summary, RBF kernel generally seems to work better for consonants vis-à-vis vowels when compared with (Bannert, 1984) but also with the Euclidean distance measure. A small improvement in the percentage of the seriously problematic consonants is confirmed – accomplished by all three RBF-based measures – compared to the Euclidean measure. The figures remain better even in the case in which only the five most problematic consonants are taken into account. The results of the RBF kernel metrics are still in a better agreement with linguistic findings in comparison to the Euclidean-based one. On the other hand for the case of vowels, the two metrics perform nearly the same based on the criteria listed in Table 3. While for instance, Θ_ℓ is better considering the total number of mismatches with theory and, in addition, misses less seriously problematic vowels according to Bannert's study, Θ_ℓ^{rbf250} has a slightly better performance when concentrating on the five most problematic vowels and $\Theta_\ell^{rbf1000}$ is mainly preferable for more L2 groups compared to the rest of the metrics. Generally speaking, RBF-kernel may be considered to outperform to a small extent the Euclidean measure, though the two measures do not have major differences and they both seem to work well and achieve positive results as they regurarly agree with Bannert's linguistic survey. It is noted that the intention of the research described in this paper was to investigate alternative measures for the perceptually-motivated PED approach and carry out experiments to explore their behavior. Moreover, the deviations from the theoretical findings that both distance measures have can, for the most part, be explained by the nature of the two studies (theoretical linguistic *vs.* computational automatic) and the methodology that was followed. Bannert studied the pronunciation problem from a pure linguistic perspective, including lots of subjective observations and analysis. The computational methods do not consider many linguistic aspects, such as context and influence from preceding or succeeding phonemes. In addition, the PED methods aim at diagnosing mispronunciations made by the examined learners and are not designed to be used for identifying general problems related to the L1 of a group of speakers as Bannert's study was. It is noted that Bannert collected data from L2 speakers that were not influenced by repeating after a native speaker. The reason was that the study was aimed at making an inventory of mispronunciations for various groups of L2 students that would be used as a reference list for the teachers of Swedish as a second language. This may partly explain why some of the seriously problematic phonemes in Bannert's study were not diagnosed likewise with the nPAD approaches.

4 Conclusions

In this paper, a RBF kernel-based similarity measure was investigated as part of a pronunciation error detection algorithm previously presented in (Koniaris and Engwall, 2011; Koniaris et al., 2013) where a Euclidean distance measure was utilized. The idea was to investigate whether it can achieve good performance in relation to relevant linguistic literature and in comparison to the Euclidean similarity measure. The experiments show that good results can be obtained using this measure. In the future, it will be interesting to extend the idea by applying support vector machines in combination to the RBF kernel measure.

References

Bannert, R. (1984). Problems in learning Swedish pronunciation and in understanding foreign accent. *Folia Linguistica*, 18(1-2):193–222.

Braun, M. L., Buhmann, J. M., and Müller, K.-R. (2008). On relevant dimensions in kernel feature spaces. *J. Machine Learn. Research*, 9:1875–1908.

Delmonte, R. (2000). SLIM prosodic automatic tools for self-learning instruction. *Speech Communication*, 30(2-3):145–166.

Flege, J. E. (1995). *Second-language speech learning: theory, findings, and problems*. Strange, W. (Ed.), Speech Perception and Linguistic Experience: Theoretical and Methodological Issues in Cross-Language Speech Research. Timonium, MD: York Press Inc.

Franco, H., Neumeyer, L., Kim, Y., and Ronen, O. (1997). Automatic pronunciation scoring for language instruction. In *IEEE Int. Conf. Acoust., Speech, Sig. Proc., Munich, Germany*, pages 1471–1474.

Guion, S. G., Flege, J. E., Ahahane-Yamada, R., and Pruitt, J. C. (2000). An investigation of current models of second language speech perception: the case of japanese adults' perception of english consonants. *J. Acoust. Soc. Am.*, 107(5):2711–2724.

Koniaris, C. and Engwall, O. (2011). Phoneme level non-native pronunciation analysis by an auditory model-based native assessment scheme. In *Interspeech, Florence, Italy*, pages 1157–1160.

Koniaris, C., Salvi, G., and Engwall, O. (2013). On mispronunciation analysis of individual foreign speakers using auditory periphery models. *Speech Communication*, 55(5):691–706.

Neumeyer, L., Franco, H., Digalakis, V., and Weintraub, M. (2000). Automatic scoring of pronunciation quality. *Speech Communication*, 30:83–93.

Neumeyer, L., Franco, H., Weintraub, M., and Price, P. (1996). Automatic text-independent pronunciation scoring of foreign language student speech. In *Int. Conf. Spoken Lang. Proc., Philadelphia, PA , USA*, pages 1457–1460.

Park, J. G. and Rhee, S. C. (2004). Development of the knowledge-based spoken english evaluation system and its application. In *ISCA Interspeech, Jeju Island, South Korea*, pages 1681–1684.

Piske, T., Flege, J., and MacKay, I. (2001). Factors affecting degree of foreign accent in an l2: a review. *J. Phonetics*, 29(2):191–215.

Raux, A. and Kawahara, T. (2002). Automatic intelligibility assessment and diagnosis of critical pronunciation errors for computer-assisted pronunciation learning. In *Int. Conf. Spoken Lang. Proc., Denver, CO, USA*, pages 737–740.

Sjölander, K. (2003). An HMM-based system for automatic segmentation and alignment of speech. In *Fonetik*, pages 93–96.

Strik, H., Truong, K., de Wet, F., and Cucchiarini, C. (2009). Comparing different approaches for automatic pronunciation error detection. *Speech Communication*, 51(10):845–852.

Tepperman, J. and Narayanan, S. (2005). Hidden-articulator markov models for pronunciation evaluation. In *Proc. ASRU, San Juan, Puerto Rico*, pages 174–179.

Tepperman, J. and Narayanan, S. (2008). Using articulatory representations to detect segmental errors in nonnative pronunciation. *IEEE Tr. Audio, Speech, Lang. Proc.*, 16(1):8–22.

Truong, K. P., Neri, A., de Wet, F., Cucchiarini, C., and Strik, H. (2005). Automatic detection of frequent pronunciation errors made by L2-learners. In *ISCA Interspeech, Lisbon, Portugal*, pages 1345–1348.

van de Par, S., Kohlrausch, A., Charestan, G., and Heusdens, R. (2002). A new psychoacoustical masking model for audio coding applications. In *IEEE Int. Conf. on Acoust., Speech, Sig. Proc., Orlando, FL, USA*, volume 2, pages 1805–1808.

Wei, S., Hu, G., Hu, Y., and Wang, R.-H. (2009). A new method for mispronunciation detection using support vector machine based on pronunciation space models. *Speech Communication*, 51(10):896–905.

Weigelt, L. F., Sadoff, S. J., and Miller, J. D. (1990). Plosive/fricative distinction: the voiceless case. *J. Acoust. Soc. Am.*, 87:2729–2737.

Wik, P. and Hjalmarsson, A. (2009). Embodied conversational agents in computer assisted language learning. *Speech Communication*, 51(10):1024–1037.

Witt, S. M. and Young, S. (2000). Phone-level pronunciation scoring and assessment for interactive language learning. *Speech Communication*, 30:95–108.

Xu, S., Jiang, J., Chen, Z., and Xu, B. (2009). Automatic pronunciation error detection based on linguistic knowledge and pronunciation space. In *IEEE Int. Conf. Acoust. Speech Sig. Proc. (ICASSP), Taipei, Taiwan*, pages 4841–4844.

Yamashita, Y., Kato, K., and Nozawa, K. (2005). Automatic scoring for prosodic proficiency of english sentences spoken by japanese based on utterance comparison. *IECE Trans. Inform. Systems*, E88-D:496–501.

Russian Error-Annotated Learner English Corpus: a Tool for Computer-Assisted Language Learning

Elizaveta Kuzmenko, Andrey Kutuzov
National Research University Higher School of Economics
lizaku77@gmail.com, akutuzov@hse.ru

ABSTRACT
The paper describes the learner corpus composed of English essays written by native Russian speakers. REALEC (Russian Error-Annotated Learner English Corpus) is an error-annotated, available online corpus, now containing more than 200 thousand word tokens in almost 800 essays. It is one of the first Russian ESL corpora, dynamically developing and striving to improve both in size and in features offered to users. We describe our perspective on the corpus, data sources and tools used in compiling it. Elaborate self-made classification of learners' errors types is thoroughly described. The paper also presents a pilot experiment on creating test sets for particular learners' problems using corpus data.

KEYWORDS: learner corpora, English as a second language, computer-assisted language learning.

Elizaveta Kuzmenko and Andrey Kutuzov 2014. Russian error-annotated learner English corpus: a tool for Computer-Assisted Language Learning. *Proceedings of the third workshop on NLP for computer-assisted language learning.* NEALT Proceedings Series 22 / Linköping Electronic Conference Proceedings 107: 87–97.

1 Introduction

The present paper describes the learner corpus composed of English essays written by native Russian speakers, namely, students of National Research University Higher School of Economics. The corpus is error-annotated and available at `http://realec.org` (REALEC is for Russian Error-Annotated Learner English Corpus).

English learner corpora have been well documented in many countries [1], but in Russian linguistics not much attention has been paid to this research area. Therefore, there are not many corpora which comprise texts written by learners with Russian as the L1, Russian subcorpus of the ICLE being the best documented and representative of Russian-speaking learners' population (Granger et al., 2009). Another example of a corpus with Russian learners' data is RusLTC (Russian Learner Translator Corpus[2], which is composed of translations made by students. This corpus is of great help while studying translation process and mistakes typical for this kind of language task. At the same time, this corpus cannot be fully representative of Russian learners' language in general as translation is a very specific task. Also there is little or no sign of integrating corpus-based applications and techniques adapted for the needs of Russian-speaking learners into the study process.

Our research aims at developing a learner corpus with pure Russian-English interlanguage data available for use to anyone interested and at investigating how the corpus data can be used to facilitate the language learning. In particular, we describe the set of training exercises which are built on the basis of our corpus data and we compare their efficiency to the traditional exercises found in books for learners of English.

The structure of this paper is as follows: in section 2 we present our views of the tasks carried out by learner corpus research, describe the goals underlying the creation and usage of our corpus and give an overview of the corpus data. In section 3 we describe the annotation scheme adopted in our corpus. Section 4 presents external tools used for the creation of our corpus – the *brat* annotation tool used for marking up errors and the *Freeling* parser used for implementing part-of-speech tagging in our corpus. In section 5 we report our attempt to use corpus-based grammar exercises in the process of language teaching. Section 6 outlines the problems encountered during the process of setting up the corpus and discusses our future work.

2 Corpus overview (our perspective on LCR)

It is a common knowledge that having access to learner corpora is of great benefit for both learners and instructors – it has already been proved over more than twenty years of research in learner corpora (Granger et al., 2013). Learner corpora can be beneficial in several ways. First of all, learner corpus data are of tremendous help when studying a learner's interlanguage. Corpus linguistics methods have proved to be very successful when applied to the field of second language acquisition (SLA) as they help to observe patterns which are impossible to notice in the research of an individual subject (which is the traditional method in the field of SLA). Secondly, learner corpora offer major pedagogical help, much more than can be expected from purely descriptive SLA studies. This is why we pay so much attention to the aspect of error-annotation – students can improve their knowledge directly from corpus data.

Also, the number of teaching applications that can be built on the basis of a learner corpus is

[1]`http://www.uclouvain.be/en-cecl-lcworld.html`
[2]`http://rus-ltc.org`

beyond counting. Almost all learners' dictionaries are based on corpus data, *Longman Essential Activator* (LEA, 1997) being the first of this kind. Grammar books can be designed on the basis of learners' data too (Granger and Paquot, 2014). Such design is extremely helpful to learners, as they are shown concrete patterns in which mistakes often arise, not abstract rules that are to remember. Virtually, we define our main research purpose when building the Russian Error-Annotated Learner English Corpus as studying inconsistencies of students' interlanguage and getting insights about methods of language learning, which can later be embodied in the form of learning applications, such as corpus-based grammar and vocabulary exercises or recommendations on how to avoid typical learners' errors.

On the other hand, we consider the task of describing the Russian-English interlanguage in terms of CIA (Contrastive Interlanguage Analysis, as in (Granger et al., 1996)) secondary with respect to our aims. There are many studies carried out in the framework of CIA, whereas works on error analysis have been far less frequent for several reasons:

1. it is hard to strictly define what an error is,

2. error-annotation is a time-consuming task,

3. there is huge influence of a human factor, as errors are mostly identified by human annotators, who can have their own concepts of errors.

Thence, we hope to contribute to the field of error analysis by trying to overcome these difficulties and to formalize the basic concepts.

It should be noted that we acknowledge that the notion of error is rather vague and from the strict point of view it would be more correct to talk about 'variations of language'. The word '*error*' itself should, of course, be used with much caution (Kachru, 1992). However, from the practical point of view, learner corpora (including ours) are used in real teaching environment, where students are supposed to acquire a level of language skills enough to pass IELTS examination or other qualification tests. Good example is Russian Learner Translator Corpus, which among other tasks is employed to create exercises aimed at prevention of frequent translation mistakes (Kutuzov and Kunilovskaya, 2014).

So, from the point of view of IELTS etc., such 'variations' are outright mistakes. Thus, we believe that learner corpus annotation should include the notion of error, and it is practically useful to consider some language variations 'erroneous'.

Let us now describe the data presented in our corpus. As of September 2014, our corpus consists of 794 pieces of students' writing, which comprise more than 225 thousand word tokens, and the corpus is steadily growing.

The contributors to the corpus are 2, 3 and 4 year students (with Russian as their L1) from National Research University Higher School of Economics, Faculty of Philology, together with students of the first year of Master's program, Faculty of Psychology. The works presented in the corpus are either routine assignments or exam-type essays. Most of the works found in the corpus have the structure similar to that of IELTS writing tasks (Moore and Morton, 2005), as the main goal of English courses at the university is preparation for the compulsory IELTS examination.

The writing pieces in the corpus are initially processed with the help of a part-of-speech tagger (see section 4), and then error-annotated by experienced annotators (mostly teachers) using linguistically advanced error classification.

However, search options applied in our corpus that we have at the moment are not always sufficient for our needs. It is possible to search for a particular error tag or a string or substring containing part of a target word (using regular expressions). In future a morphologically enriched search tool, which allows searching a specified lemma, wordform or POS-tag alongside with error tags, will be developed.

3 Annotation scheme

We consider error-annotation the most important part of learner data analysis (Izumi and Isahara, 2004) . At the dawn of second language acquisition and learner corpus research it was already stated that errors made by a learner convey a lot of information about foreign language acquisition process (Corder, 1981).

However, the process of annotating errors is generally thought of as a very complex task, whose results cannot be truly reliable due to the human factor (Izumi et al., 2005). There were other points of criticism as well: ambiguous understanding of the term '*error*', neglecting structures that the learner generated correctly, etc. Despite this criticism, we believe that error annotation not only provides evidence concerning the process of acquiring language, but also can be of major pedagogical value, as stated in the previous section. Consequently, we have developed a detailed multi-layered annotation scheme to fully describe different aspects of errors.

The process of error annotation is carried out within *brat* text annotation framework, described in the next chapter. As of September 2014, more than 10 000 error spans are annotated in our corpus. Our annotation scheme comprises 4 tiers of information about a particular error. These tiers are:

1. type of grammar rule violated by the error,
2. supposed cause of the error,
3. the degree of grammar or 'linguistic' damage caused by the error,
4. the degree of pragmatic damage caused by the error (influence on understanding).

In addition, it is marked whether the correction of the error is insertion or deletion.

Let us observe every level of the annotation scheme in detail.

Primarily, the most important component of any annotation scheme is considered to be the classification of erroneously broken grammar, lexical and discourse rules. Approaches to this level of annotation differ by granularity. In our research we adopt a rather detailed annotation for grammar rule – it amounts to 151 types of grammar rules. This tier is divided into 5 categories with further subdivision (tree structure): punctuation, spelling, grammar, vocabulary and discourse. If an error affects more than one grammar rule, the mistake area can be tagged several times.

The figure 1 gives an idea of the ratio of different mistakes types across the corpus. Grammar and vocabulary mistakes dominate, accompanied by a serious amount of mistakes which annotators were not able to link to any type.

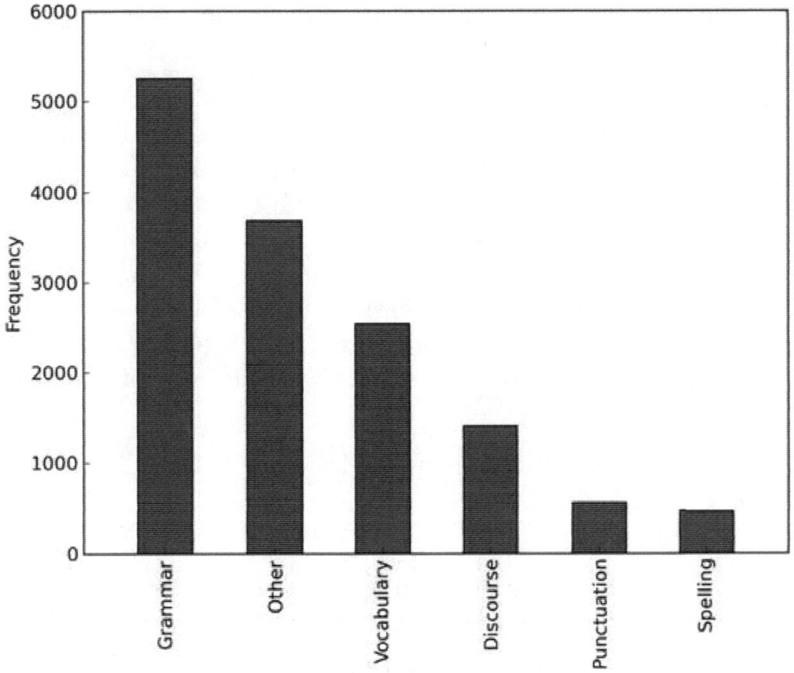

Figure 1: Mistakes types distribution over the whole corpus

The supposed causes of errors include typos and L1 interference (with a separate case of the absence of the category in L1). The evidence about typos can be of interest to psycholinguistic research, but in some cases it is not easy to distinguish typos from other errors. At the same time, the issue of transfer effects in the studied language deserve thorough consideration (Gas, 1979), so we are planning to refine this tier.

The next two levels of annotation – namely, grammar and pragmatic damage caused by the error – are by their nature scales with 3 values: 'minor damage', 'major damage' and 'critical damage'. Different types of errors are assigned a particular value of pragmatic and grammar damage according to our own classification of errors by this feature. These characteristics can be easily turned into integers and used for automated evaluation of students' work.

The unresolved problems of our annotation scheme are the following:

1. Lack of measurements for inter-rater and intra-rater agreement. Due to the lack of resources we can't have each essay annotated by several independent assessors and then compare their results, calculating inter-rater agreement. Neither did we check our assessors for intra-rater agreement by repeating annotation of the same text after some time, or by asking them to revise their own annotations. This knowledge can be of great use in assessing soundness of our error annotation.

2. Sophisticated classification by the violated rule, which reduces the possibility of direct pedagogical application as understanding tagging principles requires special training.

3. Inconsistent and subjective marking of degree of pragmatic damage (we have a more restricted principles of assigning degree of grammar damage).

Dealing with these problems will be our primary goal in the upcoming refinement of the annotation scheme.

Let us compare our scheme to other annotation schemes in use. Error categorization devised for use in the ICLE is in some ways similar to ours (Granger, 2003). It is based on linguistic error taxonomy developed in (Dulay et al., 1982) and focuses on grammatical categories being violated. The hierarchy of errors consists of 53 types divided into 8 major categories, which include standard lexical, grammatical, punctuational, syntactic errors and a number of intermediate subtypes. This scheme and ours are built according to the principle of tagging errors on the basis of the incorrect word/phrase, and not on the basis of the corrected word/phrase. Therefore, if an article stands in place for a personal pronoun as in the sentence *I saw the mother from a long distance*, this error belongs to the category *misuse of article* and not to *misuse of a possessive determiner*.

The differences between our annotation scheme and the one in the ICLE include:

1. greater detalization of error subtypes in our scheme,
2. variances in attributing particular error categories to major types (for example, errors on subordinating conjunctions are assigned to lexis in ICLE and to syntax in REALEC)
3. technical issues of juxtaposing markup and learners' texts (in ICLE markup is incorporated into the text and in REALEC texts and annotations are stored separately)

Now let us turn to another credible annotation scheme – the one deployed in Falko (Fehlerannotiertes Lernerkorpus, described in (Siemen et al., 2006)). This annotation does not seem to back on classical error taxonomies (Lüdeling et al., 2005). It is adjusted to the German language and reflects the grammatical categories which are frequently violated by the learners of German. The taxonomy itself comprises 8 types of errors: orthography, word formation, agreement, government, tense, mood, word order and expression. As well as in our corpus, annotation is carried out in the frame of the multi-layer standoff model, so that annotation is stored separately from texts. Also in Falko there is an annotation layer devoted to the description of error causes.

4 External tools

In compiling REALEC corpus we extensively used two external tools. The first is *brat*[3], open-source text annotation framework (Stenetorp et al., 2012). It allows simultaneous annotation of texts on server by multiple annotators at once using only their browsers, no matter their location. *Brat* also visualizes annotated texts in real time, making it easy to see and edit error spans and other markup.

It is very important that *brat* is highly customizable. One can adapt it to almost any type of markup (linguistic or not). Particularly, in our case it was easy to configure *brat* so that it offers our error classification as markup scheme.

One notable disadvantage of brat is its search interface which is not very rich. Although it is possible to look for particular entity (error type) in a document or in whole collection, one cannot combine several entity types in the query. Even more disappointing is the fact that *brat* does not support saving search results in any form. Due to open-source-nature of *brat*, this can be fixed, so we plan to do it.

[3]`http://brat.nlplab.org/`

Another external tool is *Freeling* suite of linguistic analyzers[4], also open-source. We employed only its lemmatizer and part-of-speech tagger module to assign POS and lemmas to word tokens in our corpus. With the help of our custom-made conversion tool, we managed to augment brat annotation files with data from *Freeling* output.

Freeling English tagger is trained on the widely known WSJ corpus, performs disambiguation and is reported to yield precision near 97-98% (Padró and Stanilovsky, 2012). It is hardly possible to somehow estimate Freeling performance on erroneous forms. Suppose we have a sentence *'The number are dropping.'* with the mistake in the verb form. *Freeling* marks *are* as a verb in plural. Context can't help disambiguation, because *are* simply does not have singular forms among its possible parsings. But we can hardly say that the tagger performs poorly here: it assigns the only possible POS tag to the token. It is suitable for us, as after that we theoretically can analyze annotated texts and look for 'strange' part-of-speech sequences.

Another case is wrong spelling. *Freeling* does not perform spell-checking before analyzing, thus it processes spelling errors as unknown words, and this is where the context comes into play. In most cases *Freeling* tagger is able to correctly assign a PoS tag to a wrongly spelled word based on word suffix and its neighbours. For example, in the sentence *'However, certain reseches disagree.'* the word **reseches* (*researchers*) is assigned a noun tag, obviously because it is preceded by an adjective and followed by a verb. To sum it up, we have not met many additional problems related to the fact that the authors of our texts are learners, not native English speakers.

Thus, we have if fact two layers of annotation: errors and POS/lemma. This provides corpus user with the possibility to search for particular parts of speech and to find all grammatical forms of query word. However, as stated before, *brat* does not allow double query constraints (for example, one can't search for verbs with word choice errors). Also, our *freeling2brat* converter is not perfect and in some cases lemmas and morphological tags are assigned to wrong words. Mostly this is because *Freeling* deals with sentences and words, while *brat* operates with character offsets from the beginning of the document. Fixing the converter is one of directions for our future work.

5 Applications for language teaching

As it was pointed out earlier, various applications for language teaching can be built using the corpus data. There is no clear evidence on which learning stage corpus-based tools should be used. On the one hand, intermediate or advanced learners eager to eliminate the traces of their non-nativeness might want to know subtle problematic cases among learners in general. On the other hand, beginners might also be interested in error patterns in order to avoid them from the very beginning of their study. It can be noted, however, that most corpus-based tools are designed for self-tuition, making them more appropriate for advanced learners.

In particular, learner corpus data are used to present mistake patterns to students and to explain them the nature of their mistakes, as in (Altenberg and Granger, 2001). Also, error-tagged data can be used to identify which erroneous patterns are frequently encountered in learners' writing and to correct one's teaching methodology correspondingly, as described in (Seidlhofer, 2002).

Now we are going to describe the corpus-based exercises and give an experimental estimation of their efficiency. We believe that this can be regarded as a preliminary attempt to apply the results of our corpus work to practical uses in the learning process.

[4] `http://nlp.lsi.upc.edu/freeling/`

We hypothesized that students acquire grammar rules better if supported by corpus-based, focused on problematic cases exercises, whereas traditional grammar drills lose their efficiency compared to corpus-based exercises. To support this insight, we performed a pilot experiment described below.

The grammar rule chosen for testing in this experiment was using commas in defining and non-defining relative clauses.

The design of the experiment was as follows: students were assigned an essay, and all essays were uploaded in the corpus and error-annotated. After that the students were divided in two groups, 20 people each. The members of the first group completed exercises built on erroneous sentence instances from the corpus. Another group of students was studying the rule with the traditional material from grammar books ((McCarter and Roberts, 2010) and (Cotton et al., 2008)). After practicing the rule, students were once again assigned an essay, and the second portion of essays was error-annotated too.

The measure used for statistical analysis was errors per word ratio. The analysis has shown that the ratio has decreased in the data of experimental group and, on the contrary, increased in the control group (cf. Table 1).

Group	Error/word ratio before	Error/word ratio after	t-test confidence
Experimental	0.005122	0.001605	0.046853
Control	0.002785	0.004274	0.082329

Table 1: Error per word ratio

The obtained data show that so far corpus-based exercises proved to be influencing learners' performance in a positive way. If supported by future experiments, it can be confirmed that corpus-based exercises suit the study process better as they focus on problematic for learners' issues. Our future plans concerning this experimental schema are to design exercises for various rules and involve the measures of grammar and pragmatic damages into calculations.

6 Future work

As there are not many learner corpora for Russian-speaking learners of English and even fewer freely available corpora, our corpus seems to be a valuable contribution into the field. We plan to maintain the corpus, expand its volume and augment it with extensive error annotation cross-validated by numerous annotators. An important aspect of our refinement is developing a uniform way of tagging errors and verifying the details of the instructions for annotators to make sure that similar types of errors are tagged with similar tags. We also need to specify the tagging principles for the following tiers of annotation: causes of an error and the pragmatic damage caused by an error.

We are working within *brat* web annotation framework, so we are heavily dependent on its capacities. We are going to improve the framework by:

1. developing robust library to convert Freeling output to brat annotation files,
2. adding automatic tagging of typical spelling and grammar/syntactic errors,
3. improving search tool (possibility to save search results, multiple constraints, etc.),

4. adding the option to show only chosen tags (invisible annotation layers),
5. providing the possibility to annotate empty spans (missing articles, for example)
6. improving access control abilities (ability to show or hide annotations depending on user role).

Also we plan to use our corpus for the following applied tasks:

1. automated error detection,
2. automated grading of students' work (based on complex metrics and taking into account the predefined structure of exam essays),
3. massive creation of corpus-based error-focused grammar exercises,
4. adjusting morphological and syntactic parsers to learner corpus data.

Another important aspect of our future work is research into the process of second language acquisition based on the corpus data. In particular, we are planning to investigate the following aspects:

1. error patterns specific for Russian-speaking learners of English,
2. types error patterns typical of different stages in the learning process,
3. common causes of errors and peculiarities of L1 transfer effects for native Russian speakers,
4. introduction of the procedures of self-editing and mutual annotation among students,
5. features of interlanguages of learners with different past exposure to English (we have correspondent metadata available to large part of texts in the corpus).

Finally, the corpus can be of great value to the research into didactic issues, such as formulating the concept of an error in general, elaborating criteria for assigning errors, or studying the rate of agreement between EFL instructors.

7 Acknowledgements

We would like to express our deep gratitude to Olga Vinogradova for inspiring this project and for guiding us through the jungle of learners' errors.

The study was implemented in the framework of the Basic Research Program at the National Research University Higher School of Economics (HSE) in 2014.

References

Altenberg, B. and Granger, S. (2001). The grammatical and lexical patterning of make in native and non-native student writing. *Applied linguistics*, 22(2):173–195.

Corder, S. P. (1981). *Error analysis and interlanguage*, volume 112. Oxford Univ Press.

Cotton, D., Falvey, D., Kent, S., Albery, D., Kempton, G., and Hughes, J. (2008). *Language Leader: Upper Intermediate*. Pearson Education.

Dulay, H., Burt, M., and Krashen, S. D. (1982). *Language two*, volume 2. Oxford University Press New York.

Gas, S. (1979). Language transfer and universal grammatical relations. *Language learning*, 29(2):327–344.

Granger, S. (2003). Error-tagged learner corpora and call: A promising synergy. *CALICO journal*, 20(3):465–480.

Granger, S., Dagneaux, E., Meunier, F., Paquot, M., et al. (2009). The international corpus of learner english. version 2. handbook and cd-rom.

Granger, S. et al. (1996). From ca to cia and back: An integrated approach to computerized bilingual and learner corpora.

Granger, S., Gilquin, G., and Meunier, F. (2013). *Twenty Years of Learner Corpus Research. Looking Back, Moving Ahead: Proceedings of the First Learner Corpus Research Conference (LCR 2011)*, volume 1. Presses universitaires de Louvain.

Granger, S. and Paquot, M. (2014). The louvain eap dictionary (lead): A tailor-made web-based tool for non-native academic writers of english.

Izumi, E. and Isahara, H. (2004). Investigation into language learners' acquisition order based on the error analysis of the learner corpus. In *Proceedings of Pacific-Asia Conference on Language, Information and Computation (PACLIC) 18 Satellite Workshop on E-Learning, Japan.(in printing)*.

Izumi, E., Uchimoto, K., and Isahara, H. (2005). Error annotation for corpus of japanese learner english. In *Proceedings of the Sixth International Workshop on Linguistically Interpreted Corpora*, pages 71–80.

Kachru, B. B. (1992). *The other tongue: English across cultures*. University of Illinois Press.

Kutuzov, A. and Kunilovskaya, M. (2014). Russian learner translator corpus. In Sojka, P., Horák, A., Kopeček, I., and Pala, K., editors, *Text, Speech and Dialogue*, volume 8655 of *Lecture Notes in Computer Science*, pages 315–323. Springer International Publishing.

Lüdeling, A., Walter, M., Kroymann, E., and Adolphs, P. (2005). Multi-level error annotation in learner corpora. *Proceedings of corpus linguistics 2005*, pages 15–17.

McCarter, S. and Roberts, R. (2010). *Ready for IELTS Coursebook*. Macmillan Education.

Moore, T. and Morton, J. (2005). Dimensions of difference: a comparison of university writing and ielts writing. *Journal of English for Academic Purposes*, 4(1):43–66.

Padró, L. and Stanilovsky, E. (2012). Freeling 3.0: Towards wider multilinguality. In Calzolari, N., Choukri, K., Declerck, T., Doğan, M. U., Maegaard, B., Mariani, J., Odijk, J., and Piperidis, S., editors, *Proceedings of the Eight International Conference on Language Resources and Evaluation (LREC'12)*, Istanbul, Turkey. European Language Resources Association (ELRA).

Seidlhofer, B. (2002). Pedagogy and local learner corpora: Working with learning-driven data. *Computer learner corpora, second language acquisition and foreign language teaching*, pages 213–34.

Siemen, P., Lüdeling, A., and Müller, F. H. (2006). Falko – ein fehlerannotiertes lernerkorpus des deutschen. *Proceedings of Konvens 2006*.

Stenetorp, P., Pyysalo, S., Topic, G., Ohta, T., Ananiadou, S., and Tsujii, J. (2012). brat: a web-based tool for nlp-assisted text annotation. In *EACL*, pages 102–107.

A VIEW of Russian: Visual Input Enhancement and adaptive feedback

Robert Reynolds[1], *Eduard Schaf*[2], *Detmar Meurers*[1,2]

(1) University of Tromsø, Department of Language and Linguistics
(2) University of Tübingen, Department of Linguistics

robert.reynolds@uit.no, eduard.schaf@student.uni-tuebingen.de,
detmar.meurers@uni-tuebingen.de

ABSTRACT

We explore the challenges and opportunities which arise in developing automatic visual input enhancement activities for Russian with a focus on target selection and adaptive feedback. Russian, a language with a rich fusional morphology, has many syntactically relevant forms that are not transparent to the language learner, which makes it a good candidate for visual input enhancement (VIE). VIE essentially supports incidental focus on form by increasing the salience of language forms to support noticing by the learner. The freely available VIEW system (Meurers et al., 2010) was designed to automatically generate VIE activities from any web content. We extend VIEW to Russian and discuss connected research issues regarding target selection, ambiguity management, prompt generation, and distractor generation. We show that the same information and techniques used for target selection can often be repurposed for adaptive feedback. Authentic Text ICALL (ATICALL) systems incorporating only native-language NLP, without the NLP analysis specific to learner language that is characteristic of Intelligent Language Tutoring Systems (ILTS), thus can support some forms of adaptive feedback. ATICALL and ILTS represent a spectrum of possibilities rather than two categorically distinct enterprises.

KEYWORDS: CALL, ICALL, ATICALL, input enhancement, noticing, consciousness raising, adaptive feedback, scaffolding, part-of-speech tagging, finite-state technology, Constraint Grammar, Russian, stress, aspect, participles, case.

Robert Reynolds, Eduard Schaf and Detmar Meurers 2014. A VIEW of Russian: Visual Input Enhancement and adaptive feedback. *Proceedings of the third workshop on NLP for computer-assisted language learning.* NEALT Proceedings Series 22 / Linköping Electronic Conference Proceedings 107: 98–112.

1 Introduction

Intelligent Computer-Assisted Language Learning (ICALL) has been characterized (Meurers, 2012) as consisting of two distinct areas, Intelligent Language Tutoring Systems (ILTS) and Authentic Text ICALL (ATICALL). In the former, researchers have focused on the challenge of analyzing learner language and providing adaptive feedback. In the latter, research employs standard NLP tools developed for native language to identify and enhance authentic texts in the target language. While this seems like a categorical difference in some respects, in this article we want to show that it can be attractive to combine aspects of both approaches. We describe how an ATICALL system can incorporate a feature typical of ILTS: adaptive feedback to learner responses. The idea is explored using language activities for Russian, a language with a rich, fusional morphology that is challenging for second language learners. We showcase four of the Russian activities that we developed on top of the freely available VIEW platform (Meurers et al., 2010).

Russian Morphological Analysis Most Russian grammar books focus primarily on morphology, a serious challenge to most learners. Russian has a highly fusional morphology, with nominal inflection for six cases, two numbers, and three genders. There are three noun declension paradigms, each containing 12 forms. Adjectival modifiers have at least 24 forms. Russian verbs represent a relatively extensive inflectional system, similar to other Indo-European languages. A related difficulty is that Russian stress is phonemic, differentiating both lexical and inflectional homographs. This causes difficulties for learners, since there is a complex system of lexically specified stress placement, yet stress is almost never marked in the written language.

In order to build an ATICALL system for Russian, we need a fast, broad-coverage morphological engine to both analyze and generate word forms. In addition to the usual demands of a general-purpose morphological engine, we also need to generate stressed word forms. No open-source state-of-the art tools we are aware of provide this functionality. Thus a Russian Finite-State Transducer (FST) was developed (Reynolds, 2014) using the two-level formalism (Koskenniemi, 1983). The transducer was originally based on Zaliznjak (1977) ($\approx$ 120 000 words), which is the foundation for most Russian computational morphologies. Additional words, especially proper nouns, are continually being added. Since Russian has systematic syncretism and widespread homonymy, a constraint grammar (Karlsson et al., 1995) implemented in the freely available CG3 system[1] is used to disambiguate multiple readings.

Most state-of-the-art part of speech taggers for Russian are based on finite-state transducers, including *AOT/Dialing* (Nozhov, 2003), and *mystem* (Segalovich, 2003). Finite-state methods make it possible to provide efficient and robust computational analyses with wide empirical coverage, while keeping a clear conceptual distinction between the linguistic system and its usage. Finite-state methods also have several characteristics that make them especially well suited for ICALL. A finite-state analysis keeps track of what it knows, which allows an ATICALL system to focus only on targets that are clearly identifiable. Since finite-state tools provide an actual linguistic model of the language being analyzed, it is possible to identify and increase the salience of linguistic characteristics known to be relevant in language learning. A good case in point is stress placement, which is lexical, yet requires syntactic disambiguation. The finite state analysis provides effective access to subsets of data for certain grammar topics (e.g., retrieve all words with a particular stress pattern), since this information is modeled in the FST source files. Mistakes and errors in the system can be diagnosed and corrected.

[1]`http://beta.visl.sdu.dk/cg3.html`

This is especially important in ICALL, where low precision in the analysis leads to unreliable output easily confusing and frustrating learners. And, importantly in the context of ATICALL involving activities with distractors, a finite-state morphological analyzer can simply be reversed to become a generator.

Visual Input Enhancement Researchers in second language acquisition agree that comprehensible input is necessary for language learning. The Noticing Hypothesis (Schmidt, 1990) extends this claim to say that noticing of grammatical categories and relations also is required for successful second language acquisition. Based on the Noticing Hypothesis and related work on Consciousness Raising (Rutherford and Sharwood Smith, 1985) and Input Enhancement (Sharwood Smith, 1993, p. 176), researchers have investigated Visual Input Enhancement (VIE) to encourage learners to notice the grammatical forms in comprehensible input. VIE refers to the graphical enhancement of written text to draw attention to targeted grammatical structures. Various modes of enhancement have been suggested, such as font manipulation (e.g., bold, italic, color), capitalization, and other notations (e.g., underlining, circling). Such textual enhancements are intended to increase the likelihood that the learner will notice the target grammatical form in its grammatical and functional context of use.

Visual Input Enhancement of the Web (VIEW) is an ATICALL system designed to automatically generate learning activities from user-selected texts on the web. A description of the system architecture can be found in Meurers et al. (2010). VIEW includes four activity types to guide the learner from recognition via practice to production. The *highlight* activity adds color to target wordforms. The *click* activity allows the learner to identify target wordforms in the text. The *multiple-choice* activity provides controlled practice, allowing the learner to choose the correct form from a multiple-choice list. The *practice* activity asks learners to type the wordforms themselves. The activities can be accessed as a web application on a webpage or through a toolbar provided as a Firefox web browser Add-on. Activities have previously been developed for English, German, and Spanish. The open-source research prototype is available at `http://purl.org/icall/view`.

The following issues were considered in developing the activities for Russian:

1. Learner needs: What are the needs of the learner?
2. Feasibility: Can the target construction be reliably identified using NLP?
3. Target selection: Which tokens of the target construction should be focused?
4. Prompt generation: What kind of prompt can sufficiently constrain the learner productions for practice? (cf. Amaral and Meurers, 2011, sec. 3.1)
5. Generation of distractors for multiple-choice activities: What forms can or should serve as distractors? How does Second Language Acquisition (SLA) research help us with this, and how does the systematicity of the linguistic system allow us to generate distractors?
6. Feedback: What kind of feedback does the learner receive for (in)correct answers, under a perspective conceiving of feedback as *scaffolding* guiding the learner in their Zone of Proximal Development (Vygotsky, 1986)?

Related work Although research in Russian NLP for language learning has not been as extensive as for English and some other languages, some significant inroads have been made. One string of research is concerned with methods for identifying Russian texts at a suitable reading level for language learners. Sharoff et al. (2008) use a Principle Component Analysis to analyze the lexical and grammatical complexity of texts in a variety of languages, including

Russian. Similarly, Karpov et al. (2014) train a variety of machine-learning models on a small corpus of texts categorized by CEFR level, with promising results.

Another set of studies has been dedicated to Russian Intelligent Tutoring Systems. The Boltun project[2] has as one of its goals to develop NLP resources for ICALL, especially for analyzing learner language (Dickinson and Herring, 2008a,b; Dickinson, 2010). Another project, KLIOS, is a Learning Management System being developed specifically for Russian foreign language learning (Gorisev et al., 2013). KLIOS apparently makes use of the existing general-purpose tagger pymorphy2[3] and parser ABBYY Compreno[4], but not enough information is currently available to draw meaningful comparisons of the activities and analyses to our work on the Russian VIEW.

Goal and Structure of the Paper The goal of this article is to explore the ability of authentic text ICALL systems to provide adaptive feedback to learners. In doing so, we also demonstrate some features of the Russian VIEW system that we are currently developing, for which a prototype can be found at `http://purl.org/icall/rusVIEW`. In section 2, we introduce exercises for four separate target grammatical topics: Stress, Noun Declension, Aspect, and Participles. For each topic, we discuss the pedagogical motivation for the exercises, as well as relevant practical and theoretical issues that arose during development. Special attention is given to factors involved in target selection since these factors become relevant in the subsequent discussion. In section 3, we show how the same technology and strategies used in target selection can be used to provide adaptive feedback. Section 4 summarizes the contributions of the article and considers options for evaluating the approach.

2 Key topics for Russian learners

The following grammar topics are generally difficult for learners, relatively ubiquitous, and they allow us to exemplify central issues in visual input enhancement and the computational modeling it is built on. Section 2.1 introduces a basic example, highlighting the morphological analysis in a noun declension activity. The discussion of target selection for this activity illustrates the need to distinguish between grammatically and referentially determined morphosyntactic properties. Section 2.2 discusses activities for word stress, where target selection is primarily lexical, but is also concerned with managing the ambiguity that arises in rule-based morphologies. Section 2.3 outlines verbal aspect activities, where target selection is complicated by limitations in determining whether the learner should be able to deduce the aspect of each token. Section 2.4 presents participles activities, which demonstrate a more complicated use of wordform generation for providing prompts to guide learners' responses in multiple-choice and cloze activities.

2.1 Noun declension

The relatively extensive nominal inflection system is one of the first major hurdles for most Russian learners. Learners whose L1 does not have similar noun declension frequently seem to ignore inflectional endings. A visual input enhancement activity has the potential to boost learning by raising awareness of those endings.

We developed activities targeting specific case distinctions known to be difficult, but in this

[2] `http://cl.indiana.edu/~boltundevelopment`
[3] `https://pymorphy2.readthedocs.org`
[4] `http://www.abbyy.ru/isearch/compreno`

article we focus on describing the multiple-choice activity developed for all cases, since that activity makes it possible to illustrate both the underlying NLP and some points regarding target selection. When learners select this activity for a web page, VIEW replaces some nouns in the text with dropdown boxes containing the original noun in all of its case forms as options.

Target selection As a rule, each noun declension paradigm has 12 cells (six cases, singular and plural), but some forms are syncretic. For example, prototypical masculine nouns have ten unique forms, feminine and neuter nouns have nine, and the soft-consonant feminine nouns have only seven unique forms. Although our constraint grammar is able to disambiguate many syncretic forms, some ambiguity still remains in our analyses. One might expect that ambiguity in the analysis would complicate target selection, but this is only true if the analysis is ambiguous with regard to number. This is because a number ambiguity may be a referential ambiguity that cannot be resolved by checking contextual clues, as illustrated in (1).

(1) He saw the ________ (dancer/dancers).

Without additional context, such as a picture, this would be a confusing exercise given that both *dancer* and *dancers* are grammatically correct. Given this potential difficulty, we do not select tokens for which number is grammatically ambiguous.

Distractor generation After selecting targets that are unambiguously singular or plural, generating distractors is very straightforward. Let us assume that a given target ковёр *kovër* 'rug' results in the two morphological analyses in (2).

(2) a. ковёр+N+Msc+Inan+Sg+Nom
b. ковёр+N+Msc+Inan+Sg+Acc

To generate the distractors, we strip the case tag and generate all six cases from that base by adding the tags (+Nom, +Acc, +Gen, +Loc, +Dat, +Ins). For the example at hand, this generates the following forms: ковёр, ковёр, ковра, ковре, ковру, ковром. Because the original token was singular, all of the generated wordforms are also singular.

The generated forms are combined with the original token, and a set of unique wordforms is supplied to the learners as options in the multiple-choice activity. Currently, all six cases are used as distractors every time, but insights from SLA and future research should make it possible to identify those subsets of distractors most facilitating learning given a specific target.

2.2 Stress

Russian stress patterns are specified lexically and cannot be predicted reliably from stem shape. Furthermore, many homographic forms of the same lemma have differential stress. This makes mastering the correct pronunciation of some words a difficult task for learners.

Four different activities were developed for stress. Unlike most 'highlight' activities in VIEW, the stress highlight activity does not make use of color, but simply adds a stress mark above every known stressed vowel in the text. For the 'click' activity, every vowel in the text becomes clickable: stressed vowels turn green and receive a stress mark; unstressed vowels turn red. The 'multiple-choice' activity selects some targets and learners try to identify the correctly stressed variant. The conventional use of the 'practice' activity is not well motivated for stress, since the entire set of possible responses is already represented in the 'multiple-choice' activity. Furthermore, typing stress marks is cumbersome for most users. Because of this, the 'practice' activity was replaced by an activity in which stressed vowels are highlighted when the cursor hovers over the token.

Target selection The morphological analyzer cannot always determine the stress of a given token. Sometimes this is because the lemma is not in the lexicon. Such tokens are never targeted, since their stress is not certain. Other times, the morphological analyzer is unable to completely disambiguate all of the readings of a given token. In such cases, the token can still be targeted if the remaining morphological ambiguity is immaterial with regard to stress. For example, the fact that the form stressed on the first syllable in (3-a) is ambiguous between accusative or nominative is not relevant in our context; what matters is that it can be distinguished from the genitive form in (3-b).

(3) a. гу́бы
gúby
губа+N+Fem+Inan+Pl+Nom or +Acc
b. губы́
gubý
губа+N+Fem+Inan+Sg+Gen

Choosing targets for multiple-choice and practice activities is an interesting pedagogical issue, since almost every multisyllabic token is a potential target. Although there are many high-frequency words with difficult stress patterns, the overwhelming majority of Russian words have fixed stress. This means that if the program randomly selects targets for the multiple-choice and practice activities, many of the targets will not be pedagogically effective.

Since stress patterns in Russian are specified lexically, the solution to the target selection problem is also lexical. We compiled a stress activity target list of lemmas that have shifting stress based on our FST resource (Reynolds, 2014).[5] We also target one other large class of words: cognate words in L1 that have a different stress position in Russian. For example, compare English *rádiator* and Russian *radiátor*. We also added proper nouns for which a single standard stress position can be defined (e.g., *Rossíja* 'Russia', *Ukraína* 'Ukraine') to the stress activity target list.[6]

Distractor generation Generating distractors for the multiple-choice stress activity is very simple at this point. Since potential responses for a stress activity are a closed set, we provide all possible stress positions as distractors. Ideally, distractors should mimic likely incorrect responses that learners would make on a parallel cloze test. The distractors should represent the kinds of mistakes that learners typically make, so one could tune the distractor set by logging user interaction with the system, possibly also using distinct classes of learner models.

[5]For nouns, in addition to Zaliznjak's stress indexes *c*, *d*, *e*, and *f*, we also include masculine nouns with index *b* (end stressed), such as *kón'* ~*kon'á* 'stallion'. For adjectives, only short-form adjectives are targeted.

[6]Many proper names have differential pronunciation for different referents, especially surnames: Ivánov vs Ivanóv. Such lemmas are not targeted.

2.3 Aspect

Most Russian verbs are either imperfective or perfective. For example, the English verb 'to say/tell' corresponds to the two Russian verbs *govorit'* (impf) and *skazat'* (perf). Imperfective verbs are generally used to express duration, process, or repetition. Perfective verbs are generally used for unique events, and they typically imply completion. The use of one aspect or the other is frequently dependent on context, as we discuss in more detail in a corpus study below.

Russian has a productive system of aspectual derivation, by which so-called aspectual pairs are formed. Although some verb pairs have no derivational relation (like *govorit' / skazat'*), many verb pairs have one of the following two relations:[7]

(4) a. IMPF: simplex verb ; PERF: prefix + simplex verb
smotret 'to watch.IMPF' / *po-smotret* 'to watch.PERF'
b. IMPF: (perfective stem) + suffix ; PERF: prefix + simplex verb
(ras-smatr)-ivat 'to examine.IMPF' / *ras-smotret* 'to examine.PERF'

Verbal aspect is arguably the single most challenging grammar topic for learners of Russian. The distinction between imperfective and perfective verbs is difficult for beginners to grasp, and even very advanced learners struggle to master the finer points. A set of ATICALL activities on aspect enables learners to focus on how aspect is used in context, which is crucial for Russian.

Target selection Since aspect in Russian is lexical, target selection also takes a lexical approach. First, not all verbs are paired with aspectual counterparts that have identical meanings. Since distractors should be equivalent in every respect other than aspect, we select only verbs that belong to an aspectual pair.[8] The list of paired verbs is compiled from three sources: 1) pairings such as (4-a) above are taken from the Exploring Emptiness database[9], 2) pairings such as (4-b) above are taken from Zaliznjak (1977), and 3) pairings without a derivational relationship (of which there are few) are extracted from electronic dictionaries.

Choice of verbal aspect is generally a matter of construal, i.e., how the speaker is structuring the discourse, and some verb tokens could be grammatically correct with either aspect. Consider the English examples *John saw Mary* and *John had seen Mary*. Even though they are likely to be used in different circumstances, both sentences are grammatically well-formed. Likewise, in Russian there are cases that allow either aspect. Meurers et al. (2010) suggested that lexical cues for English aspect and tense could be automatically identified by NLP. Indeed, many Russian grammars also indicate contexts in which one aspect or the other is impossible, or at least very unlikely. In order to identify contexts which constrain the expression of one aspect or the other, Russian grammar books were consulted, resulting in the following lexical cues.

(5) Contexts in which perfective aspect is impossible/unlikely:
a. Infinitive complement of *byt'* 'to be' (analytic future)
b. Infinitive complement of certain verbs (especially phrasal verbs, such as 'begin', 'continue', 'finish', etc.)
c. With certain adverbials denoting duration and repetition

[7]This is a simplistic sketch of Russian verbal aspect; for a proper discussion cf., e.g., Timberlake (2004).

[8]Although the notion of aspectual pairs has been shown to be somewhat problematic (Kuznetsova, 2013), this is the most robust approach available to us, and we do not expect problematic cases to be common.

[9]`http://emptyprefixes.uit.no`

(6) Contexts in which imperfective aspect is impossible/unlikely:

a. Infinitive complement of certain verbs (e.g., 'forget' and 'succeed')
b. With certain adverbials denoting unexpectedness, immediacy, etc.

A corpus study was conducted to test the usefulness of these features in an ATICALL application. The goal of the study was to determine the precision of the features, as well as their coverage, or recall. Precision was calculated as the percentage of verbs found adjacent to the appropriate lexical cues listed in (5) and (6) whose aspect was accurately predicted by that lexical cue. Recall was calculated as the percentage of all verbs whose aspect is correctly predicted by an adjacent lexical cue. From the perspective of ATICALL, precision tells us whether the student ought to know which aspect is required, which is useful for target selection. Recall tells us what percentage of verbs actually appear together with these lexical cues, and whose aspect is correctly predicted by them.

The study included two corpora, each investigated separately. The Russian National Corpus[10] (230 M tokens) is a tagged corpus with diverse genres. The annotation in the RNC frequently contains ambiguities, but since the aspect of Russian verbs is rarely ambiguous and the aspect of the contextual features is irrelevant, ambiguous readings do not significantly affect our outcomes. Since the RNC does not include syntactic relations, we rely on collocation of these lexical cues with verbs. SynTagRus[11] (860 K tokens) is a morphologically disambiguated and syntactically annotated dependency treebank of Russian. Because dependency relations are defined, identifying adverbial relations and verbal complements is straightforward. The results are given in Table 1.

	RNC	SynTagRus
Precision	0.95	0.98
Recall	0.03	0.02

Table 1: Results of the corpus study of lexical cues for aspect

The precision of these lexical cues is very high, meaning that when lexical cues are present, the verb is of the predicted aspect. This is expected, since known counterexamples such as (7) are uncommon. Given that Russian allows variable word order, it is surprising that collocation in the RNC is nearly as reliable as dependency relations in this task. Apparently these words have a very strong tendency to appear adjacent to one another.

(7) Настоящий друг всегда скажет правду.
Nastojaščij drug vsegda skažet pravdu.
True friend always will-tell.PF truth
'A true friend will always tell the truth.'

Unfortunately the recall of the lexical cues is extremely low. It correctly predicted the aspect of only one out of 50–60 verbs. Although future work is needed to explore these phenomena more thoroughly, these results seem to indicate that verbal aspect in Russian is predominantly determined suprasententially, with lexical cues playing only a very minor role.

[10] http://www.ruscorpora.ru/en/index.html
[11] http://www.ruscorpora.ru/search-syntax.html

For language learning, this result has several implications. First, it shows that learners can place their confidence in lexical cues, but these cues will not get them very far. Yet in some Russian textbooks, more space is dedicated to these lexical cues than to discourse considerations. This means that some learners may not be getting enough instruction on strategies that help in the majority of cases. Second, for the purposes of target selection, the Russian VIEW system can rely on lexical cues of aspect with some confidence. If a token is adjacent to the appropriate cues, then a learner should be expected to know the aspect of that token. However, since the lexical cues are so sparse, the system cannot make an intelligent decision for the overwhelming majority of verb tokens. One potential solution would be to implement machine-learning approaches to predict the distribution of each aspect more accurately. However, even though such models might make more accurate predictions, there is no guarantee that its output would reflect what a human second language learner should be capable of distinguishing.

If it is true that structural rules cannot provide adequate coverage of aspectual usage, then this implies that Russian verbal aspect is acquired through semantic bootstrapping. As learners are exposed to verbs of both aspects, real-world knowledge and expectations form the foundation upon which aspectual categories are built in their minds. If this is the case, it may not be feasible for an ATICALL system to predict how or whether the learner can be expected to know the aspect of a given target. The system can still provide a significant benefit to the learner by facilitating focus-on-form exercises, albeit blindly.

These last points are based on the assumption that the distribution of verbal aspect in Russian cannot be adequately accounted for with rules that are both pedagogically reasonable and technologically implementable. Our ongoing research will attempt to clarify this situation, but in the meantime, our system selects any paired verbs as targets, giving preference to forms that appear adjacent to our lexical cues.

Distractor generation Distractors for the multiple-choice activity are generated by replacing the lemma with its aspectual partner, and replacing the aspectual tag, as shown in (8-b).

(8) a. Original: читать+V+Impf+TV+Pst+Msc+Sg
b. Distractor: прочитать+V+**Perf**+TV+Pst+Msc+Sg

2.4 Participles

Russian has four kinds of adjectival participles, which are used both attributively and as relativizers. Their formation, meaning, and usage are not usually introduced to learners until more advanced levels. Although they are not used frequently in spoken Russian, participles are very common in written Russian, especially in high registers, such as literature, official documents, news, and technical writing. Many learners without parallel forms in their L1 struggle with Russian participles. All of these things make participles an excellent candidate for ATICALL visual input enhancement.

Target selection The four participles are present active, present passive, past active, and past passive. The passive participles are generally only formed from transitive verbs. Present participles are only formed from imperfective verbs, and past participles are typically formed from perfective verbs. The result of this is that not all verbs (or rather, verb pairs) can form every kind of participle. In order to select only those verbs from which a full 'paradigm' of distractors can be formed, we limit target selection to transitive verbs that are members of aspectual pairs (as described in section 2.3). We also do not target participles that have a possible lexicalized adjective reading, such as одетый *odetyj* 'dressed', or participles in the short-form.

Prompt generation Multiple-choice and cloze activities require a prompt for students to know which kind of participle is being elicited. One way to do this is to rephrase the participle using the relative determiner который *kotoryj* 'which'. For example, the present active participle дремлющий *dremljuščij* 'slumbering' can be rephrased as который дремлет *kotoryj dremlet* 'which/who slumbers'. Fortunately, it is possible to perform this rephrasing automatically, based solely on the tags of the original token. This is demonstrated in (9) and (10), where (a) gives an example of a participle in context, (b) gives the participle's grammar tags assigned by the tagger, and (c) provides the *relative-rephrase* and its readings. The bolded tags in (b) and (c) indicate the tags that are extracted from the participle reading in order to generate the relative-rephrase. The tags in (c) that are not bolded are the same for every participle of that category.

(9) Present Active

a. разлука есть гроб, заключающий в себе половину сердца
separation is tomb which-imprisons in itself half of-heart
'separation is a tomb which imprisons half of one's heart.'

b. заключающий: заключать+V+Impf**+TV+Prs**Act**+Msc+Sg**+Nom

c. который заключает 'which imprisons'
который+Pron+Rel**+Msc+Sg**+Nom
заключать+V+Impf**+TV+Prs**+**Sg**3

(10) Past Passive

a. Рассеянное молчание
which-was-scattered silence
'scattered silence'

b. рассеять+V**+Perf**+TV**+Pst**Pss**+Neu+Sg**+Nom

c. которое рассеяли 'which (they) scattered'
который+Pron+Rel**+Neu+Sg**+Acc
рассеять+V**+Perf**+TV**+Pst**+MFN+Pl

The given relative-rephrasing of passive participle in (10) is a zero person construction (неопределённо-личное предложение), in which there is no explicit subject, and the verb shows third-person plural agreement. Although this rephrasing is not always the best possible rewording of the passive, it is the alternative that works best in a wide variety of circumstances.

This method of prompt generation takes advantage of the systematicity of grammatical relations in Russian. It works because all of the morphosyntactic information needed to form the relative-rephrase is already present in the original participle's morphosyntactic tags.

3 Feedback

In contrast to Intelligent Tutoring Systems, ATICALL systems such as VIEW and reading support tools such as Glosser-RuG (Nerbonne et al., 1998), COMPASS (Breidt and Feldweg, 1997),

REAP[12], or ALPHEIOS[13] focus on the analysis of authentic native text. Where input enhancement and reading support turns into exercise generation, such as the multiple-choice and cloze activities of VIEW, the feedback currently provided by the system is very limited. If a response is correct, then it turns green. If a response is incorrect, it turns red. VIEW does not attempt to reveal *why* a response is correct or incorrect. How about providing more informative adaptive feedback, whereby VIEW becomes more similar to an Intelligent Tutoring System?

In the following, we consider the degree to which the feedback that learners receive in an ATICALL environment can be enhanced without developing new NLP tools for learner language analysis. For the feedback methods listed below, enriched feedback can be provided using only the information already used in the target selection and distractor generation processes. In other words, the information used to select a given token is frequently the same information that is needed to provide enriched feedback beyond a simple correct/incorrect indicator.

3.1 Noun declension feedback (multiple-choice activity)

Feedback for noun declension activities can be based on dependency relations established by a native-language parser. For example, in the phrase *On obyčno sidel rjadom s mamoj* 'He usually sat next to (his) mother.INS', the word *mamoj* is in the instrumental case because it is the object of the preposition *s*. This fact is explicitly represented in a dependency tree, since the preposition *s* directly dominates *mamoj*. The ATICALL system can consult the parse tree to prepare relevant feedback. If a learner selects the wrong case for this target, then the preposition *s* is highlighted to show the learner why it should be in instrumental. As in tutoring systems, miniature lessons could be prepared for specific syntactic constructions to provide related information. For example, with this preposition, the learner could be presented with the following: "*s* can govern three different cases depending on its meanings: INS='with', GEN='(down) from', and ACC='approximately'. (Use with ACC is rare.)"

This type of feedback is relevant, informative, and can easily be linked to specific syntactic constructions. Effective adaptive feedback in such a multiple-choice activity thus does not depend on learner-language NLP. The native-language NLP – both syntactic analyses and distractor generation – is providing effective feedback capabilities, even if it is not equivalent to what is possible with learner-language NLP.

3.2 Stress feedback (click and multiple-choice activities)

In the multiple-choice and practice activities for stress, targets are selected according to the stress activity target list introduced in section 2.2, which is extracted from the FST source files (Reynolds, 2014) partially based on Zaliznjak (1977). In his dictionary, every word is assigned a code signifying which stress pattern it belongs to. We combined this information with frequency data from the Russian National Corpus in order to select an exemplar for each stress type. Based on this information, a tooltip can be displayed that shows the exemplar and its paradigm when a learner gives an incorrect response. In this way, the learner is able to associate the targeted token with a word that is hopefully more familiar. This type of feedback supports both top-down and bottom-up learning, since it relies on an abstract connection to a concrete example.

[12] `http://reap.cs.cmu.edu`
[13] `http://alpheios.net`

3.3 Aspect feedback (multiple-choice activity)

As we discussed in section 2.3, determining *why* a given aspect is required in a given context is rarely possible with current technology. However, some tokens do have a clear lexical cue, which is used both to promote their selection as targets, and can also be used as corrective feedback. For example, given the sentence *On obyčno sidel rjadom s mamoj.* 'He usually sat.IMPF next to (his) mother', if the learner selects the perfective verb, then the adverb cue *obyčno* can be highlighted to show the learner *why* perfective is not appropriate. As in the previous case, the information needed to give enhanced feedback is the same information used in target selection.

3.4 Participles feedback (multiple-choice activity)

Recall that the participle activities discussed above have a prompt provided in the form of a *kotoryj* 'which/who' relative-rephrase of the participle. It was shown that the morphosyntactic properties of the participle correspond directly to the morphosyntactic properties of the relative-rephrase. These very same relations can be leveraged to provide feedback to the learner.

For example, let us say that the original token was a past active participle *napisavšij* 'who wrote' with the relative-rephrase hint (*kotoryj napisal*). If the learner selects the present active participle distractor *pišuščij*, they could be presented with feedback such as: "The word you selected means *kotoryj pišet*. Pay attention to the tense of *napisal*." This feedback is tailored to the learner's response, and encourages the learner to compare the functional meanings of the relevant morphological forms. In this case, the strategy used for prompt generation facilitates customized feedback.

Overall, the four examples sketched above show that the provision of specific types of adaptive feedback is a meaningful and natural extension of an ATICALL system such as VIEW, using the same NLP techniques employed in analysis, target selection and distractor generation. We are currently working on extending the implemented Russian activities discussed in section 2 in this direction.

4 Conclusions and Outlook

We reported practical and theoretical issues related to developing automatic visual input enhancement for Russian, with a focus on including adaptive feedback in such an ATICALL system. The selected topics demonstrate the challenges that a morphology-rich language brings with it and how a rule-based morphological analysis can be used to tackle them. In addition to providing the means for effective disambiguation, the finite state approach makes it possible to generate wordforms for distractors, prompts (participles), and stressed wordforms. We also characterized certain types of adaptive feedback, typically associated with intelligent language tutoring systems, that can be added in an ATICALL environment using the same information that is used for target selection and distractor generation. This refines the perspective distinguishing two subdisciplines of ICALL (Meurers, 2012), while keeping a clear distinction on the processing side between analyzing learner language and analyzing native language for learners.

In terms of future work, the crucial next step is to empirically evaluate the approach and the specific parameterization (activities, enhancement methods, distractors, and feedback used) in terms of learner uptake and, more generally, learning gains. While identifying a real-life educational context in which the tool can be integrated meaningfully is a complex undertaking, the computational approach presented in this article should readily support a controlled study with different intervention groups and a standard pretest-posttest-delayed posttest design. The foundational hypotheses upon which visual input enhancement is built have not been empirically evaluated to a sufficient degree (Lee and Huang, 2008), so evaluating learner outcomes is needed not only to establish the system's effectiveness, but also to validate the theories upon which it is based. As already suggested in Meurers et al. (2010), an ATICALL platform such as VIEW should make it possible to push intervention studies to a level where effects could be more readily established than in the very controlled but small laboratory settings.[14] This seems particularly relevant since there are many parameters that need to be explored, e.g., which kind of visual input enhancement works for which kind of learners and for which kind of linguistic targets presented in which contexts. We are also interested in exploring which kind of distractors (and how many) are optimal for which activities or learner levels. Finally, while it is beyond the current analysis we perform, we plan to investigate different ways of measuring *noticing* through computer interaction behaviors, and test their correlation with individual learner characteristics and learning outcomes.

On the computational side, we also plan to evaluate the performance of the NLP components used in the approach in terms of precision, recall, and speed. Here it is important to evaluate not only the general performance, but also its performance for the specific parts of speech and morphological properties that are at issue in a given activity. For the activities discussed in this article, this includes nouns for the noun declension activity, infinitive and indicative verbs for the aspect activity, participles for the participles activity, and all parts of speech for the stress activity. The performance should also be tested on different genres and reading levels, since those distinctions will affect NLP performance. Ideally, the performance should be analyzed on a corpus that is characteristic of the material that the learners or their teachers select as basis for generating activities – which is only possible in an interdisciplinary approach including both NLP research and real-life teaching and learning contexts.

In terms of making an ATICALL system useful in real-life, an important challenge arises from the fact that many texts do not contain enough of the relevant sorts of targets or contextual cues. This, for example, was apparent in the corpus study related to verbal aspect. The texts a learner chooses for enhancement and activity generation thus should be filtered in a way ensuring a sufficient number of targets in the texts. To address that need, we plan to further develop language-aware search engines (Ott and Meurers, 2010) supporting the selection of appropriate materials.

Acknowledgments

We would like to thank Elena Grishina and Andrej Zaliznjak for making the most recent version of Zaliznjak's grammar dictionary available electronically for academic purposes. We are grateful to Laura Janda and the CLEAR research group at the University of Tromsø, as well as two anonymous reviewers for their comments on our paper. All remaining faults are, of course, our own. In terms of the context making our collaboration possible, we are indebted to Trond Trosterud and Lene Antonsen at the Giellatekno research group at the University of Tromsø.

[14] In a similar vein, Presson et al. (2013) discuss the potential of experimental computer-assisted language learning tools for SLA research.

References

Amaral, L. and Meurers, D. (2011). On using intelligent computer-assisted language learning in real-life foreign language teaching and learning. *ReCALL*, 23(1):4–24.

Breidt, E. and Feldweg, H. (1997). Accessing foreign languages with COMPASS. *Machine Translation*, 12(1–2):153–174. Special Issue on New Tools for Human Translators.

Dickinson, M. (2010). Generating learner-like morphological errors in Russian. In *Proceedings of the 23nd International Conference on Computational Linguistics (COLING-10)*, Beijing.

Dickinson, M. and Herring, J. (2008a). Developing online ICALL exercises for Russian. In *The 3rd Workshop on Innovative Use of NLP for Building Educational Applications (BEA-3) at ACL'08*, pages 1–9, Columbus, OH.

Dickinson, M. and Herring, J. (2008b). Russian morphological processing for ICALL. In *The Fifth Midwest Computational Linguistics Colloquium (MCLC-5)*, East Lansing, MI.

Gorisev, S., Koynov, A., Kuzemchik, V., Lisinin, S., Mikhaleva, E., Mishunin, O., Savinov, A., Terekhin, D., Firstov, D., and Cherkashin, A. (2013). Интеллектуальный лингвопроцессорный комплекс «КЛИОС» для обучения РКИ [Intelligent language-aware tutoring system "KLIOS" for studying Russian as a foreign language]. Современные проблемы науки и образования *[Modern problems of science and education]*, 6.

Karlsson, F., Voutilainen, A., Heikkilä, J., and Anttila, A., editors (1995). *Constraint Grammar: A Language-Independent System for Parsing Unrestricted Text*. Number 4 in Natural Language Processing. Mouton de Gruyter, Berlin and New York.

Karpov, N., Baranova, J., and Vitugin, F. (2014). Single-sentence readability prediction in Russian. In *Proceedings of Analysis of Images, Social Networks, and Texts conference (AIST)*.

Koskenniemi, K. (1983). Two-level morphology: A general computaitonal model for word-form recognition and production. Technical report, University of Helsinki, Department of General Linguistics.

Kuznetsova, J. (2013). *Linguistic Profiles: Correlations between Form and Meaning*. PhD thesis, University of Tromsø. Doctoral Dissertation.

Lee, S.-K. and Huang, H.-T. (2008). Visual Input Enhancement and Grammar Learning: A meta-analytic review. *Studies in Second Language Acquisition*, 30:307–331.

Meurers, D. (2012). Natural language processing and language learning. In Chapelle, C. A., editor, *Encyclopedia of Applied Linguistics*, pages 4193–4205. Wiley, Oxford.

Meurers, D., Ziai, R., Amaral, L., Boyd, A., Dimitrov, A., Metcalf, V., and Ott, N. (2010). Enhancing authentic web pages for language learners. In *Proceedings of the 5th Workshop on Innovative Use of NLP for Building Educational Applications (BEA-5) at NAACL-HLT 2010*, pages 10–18, Los Angeles.

Nerbonne, J., Dokter, D., and Smit, P. (1998). Morphological Processing and Computer-Assisted Language Learning. *Computer Assisted Language Learning*, 11(5):543–559.

Nozhov, I. (2003). Морфологическая и синтаксическая обработка текста (модели и программы) *[Morphological and Syntactic Text Processing (models and programs)] also published as* Реализация автоматической синтаксической сегментации русского предложения *[Realization of automatic syntactic segmentation of the Russian sentence]*. PhD thesis, Russian State University for the Humanities, Moscow.

Ott, N. and Meurers, D. (2010). Information retrieval for education: Making search engines language aware. *Themes in Science and Technology Education. Special issue on computer-aided language analysis, teaching and learning: Approaches, perspectives and applications*, 3(1–2):9–30.

Presson, N., Davy, C., and MacWhinney, B. (2013). Experimentalized call for adult second language learners. In Schwieter, J. W., editor, *Innovative Research and Practices in Second Language Acquisition and Bilingualism*, pages 139—-164. John Benjamins.

Reynolds, R. (2014). A two-level finite-state transducer for Russian language-learning applications. `https://victorio.uit.no/langtech/trunk/langs/rus/`.

Rutherford, W. E. and Sharwood Smith, M. (1985). Consciousness-raising and universal grammar. *Applied Linguistics*, 6(2):274–282.

Schmidt, R. (1990). The role of consciousness in second language learning. *Applied Linguistics*, 11:206–226.

Segalovich, I. (2003). A fast morphological algorithm with unknown word guessing induced by a dictionary for a web search engine. In *International Conference on Machine Learning; Models, Technologies and Applications*, pages 273–280.

Sharoff, S., Kopotev, M., Erjavec, T., Feldman, A., and Divjak, D. (2008). Designing and evaluating a Russian tagset. In *Proceedings of LREC*, Marrakech.

Sharwood Smith, M. (1993). Input enhancement in instructed SLA: Theoretical bases. *Studies in Second Language Acquisition*, 15:165–179.

Timberlake, A. (2004). *A reference grammar of Russian*. Cambridge University Press.

Vygotsky, L. S. (1986). *Thought and Language*. MIT Press, Cambridge, MA.

Zaliznjak, A. A. (1977). Грамматический словарь русского языка: словоизменение: около 100 000 слов *[Grammatical dictionary of the Russian language: Inflection: approx 100 000 words]*. Изд-во "Русский язык".

Automatic CEFR Level Prediction for Estonian Learner Text

Sowmya Vajjala[1], *Kaidi Lõo*[2]

(1) LEAD Graduate School, University of Tübingen, Germany
(2) Department of Linguistics, University of Alberta, Canada

sowmya@sfs.uni-tuebingen.de, kloo@ualberta.ca

ABSTRACT

This paper reports on approaches for automatically predicting a learner's language proficiency in Estonian according to the European CEFR scale. We used the morphological and POS tag information extracted from the texts written by learners. We compared classification and regression modeling for this task. Our models achieve a classification accuracy of 79% and a correlation of 0.85 when modeled as regression. After a comparison between them, we concluded that classification is more effective than regression in terms of exact error and the direction of error. Apart from this, we investigated the most predictive features for both multi-class and binary classification between groups and also explored the nature of the correlations between highly predictive features. Our results show considerable improvement in classification accuracy over previously reported results and take us a step closer towards the automated assessment of Estonian learner text.

KEYWORDS: Estonian, Proficiency Classification, CEFR, Morphological Features, Machine Learning.

Sowmya Vajjala and Kaidi Lõo 2014. Automatic CEFR level prediction for Estonian learner text. *Proceedings of the third workshop on NLP for computer-assisted language learning.* NEALT Proceedings Series 22 / Linköping Electronic Conference Proceedings 107: 113–127.

1 Introduction

People learn a foreign language for many reasons like: living in a new country, having a general interest in the language etc., In many of these scenarios, language learners also undertake exams to get certified for their proficiency in a foreign language. Language proficiency is typically measured using some standardized scale like the CEFR (Council of Europe, 2001) in European nations. Evaluating free text responses like essays is one of the standard ways of assessing the language proficiency of a learner. Traditionally, these student essays were evaluated by experienced human graders trained for doing the task. With the ever increasing number of people taking language tests and with the advent of computational tools that can process language, automatic approaches that reduce human grading effort became a standard way to assess language proficiency. Automated essay grading is already being used along with human grading in several assessment exams like Graduate Record Examination (GRE) and Graduate Management Admission Test (GMAT). It can also be useful in a placement test that one may take at a language teaching institute before starting to learn a language at a certain level or serve as a guiding tool for language learners in self-assessment. Apart from this, automated approaches can also enable us to identify distinctive features at a proficiency level, thereby providing us with insights about the process of language acquisition.

While automated assessment is an active area of research for English, approaches for the automatic proficiency classification of learner essays according to the European CEFR scale were recently proposed for German (Hancke and Meurers, 2013), Swedish (Östling et al., 2013) and Estonian (Vajjala and Lõo, 2013). In this paper, we focus on the proficiency classification of Estonian learner essays. We started with the feature set described in Vajjala and Lõo (2013) and added more features to the list. We also used a more fine-grained subset of the same base corpus, consisting of four CEFR proficiency levels. We show that our approach improves the overall classification accuracy for this task reaching up to 79% for a four-level classification. We compare this approach with modeling the problem as regression and show that classification performs better in terms of accuracy and the direction of error. Apart from these, to gain a better understanding of the modeling process, we also studied the issues of feature selection, most predictive features for classification between categories and for overall classification, and correlations between features. In sum, we investigate proficiency classification both from a prediction as well as an interpretational perspective.

Rest of this paper is organized as follows: we start with an overview of contemporary research in proficiency classification of free text responses in Section 2 and describe the corpus and features we used in Section 3. Section 4 describes our experimental setup and explains the classification and regression experiments we performed along with our results. Section 5 briefly discusses feature selection and correlational analysis with all the features. Section 6 concludes the paper with pointers to future work.

2 Background

Automated Assessment (AA) of learner essays can be useful either as a method of scoring them by their proficiency or for understanding the distinctive features of language at a given proficiency level. AA has been active area of research in the field of language testing for a few decades now. Several assessment exams like GRE, GMAT that have language proficiency as a component have been using automated assessment systems as one of the scoring methods along with human graders. These AA systems that are primarily developed for English use a wide range of linguistic and structural features to score student essays (e.g., Burstein, 2003;

Zhang, 2008; Williamson, 2009; Burstein and Chodorow, 2010; Yannakoudakis et al., 2011; Crossley et al., 2011).

Apart from these approaches whose primary purpose is to predict the learner proficiency, there have been studies that did a qualitative analysis of distinctive features between proficiency levels in Second Language Acqusition (SLA) literature. Kyle and Crossley (2014) used a range of lexical sophistication indices and showed that the measures explain 47.5% of the variance in holistic scores of lexical proficiency of second language English learners. Characteristics like lexical richness, syntactic complexity, error patterns of learners and other characteristics too were studied in the recent past (e.g., Tono, 2000; Lu, 2010, 2012; Vyatkina, 2012). Although this strand of research is primarily focused on English, recent research has started to focus on other languages as well (Gyllstad et al., 2014).

With the creation of learner corpora in various European languages, automatic approaches for classifying learner essays into various proficiency levels began to emerge. Approaches for morphologically-rich languages also made use of language specific morphological features, which were not explored before in the case of English. Östling et al. (2013) reported on a proficiency classification approach for Swedish based on a corpus of 1,700 learner essays spanning four levels, obtained from the high-school exams conducted at a national level in Sweden. Along with the features like word length, sentence length, POS tag densities and corpus based entropy features, they also used spelling and compound splitting error based features for this task and achieved an overall accuracy of 62% for four level classification. Hancke and Meurers (2013); Hancke (2013) described a proficiency classification approach for German based on European CEFR standards using a broad range of lexical, syntactic and morphological features, considering German language structure into account. For a five level graded corpus with about 200 texts per level, they achieved a classification accuracy of 64.5%.

Vajjala and Lõo (2013) developed a proficiency classification approach for Estonian learner corpus and achieved an accuracy of 66% for a three level (A,B,C) corpus consisting of 250 texts per level, using a collection of POS and morphological features. We extended this work by adding more features and working with a fine-grained corpus spanning four levels on the CEFR scale. Further, we modeled the problem as both classification and regression and compared their performance. We also explored predictive features between categories and inter-feature correlations.

3 Corpus and Features

3.1 Corpus

Our experiments are based on the Estonian Interlanguage Corpus (EIC)[1] released online by Talinn University. It is a corpus of texts written by learners of Estonian as a second or foreign language. Most of the texts are originally obtained from language examinations conducted by various government bodies in Estonia. These texts include essays, personal and official letters and answers to language exercises. The learners come from diverse language backgrounds, although majority of them are native speakers of Russian. The corpus currently consists of around 12,000 documents in total[2]. The grading of this corpus is an ongoing project. In our analysis, we only used a subset of the whole corpus that is currently annotated with proficiency level. The version used in this paper was crawled from the EIC website in July 2014. As the

[1] `http://evkk.tlu.ee/`

[2] `http://evkk.tlu.ee/statistics.html`

corpus annotation is still under development, the latest version that is available on the web may have more texts than the version we used[3].

The corpus we used in this paper consists of 879 texts in total, belonging to four proficiency levels A2, B1, B2, C1. Since only one document each was annotated as A1 and C2 respectively in the corpus, we removed those levels from our experiments. According to the CEFR definitions, A2 represents a basic language user, B1 and B2 represent independent user and C1 represents a proficient user.

This corpus was used for Estonian proficiency classification earlier in Vajjala and Lõo (2013). However, we could not use the same version as the assigned grades changed for the current version. In the previous version of the corpus, proficiency levels were estimated based on the meta information collected from teacher or based on the subjective opinion of the data enterer (Eslon, 2014). The current version of the corpus has proficiency levels estimated by three qualified professional graders and divided into six CEFR categories instead of three levels A,B,C as in the older version. Thus, the proficiency level of certain texts got modified in the process and the current version of proficiency annotation of the corpus is considered precise and accurate (Eslon, 2014). However, it has to be noted that we do not have access to the individual grades given by the three graders. We only have the final grade assigned to the text. We also do not have any information about the inter-annotator agreement about the grades per text.

The crawled corpus consisted of HTML documents, which were parsed using HtmlUnit[4] and plain-text of the learner writing was extracted using Xpath expressions. Figure 1 shows some basic statistics about the corpus we used, in terms of the number of texts per category, average and the range for number of words per text. It can be noticed that the corpus is not evenly distributed across all levels. Hence, while modeling as classification, we consider this aspect and report our experiments with two versions of the dataset - one, a balanced version with equal training samples for all categories, the other an unbalanced version. Further, there is a broad range for all the categories. We used a normalized version of the dataset for our experiments.

Proficiency Level	**#Docs**	**Avg. #words**	**Range**
A2-level	196	145.9	[23, 636]
B1-level	384	226.3	[39, 1267]
B2-level	207	368.5	[30, 1749]
C1-level	92	704.1	[180, 4508]

Table 1: The Estonian Interlanguage Corpus

3.2 Preprocessing

These texts were POS-tagged using TreeTragger [5], (Schmid, 1994) a probabilistic part of speech tagger which has Estonian parameter files to tag Estonian data. The tag set was derived from the Tartu Morphologically Disambiguated Corpus tag set[6] and consists of morphological information

[3]We can share our version of the corpus with anyone who wants to replicate the experiments.

[4]http://htmlunit.sourceforge.net

[5]`http://www.ims.uni-stuttgart.de/projekte/corplex/TreeTagger/`

[6]`http://www.cl.ut.ee/korpused/morfkorpus/`

along with basic POS information. All the features reported in this paper are calculated based on TreeTagger's output.

Table 2 shows an example output from TreeTagger for the sentence *Tänapäeva meediat valitseb suur spekter erinevaid tehnilisi abivahendeid, on arvuti, internet ja selle kõrval ka muu digitaalne kommunikatsioon*, taken from a C1 level essay in the corpus. (The sentence means: "*Today's media is dominated by a large spectrum of different technical tools, computer, internet, in addition to other digital communication.*")

word	tag	lemma
Tänapäeva	S.com.sg.gen	täna_päev+0
meediat	S.com.sg.part	meedia+t
valitseb	V.main.indic.pres.ps3.sg.ps.af	valitse+b
suur	A.pos.sg.nom	suur+0
spekter	S.com.sg.nom	spekter+0
erinevaid	A.pos.pl.part	erinev+id
tehnilisi	A.pos.pl.part	tehniline+i
abivahendeid	S.com.pl.part	abi_vahend+id
,	Z.Com	,
on	V.main.indic.pres.ps3.sg.ps.af	ole+0
arvuti	S.com.sg.nom	arvuti+0
,	Z.Com	,
internet	S.com.sg.nom	internet+0
ja	J.crd	ja+0
selle	P.sg.gen	see+0
kõrval	K.post	kõrval+0
ka	D	ka+0
muu	P.sg.gen	muu+0
digitaalne	A.pos.sg.nom	<unknown>
kommunikatsioon	S.com.sg.nom	<unknown>
.	Z.Fst	.

Table 2: TreeTagger Output: An Example

As we can see from the table, the output is rich in terms of the morphological information. For example, the tag *A.pos.pl.part* indicates - *Adjective-Positive-Plural-Partitive Case*. More detailed information on what each tag means can be found on the morpho-syntactic categories description for the Tartu Morphologically Disambiguated Corpus[7]. While suffixes are indicated in the lemma column separated by a "+" symbol, compound words are separated by an underscore. For example, in the above sentence, there are two compound words - *Tänapäeva* (täna + päev ⇒ today + day = nowadays) and *abivahend* (abi + vahend ⇒ help + tool = helping tool/aid)

3.3 Features

We started with the feature set described in Vajjala and Lõo (2013) and added a few additional features, primarily lexical richness features from Lu (2012). In total, our feature set consists of

[7]`http://www.cl.ut.ee/korpused/morfliides/seletus`

78 features.

First, several surface features, such as number of words, number of sentences in a document, mean word and sentence length in a document were considered. However, as can be seen from Table 1, the number of words in documents is unequally distributed across the classes. C1 level documents have almost five times more words than A2 on an average. This may create a bias towards this feature. While this is perfectly valid in a predictive algorithm, we wanted to understand how much can the morpho-syntactic features contribute to the task without surface measures. Hence, we excluded these surface features from the feature set. We used sentence length while doing a replication and comparison with previous work though. We also briefly present about the variation in accuracy upon including the surface features, in the results section.

Vajjala and Lõo (2013) described several features considering the morphological complexity of Estonian. These consist of the average number of nouns and adjectives in a text belonging to each of the 15 cases that exist in Estonian, average number of verbs belonging to the five moods (indicative, conditional, imperative, quotative and justive), two tenses (present, past), two voices (personal, impersonal), three persons (first, second, third), polarity (positive, negative) and other morphological features. A description of various declensions and conjugations in Estonian can be found in the Estonian Morphology guide [8]. In addition to all these features, we added the number of compound words per text and number of different cases present in the text as additional features in this category.

Vajjala and Lõo (2013) had some of the lexical variation measures from Lu (2012) (lexical variation, noun, adjective, adverb and modifier variation). We additionally implemented the other lexical richness measures described in Lu (2012) that covered the aspects of lexical density and diversity. Although these formulae are actually for English, since they are only depended on the various word counts and since we are not aware of any equivalent formulae for Estonian, we used the same formulae for Estonian as well. These measures were shown to be good predictors of learner language quality in English as second language oral narratives. Apart from this, we used the proportion of various POS tags in the text following previous work.

We also explored word and POS language models initially but since we only reached baseline performance with them, we discarded that feature set for further experiments. One reason for the poor performance of word models could be the morphological richness of Estonian which results in data sparsity for building good language models. For the POS models, we faced two issues: while using only the base POS tags resulted in all categories looking alike, using the entire morphological tag resulted in data-sparsity. We did not explore lemma/stem based language models and factored language models yet. A short experiment considering only a feature set consisting of morphological suffixes did not result in an improvement in the result. So, we discarded this feature set too, for the subsequent experiments reported in this paper.

Finally, we did not implement any syntactic features in our approach since we are not aware of any state-of-the-art parsers for Estonian. We also did not implement any features based on spelling and grammar error patterns as we are not aware of any off-the-shelf tool we can use for automatic annotation of learner errors. We also did not verify the output of the Treetagger for possible errors in tagging, as we are not aware of an automatic approach to detect them.

[8] http://lpcs.math.msu.su/ pentus/etmorf.htm

4 Experiments

Our corpus is a collection of texts spanning multiple proficiency levels. The proficiency levels can be assumed to be discrete or continuous, and with varying degree of difference between succeeding levels (i.e., difference between A2 and B1 may be less than that of B1 and B2). This allows us to conceptualize the problem of proficiency classification as belonging to nominal or interval or ordinal scales. Accordingly, we investigated this dataset by considering the problem as classification and regression. We did not explore ordinal representation yet. We used WEKA (Hall et al., 2009) for training the machine learning models and for feature selection.

4.1 Evaluation Measures

We used multiple evaluation measures based on the choice of learning approaches. We evaluated classification performance in terms of its prediction accuracy. Additionally, we report the confusion matrices and F-scores per class to compare the performance with balanced and unbalanced datasets. For linear regression, we report Pearson correlation and Root Mean Square Error (RMSE) as evaluation measures. All the evaluation was performed in a 10-fold Cross Validation setting.

We are not aware of any direct measure of comparison between classification and regression approaches using the same data. Hence, we used three measures after rounding off the regression prediction to the nearest integer value:

1. Percentage of exact matches (This is the same as accuracy for classification.)
2. Percentage of instances where the prediction is within one-level of the actual value (This is closely related to the prediction error and adjacent accuracy in regression models.)
3. Percentage of errors where the prediction is higher than the actual level. This measure was considered with the assumption that in a placement testing scenario, assigning a learner actually belonging to A2 as say, B2 is more undesirable compared to assigning a B2 learner to A2 level.

4.2 Modeling as Classification

We used the Sequential Minimal Optimization (SMO) implementation in WEKA (Platt,1998) in all our classification experiments for easy comparison with previous work with these features. Since the training corpus used in this paper differs from that used in Vajjala and Lõo (2013) in terms of the grades assigned to the texts, a direct comparison of results is not possible. Hence, we started with a replication of the classification experiment with the feature set used in their paper using the new four-level corpus described in Table 1. This resulted in a classification accuracy of 73.7% (F-score 0.74) using an unbalanced dataset and 72.3% (F-score 0.72) using a balanced dataset consisting of 92 texts per category. We consider these as our baseline measures for the rest of this paper.

After establishing this baseline, we tested the model with all our features. The model with all the features received 79% accuracy for the unbalanced corpus and 76.9% for the balanced corpus, which is clearly an increase of about 5% over the previously reported feature set. Table 3 shows the confusion matrices for both unbalanced (left) and balanced (right) versions and Table 4 shows the F-scores per category for both the versions.

(a)class. as →	A2	B1	B2	C1
A2	150	46	0	0
B1	16	340	27	1
B2	1	58	136	12
C1	0	3	21	68

(b) class. as →	A2	B1	B2	C1
A2	79	11	2	0
B1	9	66	16	1
B2	3	15	60	14
C1	0	1	13	78

Table 3: Confusion matrices for Unbalanced and Balanced training datasets

Category	F-score in un-balanced dataset	F-score in balanaced dataset
A2	0.83	0.86
B1	0.82	0.72
B2	0.70	0.65
C1	0.79	0.85

Table 4: F-scores per category, for Balanced and Unbalanced training datasets

It is interesting to note that the unbalanced corpus did not create a particular bias for or against any one level. However, the balanced version resulted in a drop in accuracy by ~2%. Though the prediction accuracy for A2 and C1 clearly increased in the balanced version, this also resulted in reducing the F-score for both B1 and B2. It is difficult to decide which version of the corpus is better for classification - balanced or unbalanced, in this case. However, since the model trained on the unbalanced version results in better accuracy without completely being skewed towards majority classes, we can perhaps consider it as the better performing model between the two. While the increase in accuracy compared to what was reported in Vajjala and Lõo (2013) (67%) can be attributed to the fine-grainedness of the dataset we use now, the performance improvement between their feature set and ours on the new dataset shows that the increased accuracy is not entirely a data artifact.

We also trained binary classifiers for all the class combinations to understand if it is easy or difficult to classify between pairs of classes. Table 5 summarizes the experiments, performed considering equal instances from both classes in each case, in terms of classification accuracy.

Classes Used	Classification Accuracy
A2 vs B1	83.2%
A2 vs B2	92.4%
A2 vs C1	98.4%
B1 vs B2	77.2%
B1 vs C1	95.1%
B2 vs C1	86.3%

Table 5: Binary Classification Accuracy

As the table shows, all the binary classifiers achieved accuracies much higher than the four-class classification accuracy for the balanced corpus (76.9%), excepting (B1 vs B2). This encourages us to explore a multi-level classification approach like the cascades used in Vajjala and Lõo (2013) in future, which could result in an improvement over the current accuracy.

Finally, we also verified if adding the surface features (word length and sentence length)

contributes to improving the classification performance. There was a slight drop (~0.2-0.5%) in accuracy for both unbalanced and balanced datasets and the drop was not statistically significant.

4.3 Modeling as Regression

Another way besides classification is to look at proficiency level prediction as regression. As mentioned earlier, these proficiency levels can be seen as scores on a numeric scale too, since proficiency is a continuous variable though the levels assigned are discrete. Further, regression also allows us to output a prediction on a scale, where it is possible to see predictions that lie between two discrete levels. Hence, we also modeled proficiency prediction as regression. We trained a Linear Regression model in WEKA, with default settings[9]. This regression model achieved a Pearson correlation of 0.85 and an RMSE of 0.49. For the feature set of Vajjala and Lõo (2013), the numbers were 0.77 and 0.58 respectively. Since a majority of previous research on this problem treated it as classification, we have no comparable results on regression. One related result is that of Hancke (2013), who reported a Pearson correlation of 0.78 and RMSE of 0.68 for a German proficiency assessment dataset consisting of 5 levels.

4.4 Comparing Classification and Regression

As mentioned in Section 4.1, we compare classification and regression in terms of exact and within one level prediction accuracy and in terms of the direction of error. Table 6 shows the comparison between the performance of classification and regression in terms of these measures. As it can be seen from the table, both classification and regression perform comparably in terms of within one level accuracy. However, classification seems to work slightly better than regression in terms of exact accuracy as well as the direction of error.

Model	**Exact Acc.**	**Within 1-Level Acc.**	**% errors where Predicted > Actual**
Classification	79%	99.43%	46.5%
Regression	76%	99.2%	50.7%

Table 6: Classification Vs Regression - Comparison

5 Feature Selection

While the above experiments will let us conclude about the efficiency of the features to predict CEFR levels accurately, understanding what features play a significant role in distinguishing between levels is interesting from a general linguistic perspective. Further, the question of how much can we predict with how few interpretable features is interesting from an application perspective. Hence, we investigated feature selection approaches and correlations between features. We used three feature selection methods implemented in WEKA and built classifiers with these extracted feature subsets. The three methods differ in their approach to feature selection. They are:

1. Information Gain - evaluates an attribute in terms of its information gain with respect to the class. Hence it considers attributes individually, irrespective of the correlations between them.

[9]M5 attribute selection, eliminateCollinearAttributes option set to TRUE

2. CfsSubsetEval (Hall, 1998) - chooses a feature subset such that the amount of redundancy between the features in the selected subset is less and together, they have a higher predictive ability with respect to the class.

3. ReliefFAttributeEval (Kira and Rendell, 1992; Kononenko, 1994) - selects individual features by repeated sampling of instances and comparing the value of the feature for the sampled instance and the nearest instances belonging to same and different classes.

Table 7 shows the classification accuracies with all the three feature selection methods, using the unbalanced dataset. Since there was no specific bias against any class and since model with unbalanced dataset gave a higher accuracy, we report all the further results only with that dataset. As the table shows, CfsSubsetEval attains almost the same classification accuracy (78.3%) as the best performing model so far (79%) with a much smaller feature set. The difference was found to be statistically insignificant (using the Corrected Paired T-Tester implementation in WEKA).

Method	# Features	Accuracy
Information Gain	10	73.5%
CfsSubsetEval	27	78.3%
ReliefFAttributeEval	10	74.5%

Table 7: Classification Accuracy with Feature Selection

From the group of 27 features of CfsSubsetEval, Table 8 shows the top-10 features from the CfsSubsetEval set, ranked by their Information Gain. Features indicated with an asterisk (*) are the ones that were not used for this task before.

Feature	Group
Corrected Type Token Ratio (CTTR*)	LexVar
Root Type Token Ratio (RTTR*)	LexVar
# 2nd person inflected verbs/# words (numPs2)	Morph
# sub-ordinating conjunctions/# words (numSubC)	Morph
# verbs in active voice/# words (numActive)	Morph
Squared Verb Variation (SVV1*)	LexVar
# distinct cases used in the document (CaseNr*)	Morph
Corrected Verb Variation (CVV1*)	LexVar
# conjunctions/# words (numConj)	Morph
# interjections/# words (numInterj)	Morph

Table 8: 10 Predictive Features (CfsSubset, ranked by Information Gain)

Five of the 10 features in this list are the ones not used in previous research for this task. However, some feature pairs in this list like (CTTR,RTTR), (SVV1,CVV1) are still variations of the same ratio and are expected to be highly correlated with each other. While this correlation between features may not affect the prediction performance as such, studying the correlations may be more useful from the perspective of understanding the process of proficiency acquisition and will also be useful in building models where less number of features explain can more variation in the data without repetition.

5.1 Correlations between Features

Table 9 lists the correlations between some pairs of features from the top-10 features listed in Table 8.

Feature 1	Feature 2	Correlation
CTTR	RTTR	0.999
CVV1	SVV1	0.976
RTTR	SVV1	0.804
CTTR	SVV1	0.804
RTTR	CVV1	0.795
CTTR	CVV1	0.795
numSubC	numConj	0.764
RTTR	CaseNr	0.719
CTTR	CaseNr	0.719
numConj	numInterj	-0.623

Table 9: The Most Correlated Features

Several features in the most predictive features have a high degree of correlation between each other, as shown in the table. It would perhaps be sufficient to use only one of them to achieve the same amount of predictability. Further analysis is needed to choose a refined feature set that can be as predictive in terms of modeling but also more interpretable in linguistic terms.

5.2 Predictive Features between Categories

As a final experiment, we investigated the most predictive features between categories. The motivation for this exploration has been to understand if there is a change in the features that are more useful, as the proficiency increased. One hypothesis could be that the morphological features are more predictive between lower proficiency levels and lexical richness features like TTR will be more predictive at higher proficiency levels. While beginning to learn Estonian, learners may have issues with its morphological complexity. But, as they become more familiar and proficient with the language, the effect of morphology may diminish and that of lexical richness may grow. Table 10 lists the top-5 most predictive features for binary classification between proficiency levels going from least to highest ranked in terms of their Information Gain.

A2 vs B1	B1 vs B2	B2 vs C1
numInterj	RTTR	numPs2
numPs2	CTTR	# imperatives/# words
numConj	SVV1	# abessive case/# words
numSubc	CVV1	CaseNr
# affirmative verbs/# words	# compound words/# words	# compound words/# words

Table 10: Most Predictive Features Between Categories

Interestingly, all the top-5 features are morphological features in the comparisons between (A2,B1) and (B2,C1). But, the comparison between the middle levels (B1,B2) is dominated by the lexical richness features. While we do not have any intuitions about the reasons for this morphology -> lexical richness -> morphology turn with the increase in proficiency, SLA research may be able to offer some perspectives on this. It would be interesting to combine computational modeling with SLA to develop an interpretable model of proficiency assessment, for which this research could a good starting point. We did not check whether this list of top-5 features varies depending on the size of the sample chosen for the analysis. To estimate the top features in this case, we used all the data available for the chosen categories.

6 Conclusions and Outlook

To conclude, we built models for automatic proficiency classification of Estonian learner texts based on the CEFR scale. We used a collection of morphological and POS tag density based features including lexical richness measures from English SLA research. The best model reported in this paper reaches a prediction accuracy of 79%. Our results show a substantial improvement over the previously reported results for Estonian and are also considerably higher than the accuracies reported on this task for other languages (German and Swedish). We can conclude from our experiments that this linguistic modeling of proficiency holds promise in the direction of developing an automatic proficiency assessment system for Estonian.

The nature of the CEFR categories allows us to model the problem as being on different scales. So, we considered nominal and interval scales and modeled the problem as both classification and regression. Comparing both of them in terms of 3 evaluation measures, we concluded that we get slightly better results by treating proficiency assessment on CEFR scale as classification instead of regression.

We experimented with feature selection strategies to understand how far can we get with how few features and found that we can reach almost the same accuracy with a small subset of 27 features. Along with this, we also did a correlational analysis between features and our experiments showed that most of the features are highly correlated with each other. We are yet to develop a solution to deal with this issue.

It has to be noted that we looked at only one dimension of proficiency in this set of experiments, ignoring aspects of syntax, discourse, learner errors, relation of the text to the question asked etc. Also, since we ignored the possibility of tagging errors by TreeTagger, we need to caution that the results need to be interpreted keeping the tool in context. However, despite these two limitations, we believe our experiments still demonstrate the value of using language specific linguistic information for performing proficiency classification of Estonian learner text.

6.1 Outlook

We are currently working on assessing what models are statistically different from each other using significance testing and by studying the fold-wise difference in a 10-fold cross-validation setup along with average performance difference between models. This may provide us a better way to compare various prediction models when the performance difference is small and also understand the effect of sampling of instances per fold on the performance of the models.

The dataset is still under development and it would be interesting to see how far can we get with the current feature set, when more annotated data becomes available in future. Although the results appear very promising at the moment, there is a lot of scope for improvement and exploration of new feature groups. Our initial experiments with n-gram models failed, but exploring factored language models and using data-driven word-frequency, spelling error and suffix-frequency features may perhaps be more useful for the task. Further, subject to the availability of required tools, we plan to explore the role of syntactic features of texts in proficiency classification.

From a modeling perspective, exploring cascade approaches like the ones in (Vajjala and Lõo, 2013) may help in improving the accuracies further. Investigating other learning algorithms and considering the dataset as ordinal - are other interesting directions that could be explored. Finally, since the results clearly establish the impact of morphological features for this task, it would be interesting to verify if this is the case for other morphologically rich languages where such learner corpora are available.

Acknowledgments

We thank the anonymous reviewers for their comments and Dr Detmar Meurers for his useful suggestions. This research is partially funded by LEAD Graduate School (GSC 1028, http://purl.org/lead), a project of the Excellence Initiative of the German federal and state governments. Sowmya Vajjala is a doctoral student of the LEAD Graduate School.

References

Burstein, J. (2003). *The e-rater Scoring Engine: Automated Essay Scoring with Natural Language Processing*, chapter 7, pages 107–115. Hillsdale, NJ: Lawrence Erlbaum Associates, Inc.

Burstein, J. and Chodorow, M. (2010). *Progress and New Directions in Technology for Automated Essay Evaluation*, chapter 36, pages 487–497. Oxford University Press, 2nd edition.

Council of Europe (2001). *Common European Framework of Reference for Languages: Learning, teaching, assessment*. Cambridge University Press, Cambridge.

Crossley, S. A., Salsbury, T., McNamara, D. S., and Jarvis, S. (2011). Predicting lexical proficiency in language learners using computational indices. *Language Testing*, 28:561–580.

Eslon, P. (2014). Eesti vahekeele korpus (Estonian Interlanguage Corpus). *Keel ja Kirjandus*, 6:436–451.

Gyllstad, H., Grandfeldt, J., Bernardini, P., and Källkvist, M. (2014). Linguistic correlates to communicative proficiency levels of the CEFR: The case of syntactic complexity in written l2 english, l3 french and l4 italian. *EUROSLA Yearbook*, 14(1):1–30.

Hall, M., Frank, E., Holmes, G., Pfahringer, B., Reutemann, P., and Witten, I. H. (2009). The WEKA data mining software: An update. *The SIGKDD Explorations*, 11(1):10–18.

Hall, M. A. (1998). *Correlation-based Feature Subset Selection for Machine Learning*. Hamilton, Newzealand.

Hancke, J. (2013). Automatic prediction of CEFR proficiency levels based on linguistic features of learner language. Master's thesis, International Studies in Computational Linguistics. Seminar für Sprachwissenschaft, Universität Tübingen.

Hancke, J. and Meurers, D. (2013). Exploring CEFR classification for german based on rich linguistic modeling. In *Learner Corpus Research 2013, Book of Abstracts*, Bergen, Norway.

Kira, K. and Rendell, L. A. (1992). A practical approach to feature selection. In *Ninth International Workshop on Machine Learning*, pages 249–256.

Kononenko, I. (1994). Estimating attributes: Analysis and extensions of RELIEF. In *European Conference on Machine Learning*, pages 171–182.

Kyle, K. and Crossley, S. A. (2014). Automatically assessing lexical sophistication: Indices, tools, findings, and application. *TESOL Quarterly*, –:–.

Lu, X. (2010). Automatic analysis of syntactic complexity in second language writing. *International Journal of Corpus Linguistics*, 15(4):474–496.

Lu, X. (2012). The relationship of lexical richness to the quality of ESL learners' oral narratives. *The Modern Languages Journal*.

Östling, R., Smolentzov, A., Tyrefors Hinnerich, B., and Höglin, E. (2013). Automated essay scoring for swedish. In *Proceedings of the Eighth Workshop on Innovative Use of NLP for Building Educational Applications*, pages 42–47, Atlanta, Georgia. Association for Computational Linguistics.

Schmid, H. (1994). Probabilistic part-of-speech tagging using decision trees. In *Proceedings of the International Conference on New Methods in Language Processing*, pages 44–49, Manchester, UK.

Tono, Y. (2000). A corpus-based analysis of interlanguage development: analysing pos tag sequences of EFL learner corpora. In *PALC'99: Practical Applications in Language Corpora*, pages 323–340.

Vajjala, S. and Lõo, K. (2013). Role of morpho-syntactic features in Estonian proficiency classification. In *Proceedings of the 8th Workshop on Innovative Use of NLP for Building Educational Applications (BEA8), Association for Computational Linguistics*.

Vyatkina, N. (2012). The development of second language writing complexity in groups and individuals: A longitudinal learner corpus study. *The Modern Language Journal*.

Williamson, D. M. (2009). A framework for implementing automated scoring. In *The annual meeting of the American Educational Research Association (AERA) and the National Council on Measurement in Education (NCME)*.

Yannakoudakis, H., Briscoe, T., and Medlock, B. (2011). A new dataset and method for automatically grading ESOL texts. In *Proceedings of the 49th Annual Meeting of the Association for Computational Linguistics: Human Language Technologies - Volume 1*, HLT '11, pages 180–189, Stroudsburg, PA, USA. Association for Computational Linguistics. Corpus available: `http://ilexir.co.uk/applications/clc-fce-dataset`.

Zhang, B. (2008). Investigating proficiency classification for the examination for the certificate of proficiency in english (ECPE). In *Spaan Fellow Working Papers in Second or Foreign Language Assessment*.

You get what you annotate:

a pedagogically annotated corpus of coursebooks for Swedish as a Second Language

Elena Volodina[1], Ildikó Pilán[1], Stian Rødven Eide[2], Hannes Heidarsson[3]

(1) Swedish Language Bank, Department of Swedish, University of Gothenburg, Sweden
(2) Department of Philosophy, Linguistics and Theory of Science, University of Gothenburg, Sweden
(3) Department of Swedish, University of Gothenburg, Sweden

elena.volodina@svenska.gu.se, ildiko.pilan@svenska.gu.se, stian@fripost.org, hannes.heidarsson@live.se

Abstract

We present the COCTAILL corpus, containing over 700.000 tokens of Swedish texts from 12 coursebooks aimed at second/foreign language (L2) learning. Each text in the corpus is labelled with a proficiency level according to the CEFR proficiency scale. Genres, topics, associated activities, vocabulary lists and other types of information are annotated in the coursebooks to facilitate Second Language Acquisition (SLA)-aware studies and experiments aimed at Intelligent Computer-Assisted Language Learning (ICALL). Linguistic annotation in the form of parts-of-speech (POS; e.g. nouns, verbs), base forms (lemmas) and syntactic relations (e.g. subject, object) has been also added to the corpus.

In the article we describe our annotation scheme and the editor we have developed for the content mark-up of the coursebooks, including the taxonomy of pedagogical activities and linguistic skills. Inter-annotator agreement has been computed and reported on a subset of the corpus. Surprisingly, we have not found any other examples of pedagogically marked-up corpora based on L2 coursebooks to draw on existing experiences. Hence, our work may be viewed as "groping in the darkness" and eventually a starting point for others.

The paper also presents our first quantitative exploration of the corpus where we focus on textually and pedagogically annotated features of the coursebooks to exemplify what types of studies can be performed using the presented annotation scheme. We explore trends shown in use of topics and genres over proficiency levels and compare pedagogical focus of exercises across levels.

The final section of the paper summarises the potential this corpus holds for research within SLA and various ICALL tasks.

Keywords: L2 coursebook corpus, annotation scheme, CEFR proficiency levels, SLA-aware ICALL, inter-annotator agreement

Elena Volodina, Ildikó Pilán, Stian Rødven Eide and Hannes Heidarsson 2014. You get what you annotate: a pedagogically annotated corpus of coursebooks for Swedish as a Second Language. *Proceedings of the third workshop on NLP for computer-assisted language learning.* NEALT Proceedings Series 22 / Linköping Electronic Conference Proceedings 107: 128–144.

1 Background

1.1 Corpora in CALL and ICALL

Corpora have become a useful and often central component in Computer-Assisted Language Learning (CALL) applications and especially in Intelligent CALL, i.e. CALL based on Natural Language Processing and Speech Technologies. Primarily, corpora of two types are being employed in such applications: native speaker (NS) corpora (e.g. Vajjala & Meurers, 2013) and corpora consisting of L2 learner production, such as essays (e.g. Hancke & Meurers, 2013). In both cases variation can be observed in the mode of language, i.e. written vs spoken language. NS corpora are primarily used for automatic selection and generation of learning materials (e.g. Volodina et al., 2014), while L2 learner corpora are used for development of different types of grammar and writing support (e.g. Attali & Burstein, 2006).

However, a number of tasks that need to be modelled for the automatic generation of L2 materials, such as text readability classification for the automatic selection of appropriate texts, depend on access to a special type of language which cannot be classified as *typical* NS or L2 learner language in the full sense of this word. NS corpora are unable to provide a reliable basis for modelling for instance text difficulty at the beginner or lower intermediate levels, since NS corpora exhibit a mixture of easy and complex linguistic phenomena, such as vocabulary, grammar, sentences, texts. L2 corpora, on the other hand, contain errors and hence cannot be used to model the language that L2 learners should be exposed to. However, reading and coursebook materials used for L2 courses can – hypothetically – be used as a subset of NS language that is appropriate for modelling L2 learner levels, for example for identifying texts understandable at each of the proficiency levels.

Corpora of coursebook (CB) texts is no novelty in itself, see Meunier & Gouverneur (2009) for an overview. A number of recent projects dealing with collection and annotation of coursebooks indicate a rise in interest in textbook analysis for various applied and theoretical studies (e.g. Gamson et al., 2013). However, CB corpora research has dominated the area of Second Language Acquisition (mainly English as a Foreign Language, EFL) to a larger extent than ICALL-driven research. L2 researchers usually pursue a narrowly defined aim, e.g. teaching of grammar/vocabulary in EFL coursebooks (Anping, 2005) or teaching phraseology at advanced EFL levels (Meunier & Gouverneur, 2007). To our knowledge, there are very few electronic CB corpora that have been compiled (e.g. Römer, 2006), with numerous studies carried out using paper copies of CBs (e.g. Reda, 2003). Systematic studies of textbooks from different angles (textual, pedagogic, didactic, linguistic) have so far been outside of research focus, which partly depends upon the lack of richly annotated electronic CB corpora.

1.2 CEFR and L2 coursebook corpora

The corpus described in this article is an electronic collection of textbooks used for teaching of L2 Swedish at CEFR-based courses. CEFR – Common European Framework of Reference for Languages (COE, 2001) – is an influential cross-national initiative that aims at providing language course syllabuses and assessment according to the same model of proficiency levels. CEFR contains 6 levels - A1, A2, B1, B2, C1, C2 – where A1 is the beginner level and C2 is the full proficiency level.

Our interest towards studying CEFR descriptors has resulted from the lack of systematic description of the CEFR levels for Swedish in concrete linguistic terms that could be useful for ICALL applications. The CEFR descriptors, that are intentionally very general to cover different languages, provide very vague guidelines on e.g. text complexity, vocabulary and grammar scope, as can be seen from Figure 1. Subject to interpretation would be: how short should "short pieces of information" and "short written passages" be? What does "collate" mean? What is meant by "in a simple fashion"?

Can collate short pieces of information from several sources and summarise them for somebody else. Can paraphrase short written passages in a simple fashion, using the original text wording and ordering.

FIGURE 1. CEFR descriptor for B1, for ability to process text. (COE, 2001:96).

Our assumption is that the necessary basis for interpretation of (a part of) the CEFR descriptors can be obtained from texts used for practical teaching, e.g. coursebooks. A corpus of CB texts linked to the CEFR levels can, firstly, facilitate pedagogical text studies which would help (1) establish a relationship between how texts selected for reading influence productive writing skills, and thus facilitate SLA research; (2) break down CEFR descriptors into concrete linguistic constituents based on the evidence of the corpus of "input" (i.e. normative) texts - thus attempting at the standardization of CEFR descriptors. Secondly, from the ICALL perspective, CEFR-linked CB corpus can provide basis for comprehensive analysis of normative language that students at CEFR courses are being exposed to. This would, among other things, entail studies of vocabulary and grammar scopes per level; text and sentence readability experiments. Depending on the type of annotation, other studies might also be possible, for instance investigation of development in genre features and use of topics; change in type and format of exercises across levels; shifts in the focus on language skills across levels. Besides, experiments on topic modelling, automatic genre identification, analysis of text questions and text question generation, etc. could also become feasible.

However evident the value of such data for ICALL and SLA might seem, there are very few attempts undertaken to compile corpora of (CEFR-based) coursebooks. François (2011) describes the only known to us CB corpus of CEFR-based texts stretching over all levels of proficiency. The main aim with François' corpus is to use it for NLP-based CALL applications for L2 French. The corpus consists of 21 coursebooks distributed over the 6 proficiency levels, see Table 1:

	A1	A2	B1	B2	C1	C2	Total
Nr textbooks	10	8	8	4	3	3	36
Nr texts	452	478	681	198	184	49	2042

TABLE 1. Overview over the French CB corpus (François, 2011)

All CBs have been published after 2001, have an explicit link to the CEFR levels of proficiency and are aimed at general L2 French (as opposed to French for specific purposes). After scanning, only reading materials (i.e. texts properly) have been extracted, leaving aside exercises, lists, instructions, etc. found in the coursebooks. Texts have been labelled with the proficiency level of the (chapter of the) book where texts came from, and assigned a genre (e.g. dialogue, recipe, poem) and linguistic annotation (POS, lemmas). The corpus compiled by François has up to date been used for readability studies of L2 French texts and for extraction of a graded lexicon aimed at L2 learners of French (François, 2011; François et al., 2014).

2 COCTAILL: collection and annotation

Work on COCTAILL (**C**orpus **o**f **C**EFR-based **T**extbooks **a**s **I**nput for **L**earner **L**evels' modelling) was initiated in 2013 and has been funded partly by the Department of Swedish at the University of Gothenburg (UGOT), and partly by the Center for Language Technology, UGOT. The process of corpus compilation consisted of several stages, shortly presented in Figure 2 below:

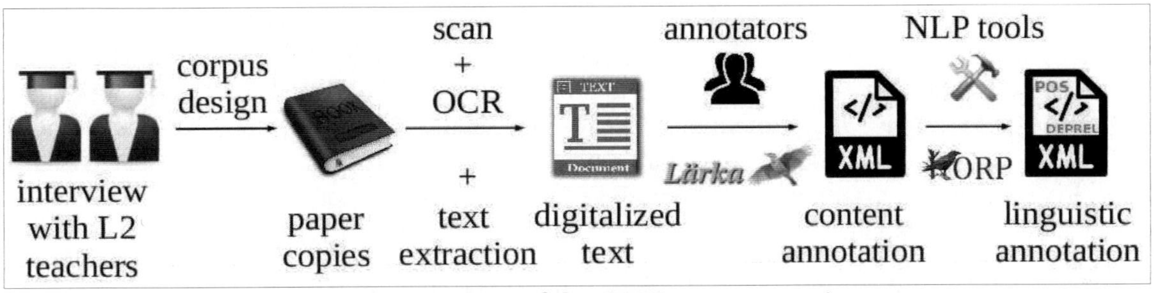

FIGURE 2. Overview of the CEFR-corpus creation

- *Interviews with L2 teachers.* To identify candidate coursebooks, we have carried out interviews with teachers engaged in CEFR-based courses as well as studied course plans for such courses. Altogether, 7 teachers at different levels, schools and institutions have agreed to have an interview. A number of CBs have been named as being used at more than one level. In such cases, to decide the border between levels, we organized a CB workshop where trained teachers discussed such coursebooks with each other and suggested division.

- *Corpus structuring & purchase of coursebooks.* Books that have been suggested by at least two teachers have been selected as core material. We have aimed at a balanced representation at each level with respect to the number of coursebooks per level. However, very few courses are offered at C1 and none at C2 levels that we know of, so the number of coursebooks at these levels differ from the others: 2 titles at C1 and none at C2, see section 2.1 for an overview of the corpus structure. Before books were purchased, we explored the possibility of getting electronic versions from the publishers, but only the publishing house *Liber* was willing to cooperate. However, the titles that Liber could provide have been named by only one teacher, and consequently have not been included into the final corpus.

- *Optical scanning & extraction of raw text.* Once the books were purchased, optical scanning was ordered from an outside contractor. PDF alongside XML files were delivered as resulting output data. Raw text extracted from the XML files was used as the input for the next stages.

- *Implementation of a coursebook editor.* At this stage we defined a taxonomy of textual and pedagogical features for annotation, as well as the format of the output data. Previously, no richly (pedagogically) annotated L2 coursebook corpora have been compiled. Therefore, there were no available editing tools to reuse. After experimenting with XML editors and DTD schemas, we have opted to develop our own editor as described in subsection 2.3.

- *Annotation for pedagogical and textual features* involved manual work. Altogether, four people have been involved in the content annotation. Initial annotation of the first two CBs was performed to test the editor and to establish an acceptable taxonomy of textual and pedagogical variables, see section 2.2. In the next round, one more annotator was trained, and as a result, a number of revisions were suggested to improve the taxonomy of pedagogical and textual features. The introduced changes led to a necessity to revise the two initially annotated coursebooks. By the end of this round, annotation guidelines have been produced. Finally, two more annotators have been trained. This stage was concluded by an inter-annotator agreement experiments, which entailed revisions to the annotation guidelines and highlighted the need of another round of revision of the already annotated books, as described in section 2.4.

- *Linguistic annotation* in the form of parts-of-speech, syntactic relations and lemmas has been automatically added using Korp web services (Borin et al., 2012). Whereas annotation of text passages and activity instructions holds good quality, we would need to assess annotation quality of all other types of information. The reason for that is the fact that tasks, lists, and language examples have an unpredictable structure – often incomplete sentences, or lists of mixed linguistic units, which tends to get a very low-level accuracy when it comes to e.g. parts of speech and dependency annotation.

- *Release of the corpus.* Unfortunately, the corpus as a whole cannot be made freely available for download for copyright reasons, however, it is browsable for research purposes via Korp (Borin et al., 2012) with password protection. Besides, parts of the corpus in the form of a bag of sentences (as opposed to connected texts) for each proficiency level are released as downloadable data[1].

2.1 Corpus overview

The COCTAILL consists of 12 coursebooks, 5 of which are used at more than one level. The corpus is balanced in the number of coursebooks per level (4 titles/level), except level C1 (2 titles/level). C2 level is not included in this corpus since it represents full language proficiency when learners "can understand with ease virtually everything heard or read" (COE, 2001:24), hence, from the point of view of linguistic modelling it corresponds to regular NS language. The summary of the corpus is presented in Table 2.

CEFR level	Nr. of books	Nr. of authors	Nr. of lessons	Nr. of texts	Nr. of tasks	Nr. of sentences (texts)	Nr. of tokens (texts)
A1	4	10	37	101	160	1581	11132
A2	4	10	105	232	244	4217	37259
B1	4	12	83	345	389	6510	79402
B2	4	8	31	314	368	8527	101583
C1	2	2	22	115	333	5085	71991
Total	18 (12 titles)	42 (26 different names)	278	1106	1494	25920	301367

TABLE 2. Overview of the Swedish CEFR corpus

[1] Contact Elena Volodina <elena.volodina@svenska.gu.se> or Ildikó Pilán <ildiko.pilan@svenska.gu.se> to get access to the files.

The COCTAILL comprises a total of 708 589 tokens, about half of which belong to texts, the rest to activity instructions, tasks, lists and language examples. The columns "Nr. of sentences (texts)" and "Nr. of tokens (texts)" refer to sentences in texts only, other elements were excluded from these counts since they often contain smaller linguistic units than a full sentence. The amount of tasks in the corpus (a total of 1494) outnumbers the number of texts (1106). The largest amount of material in terms of texts and tasks is available for B1 and B2 levels.

The values in Table 2 are meant primarily to give an idea of the size of the corpus, rather than present data from which generalizations about the CEFR levels can be made, since authors' choice varied to a great extent as far as the division into lessons and the number of texts and tasks included per level are concerned.

2.2 Coursebook content annotation

An overview over the taxonomy of textual and pedagogical annotation is provided in Figure 3. XML elements are shown on the left with their corresponding attributes on the right:

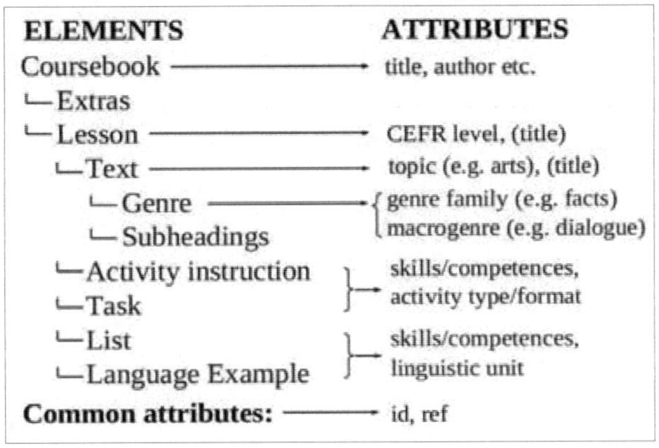

FIGURE 3. Overview over the textual and pedagogical annotation: XML elements and their attributes

Structurally, each coursebook is divided into extras (contents, foreword, copyright note, etc) and lessons (chapters). The running text in each lesson has been manually split into texts aimed at reading comprehension and other types of information typical of coursebooks, such as activity instructions, tasks, lists and language examples, whereby reading comprehension materials have been annotated for *textual features* (section 2.2.1), and the rest of information for *pedagogically relevant features* (section 2.2.2).

2.2.1 Textual annotation

By *textual* annotation we understand mark-up of text passages for *topics* and *genres.*

We have listed 28 text *topics* (Table 3) which follow the CEFR guidelines (COE, 2001) in the first place, with modifications introduced as a result of our practical work on the first coursebooks (Volodina & Johansson Kokkinakis, 2013).

In general, we followed the recommendation to opt for a broader topic, e.g. if a text is about a political crisis in some country, including military actions, Politics and power would probably be the best choice. In most cases, more than one topic has been applicable, in which case two or more topics have been assigned. In case there were no topics that corresponded to the text, we considered adding new ones, see Table 3 for the alphabetic list of the topics we have been using so far.

• Animals	• Food & drink	• Relations with other people
• Arts	• Free time, entertainment	• Religion, myths & legends
• Clothes & appearances	• Greetings/introductions	• Science & technology
• Crime & punishment	• Health & body care	• Services
• Culture & traditions	• House & home, environment	• Shopping
• Daily life	• Jobs & professions	• Sports
• Economy	• Languages	• Travel
• Education	• Personal identification	• Weather & nature
• Family & relatives	• Places	
• Famous people	• Politics & power	

TABLE 3. List of topics

The taxonomy of *genre families* is comprised of four elements: Narration, Facts, Evaluation and Other, following the taxonomy described in Johansson and Sandell Ring (2010) with slight modifications as a result of the work on the first annotated coursebooks (Volodina and Johansson Kokkinakis, 2013). Such a modification is the addition of the genre family Other which contains text genres (e.g. puzzle) that were difficult to place into the other three Narration, Facts or Evaluation families. Further subdivision of genre families into macrogenres is shown in Table 4.

Narration	**Facts**	**Evaluation**	**Other**
Description	Autobiography	Advertisement	Anecdote, joke
Fiction	Biography	Argumentation	Dialogue
News article	Demonstration	Discussion	Language tip
Personal story	Explanation	Exposition	Letter
	Facts	Interpretation, exegesis	Lyrics
	Geographical facts	Personal reflection	Notice, short message
	Historical facts	Persuasion	Puzzle
	Instruction	Review	Questionnaire
	Procedures		Quotation
	Report		Recipe
	Rules		Rhyme

TABLE 4. List of genre families and macrogenres

It can be discussed whether some of the Other macrogenres can be moved to any of the other three genre families (e.g. Anecdotes to the Narration family).
In a lot of cases, where there were no clear-cut genres, a combination of genres became an optimal solution, see Figure 4.

```
- <text id="text_8_8" title="Jag borde sluta röka" topic="daily life,food and drink,free
time; entertainment">
  - <genre>
      <other>dialogue</other>
    </genre>
  - <genre>
      <facts>explanation</facts>
    </genre>
    John: Får man röka här? Pia: Nej, man får inte röka på några restauranger eller kaféer i
    Sverige längre. Det är bra, tycker jag. Men om du måste röka får du gå ut. John: Nej,
    usch. Det är så kallt. Och jag borde faktiskt sluta röka. Ska vi betala? Måste man ge
    dricks på restauranger i Sverige, förresten? Pia: Nej, man behöver inte ge dricks, men
    man brukar lämna lite extra om servicen är bra.
  </text>
```

FIGURE 4. An example of textual annotation, text at level A1

2.2.2 Pedagogical annotation of coursebooks

Pedagogical annotation in this corpus is understood as mark-up assigned to all types of information found in coursebook lessons except texts used for reading comprehension. All books are structured by `lessons` (i.e. chapters in coursebooks), which are assigned a proficiency level, which then applies to all texts and activities in the lesson. The taxonomy of the pedagogical mark-up within each `lesson` is presented by `lists`, `language examples`, `tasks` and `activity instructions`.

Activity instructions, Tasks, Language examples, Lists	Activity instructions, Tasks	Activity instructions, Tasks	Language examples, Lists
Target skills: Listening Reading Writing Speaking **Target competences:** Grammar Pronunciation Spelling Vocabulary	**Activity types:** Brainstorming Composition/essay writing Dialogue/interview Dictation Discussion Error correction Form manipulation Information search Monologue Pre-reading Question answering Reading aloud Role-playing Summary Text questions Translation	**Activity formats:** Category identification Category substitution Free/short answers Free writing Gaps Matching Multiple choice Narration, retelling, presentation Reordering/ Restructuring Sorting True-false/Yes-no Wordbank	**Linguistic units:** Characters Dialogues Full sentences Incomplete sentences Numbers Phrases Question-answer Single words Texts/examples of text writing

TABLE 5. Overview over the taxonomy of the pedagogical mark-up

Further, each of the pedagogically-relevant elements is associated with the target `skills/competences` (e.g. reading) they are aimed at. `Lists` and `language examples` are assigned `linguistic units` (e.g. single words), and all `tasks` and `activity instructions` are associated with `format` and `type` of exercises (e.g. gaps), see Table 5 for an overview. In the terms of the output XML data, the table headings represent XML elements, the text in bold corresponds to XML attributes, and the running text stands for a set of attribute values.

An example of pedagogical annotation follows below (Figure 5)

```
-<lesson id="1" level="A1" title="Presentation: hälsa, land, arbete, studier, familj, språk.
 Klassrumsfraser. Alfabetet.">
   <activity_instruction id="ai_1_1" skill="vocabulary" format="matching"> 1 A Kan du
   svenska? Kombinera. </activity_instruction>
 -<list id="list_1_1" ref="#ai_1_1" type="vocabulary" unit="single_words">
     banan papper radio kaffe telefon hamburgare teve teater psykolog te
   </list>
```

FIGURE 5. An example of pedagogical annotation, level A1

2.3 Online coursebok editor

To simplify the process of inserting XML-annotation into the OCR-ed raw texts, an online coursebook editor has been developed early in the project (Volodina & Johansson Kokkinakis, 2013).[2]

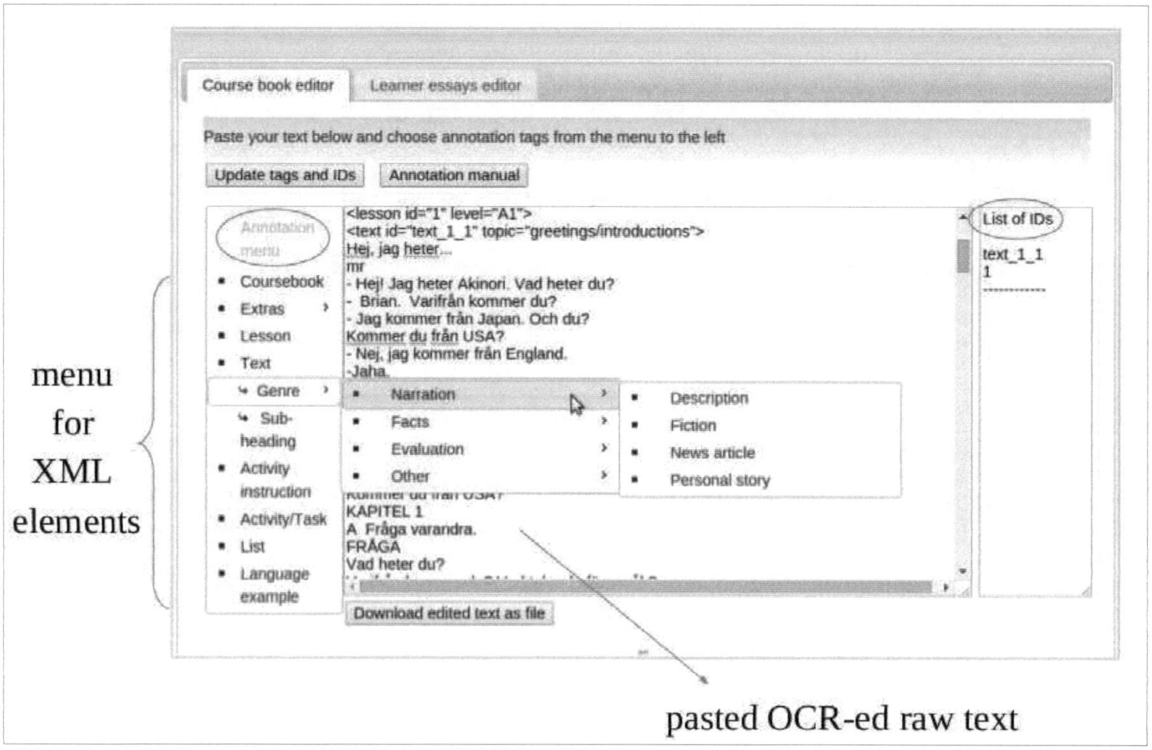

FIGURE 6. The online corpus editor.

[2]http://spraakbanken.gu.se/larka/larka_cefr_editor.html

The annotation scheme for content annotation described in section 2.2 has been implemented in the form of user-friendly menus (Figure 6, on the left). In the centre (Figure 6) is an editable text area where text for annotation is pasted, and on the right is a field for an overview of all inserted `IDs`. Link to annotation guidelines and an option of downloading the annotated text as a file are also offered.

Each menu element is accompanied with a pop-up dialogue, which prompts what information should be added, for example `IDs`, or `references` to previously used `IDs`, or `titles`. For categories where lists of options exist, such as `topics`, `genres` or `skills`, options are offered as multi-select drop-down menus. Besides, there are sub-menus for inserting `subheadings` and `extra` information, such as text author, source of information, etc. Each new inserted XML element closes the previously opened one, except in cases of `lessons`, `extras`, `genres` and `subheadings`.

Meta-information about each coursebook is collected once before the annotation of the rest of the book starts, and includes `title`, `author`, `publication year`, `publisher`, `ISBN`.

The editor is language independent, freely accessible over internet and can be easily reusable in other L2 coursebook annotation projects.

2.4 Text-level annotation: inter-annotator agreement

Inter-annotator agreement is the degree of agreement among annotators about assigning categories to the same objects (Artstein and Poesio, 2008). Our intention with the inter-annotator agreement experiment was to estimate the quality of the text-level (textual) annotation on the one hand, and to detect categories causing large number of disagreements and inconsistencies, on the other.

We have investigated randomly chosen parts of the CEFR corpus, targeting at least one chapter (lesson) per level. The controlled subset of the corpus comprised 21630 tokens at the five proficiency levels, divided between 32 texts and a number of accompanying coursebook activities. Our focus has been on texts: text topics, genre families and macrogenres. Three annotators have been involved in this experiment with knowledge of linguistics, language teaching and computational linguistics.

Agreement measure	MASI distance			Jaccard distance		
	Topic	Genre family	Macrogenres	Topic	Genre family	Macrogenres
Fleiss' kappa	0.61	0.62	0.40	**0.70**	0.67	0.52
Krippendorff's alpha	0.59	0.45	0.27	**0.67**	0.48	0.34

TABLE 6. Results of the inter-annotator agreement for topics, genre families and macrogenres

We report inter-annotator agreement in terms of Fleiss' multi-kappa (Davies and Fleiss, 1982) and Krippendorff's alpha (Krippendorff, 1980) being that the task involved multiple (i.e. three or more) annotators. Both measures take into account chance agreement (Artstein and Poesio, 2008). Each annotator could assign more than one category to each text object, i.e. multiple topics out of 28 possible ones, multiple genre families out of 4 choices and multiple macrogenres out of 34 options, therefore, we used distance measures that would calculate the dissimilarity between sets of multiple values. We considered both Jaccard's distance metric (Jaccard, 1908) and MASI (Measuring Agreement on Set-valued Items; Passonneau, 2006) when calculating agreement with the previously mentioned measures. Both metrics are based on the union and the intersection between sets, MASI including also an additional term, M, which equals 1 if the sets are identical, 2/3 in case of subsumption, and 1/3 if there is at least one element in common between the two sets (Passonneau, 2006). For both the distance[3] and the agreement[4] measures the NLTK Python module has been used (Bird, 2006). Results are shown in Table 6.

Fleiss' kappa within the range between 0.61-0.80 means substantial agreement, which given our type of annotation is a very encouraging result. However, the original results for Fleiss' kappa were lower than the ones reported in Table 6 (e.g. Fleiss' kappa for topics 0.52 with Jaccard distance and 0.37 with MASI). The reason for that proved to lie in the fact that some of the texts had substantial difference in the number of assigned values, with the intersection being a good common ground. This has led us to the conclusion that we should set a maximum number of values that may be assigned to each text object. To simulate that, we have calculated inter-annotator agreement based on the intersection of values (i.e. considering only values that were common between at least two of the three annotators, leaving out the ones that have been assigned only once, except when only one label was provided), as reported in the table above. The results have improved substantially. Following this experiment, in the near future, a revision of the corpus annotation is planned where we will consider reducing the number of assigned topics to a maximum of 3 and macrogenres – to a maximum of 2.

To exemplify cases with different interpretations, look at Figure 7 where a text with a horoscope is given in the original language and translated into English in Figure 8.

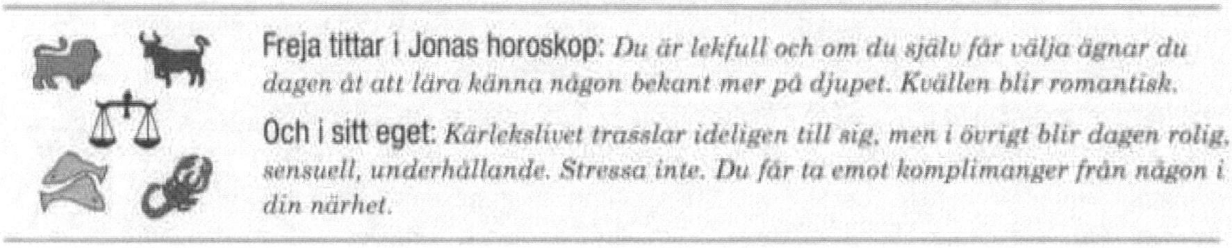
Freja tittar i Jonas horoskop: *Du är lekfull och om du själv får välja ägnar du dagen åt att lära känna någon bekant mer på djupet. Kvällen blir romantisk.*

Och i sitt eget: *Kärlekslivet trasslar ideligen till sig, men i övrigt blir dagen rolig, sensuell, underhållande. Stressa inte. Du får ta emot komplimanger från någon i din närhet.*

FIGURE 7. Text on horoscope, level B2.

***Freja looks into Jonas's horoscope**: You are playful, and if you can choose, you'd spend the day getting to know better somebody you are acquainted with. The evening will be romantic.*
***And then into her own**: The love life is a mess, but otherwise, the day will be funny, sensual and entertaining. Don't work yourself up. You will receive compliments from somebody in your surrounding.*

FIGURE 8. Translation of the text into English

Figure 9 provides the three annotations that have been provided to this text.

The first annotator assigned 4 topics: (1) culture and traditions, (2) daily life, (3) relations with other people, (4) religion; myth and legends. The second annotator assigned topic (4), whereas the third annotation assigned topics (2) and (3).

[3]http://www.nltk.org/_modules/nltk/metrics/distance.html
[4]http://www.nltk.org/_modules/nltk/metrics/agreement.html

```
<text id="text_5_8" ref="#task_5_6"
topic="culture and traditions,daily
life,relations with other
people,religion; myths and legends">
<genre><narration>fiction</narration></
genre>
Freja tittar i Jonas horoskop: Du är
lekfull och om du själv får välja ägnar
du dagen åt att lära känna någon bekant
mer på djupet. Kvällen blir romantisk.
```

```
<text id="text_1_10" topic="religion;
nyths and legends">
<genre><narration>fiction</narration></
genre>
<subheading>Freja tittar i Jonas
horoskop</subheading>
Du är lekfull och om du själv får välja
ägnar du dagen åt att lära känna någon
bekant mer på djupet. Kvällen blir
romantisk.
```

```
<text id="text_1_10" topic="daily
life,relations with other people">
<genre><narration>fiction</narration></genre>
<subheading>Freja tittar i Jonas horoskop: </
subheading>
 Du är lekfull och om du själv får välja
ägnar du dagen åt att lära känna någon bekant
mer på djupet. Kvällen blir romantisk.
```

FIGURE 9. Annotation of the text for topics and genres

For the experiments we used triples of values (annotator-code, text-code, list of assigned values), in Table 7 shown with the original set-up in the first column, and with an intersection set-up in the second column.

Original experiment	Intersection-based experiment
• (ann1, text_5_8, [1,2,3,4]) • (ann2, text_5_8, [4]) • (ann3, text_5_8, [2,3])	• (ann1, text_5_8, [2,3,4]) • (ann2, text_5_8, [4]) • (ann3, text_5_8, [2,3])

TABLE 7. Original versus "intersection"-based triples

As can be seen, the value "1" has been removed from the list of assigned values from annotator 1, since this value has not been used by any other annotator. We can see here that annotator 1 has agreed with both annotators 2 and 3, whereas there was no agreement between annotator 2 and 3.

Summarizing the results of the experiment on inter-annotator agreement, we can say that categories causing a lot of disagreement proved to be the difference in number of assigned values, rather that the values themselves, which is the reason for planned revisions in the annotation guidelines and in the annotated files. However, the experiment has also shown that the annotation is reliable and can be used for experiments as it is, in the sense that among the multiple values there has always been a central overlap between different annotators. Non-overlapping topics and genres can be considered peripheral adding an extra value to text characteristics.

3 Initial quantitative explorations of the COCTAILL

We carried out an initial quantitative analysis of the corpus observing variables such as text genres, topics as well as skills and competences targeted by tasks at each CEFR level.

Texts showed a substantial variation both in genre and in topics across proficiency levels. About half of the texts were dialogues at A1 level, but this amount steadily decreased at each CEFR level, C1 level coursebooks containing barely any. Factual texts were presented at all levels, but at higher proficiency levels they were almost twice as common. The percentage of dialogues and factual texts at each level is presented in Figure 10.

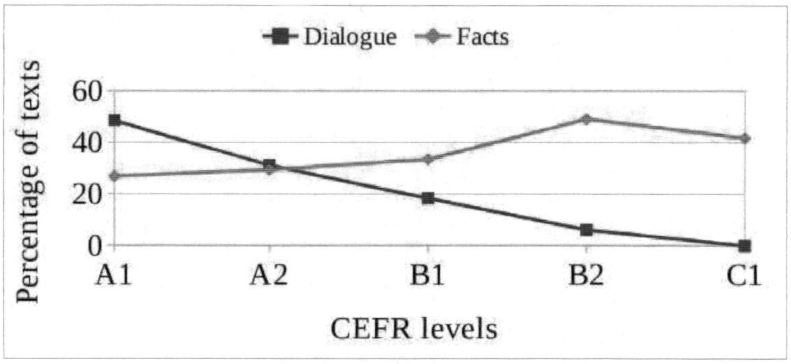

FIGURE 10. Percentage of dialogues and factual texts per CEFR level

Not only genres, but also certain topics showed large difference in distribution at different CEFR levels, as Figure 11 below shows.

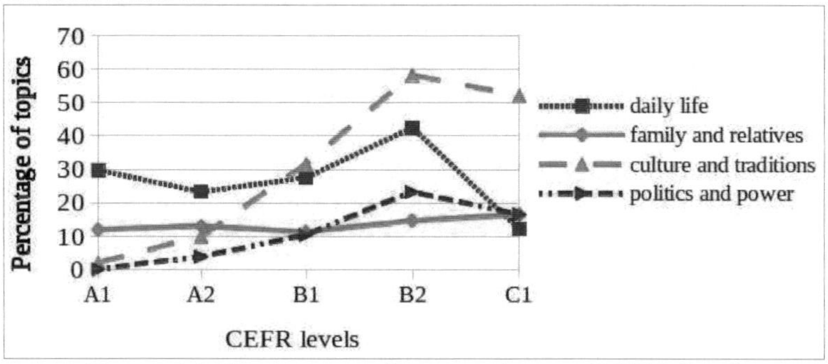

FIGURE 11. Percentage of text topics per CEFR level

The topics "culture and tradition" and "politics and power" are either not present or appear to a very limited extent at A1 level, but at higher proficiency levels their proportion increases substantially. The topic of "daily life", although appears at all CEFR levels, seems to be less common at C1 level. Interestingly, the percentage of texts focusing on "family and relatives" remains the same across all levels. Such topics would be particularly suitable for the analysis of how linguistic complexity changes at different proficiency levels within the same topic.

Further, we retrieved some quantitative data from a more pedagogical perspective aiming at tracing how the proportion of skills and competences targeted by tasks change at various levels. This information is presented in Figure 12.

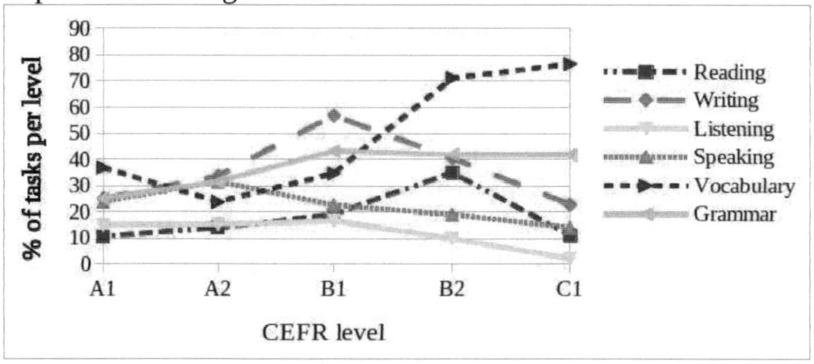

FIGURE 12. Target skills and competences per CEFR level

At A1 and A2 levels, the focus is primarily on the productive skills of speaking and writing, each of which accounted for about one fourth of the exercises at this level. Tasks involving the receptive skills of reading and listening are about 10% less frequent at this initial stage. The corpus also shows a shift in focus from oral language use to the written one at B1 and B2 levels. More than half of the tasks are writing exercises at B1 level, and the highest percentage of reading tasks (35%) appears at B2 level. The proportion of grammar exercises increases until B1 level, then it keeps its rather dominant presence (about 40%) at all further stages. Vocabulary teaching is a primary target skill of tasks at A1 level, but less so at A2 level, whilst from intermediate (B1) level on, vocabulary exercises dominate the items proposed for students, which is especially obvious at C1, which supports Singleton's (1995) hypothesis that vocabulary doesn't have a critical period at which it should be taught or learnt.

Another interesting piece of statistics we have looked at is average sentence length per CEFR level (Figure 13). Numbers have been calculated upon sentences retrieved from texts aimed at reading comprehension.

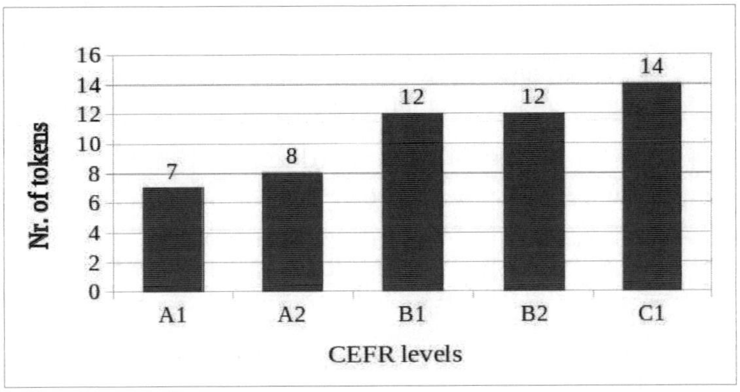

FIGURE 13. Average sentence length per CEFR level.

The graph shows that sentence length grows steadily from lower levels to more advanced ones, the largest increase being observed between A2 and B1 with no difference between B1 and B2. The most feasible explanation for the less drastic increase in sentence length starting from B1 is that texts at the higher levels contain a broader mixture of sentence types – both typical of the level itself, and of all the lower levels, e.g. B2 texts hypothetically contain sentences typical of levels A1, A2, B1 and B2. The sentence length typical of the lower levels would in that case influence the calculations of the average length at B2. Another potential explanation might be connected to the number of texts of certain genres: to take one example, dialogues that tend to contain very short sentences, dominate at A1 and A2 levels and decrease in number from B1.

These numbers show some similarity in the tendency of increase to the reported average sentence length in the L2 French corpus (François, 2011) , as shown in Table 8:

A1	A2	B1	B2	C1	C2
9,1	14,54	16,85	18,6	19,36	21,43

TABLE 8. Average sentence length in L2 French corpus (François, 2011:359)

There is a steady increase in the average sentence length over the levels in both languages. However, there is a larger increase between A1 and A2 in L2 French coursebooks, and more moderate growth between the rest of the levels. Differences in the average values between the two languages can be accounted for by linguistic characteristics of the two language, by differences in tokenization and segmentation tools, as well as by the variety of text genres present in the two corpora. In general, this piece of statistics raises interesting questions about linguistic complexity of each proficiency level and asks for deeper investigations of the problem.

4 Concluding remarks

We have presented our work on COCTAILL, a corpus of L2 coursebooks, richly annotated for textual, pedagogical and linguistic variables. The corpus is innovative in a number of ways: there are no other existing electronic corpora that have pedagogical annotation alongside proficiency level-labelling, textual annotation, and linguistic annotation covering all the spectrum of proficiency levels interesting for linguistic modelling of learner levels. We pioneered in the development of a taxonomy of pedagogical variables for L2 coursebook annotation, which up-to-date remains the only one we are aware of. Besides, unlike a number of other coursebook projects, where only reading materials are selected or only a subset of CB language is analysed, we present a possibility to study coursebooks in their entirety with important implications for correlating proficiency levels, L2 input as well as various pedagogical and textual variables, such as target skills and competences. COCTAILL is available for browsing with password protection and is downloadable as a bag of sentences labelled with coursebook levels.

In the future, we plan several iterations on the improvement of COCTAILL content annotation. This will include the revision and a potential decrease in the number of assigned topics and macrogenres. Besides, the topic and genre taxonomy may need to be revised to contain fewer, but more general categories, i.e. going from a more detailed taxonomy to one with broader categories.

Certain parameters have yet been outside the inter-annotator agreement experiment. In future we plan to focus on

(1) activity instructions and tasks, where we will calculate agreement in assigning target skills and exercise formats; and

(2) lists and language examples, where the main focus will be on the annotation of target skills and linguistic units

We can foresee that results of the inter-annotator experiments will yield another round of annotation revision.

Availability of the corpus opens prospects to engage in numerous SLA-aware ICALL-relevant studies, such as CEFR profiling, vocabulary and grammar profiling, studies on sentence and text readability, question generation, automatic genre identification, automatic topic modelling – to name just a few potential directions of research.

The taxonomy of textual and pedagogical variables present in COCTAILL provides the key to various empirical studies of coursebooks, which can help critically assess and reflect on the relation between coursebook design and SLA research. Pedagogically annotated coursebook corpora such as COCTAILL, have a potential to become a crystallized form of what should be taught, at which level and in which format, which is crucial for various ICALL tasks, such as material generation. We expect that these insights, implemented into ICALL applications, will facilitate generation of pedagogically appropriate learning materials. To put it simply, you get what you annotate.

References

Anping He. (2005). Corpus-Based Evaluation of ELT textbooks. Paper presented at the joint *conference of the American Association of Applied Corpus Linguistics and the International Computer Archive of Modern and Medieval English,* 12-15 May 2005, University of Michigan.

Artstein Ron & Massimo Poesio. (2008). Inter-coder agreement for computational linguistics. *Computational Linguistics*, 34(4): 555-596.

Attali Yigal & Jill Burstein. (2006). Automated essay scoring with e-rater v.2. *The Journal of Technology, Learning and Assessment*, 4(3).

Bird Steven. (2006). NLTK: the natural language toolkit. In Proceedings of the COLING/ACL on Interactive presentation sessions, pp. 69-72.

Borin Lars, Markus Forsberg & Johan Roxendal. (2012). Korp – the corpus infrastructure of Språkbanken. *Proceedings of LREC 2012*. Istanbul: ELRA. 474–478.

Council of Europe (COE). (2001). *The Common European Framework of Reference for Languages: Learning, Teaching, Assessment*. Cambridge University Press.

Davies Mark & Joseph L. Fleiss. (1982). Measuring agreement for multinomial data. *Biometrics*, 38(4): 1047–1051.

François Thomas. (2011). *Les apports du traitement automatique du langage à la lisibilité du français langue étrangère*, Ph.D. Thesis, Université Catholique de Louvain. Thesis Supervisors : Cédrick Fairon and Anne Catherine Simon.

François Thomas, Nuria Gala, Patrick Watrin & Cédrick Fairon. (2014). FLELex: a graded lexical resource for French foreign learners. In the 9th *International Conference on Language Resources and Evaluation (LREC 2014)*. Reykjavik, Iceland, 26-31 May.

Gamson David A., Lu Xiaofei, & Eckert Sarah Anne. (2013). Challenging the research base of the common core state standards: A historical reanalysis of text complexity. *Educational Researcher*, 42(7):381-391.

Jaccard Paul. (1908). Nouvelles recherches sur la distribution florale. *Bulletin de la Societe Vaudoise des Sciences Naturelles*, 44: 223-270.

Hancke Julia & Detmar Meurers. (2013). Exploring CEFR classification for German based on rich linguistic modeling. *Learner Corpus Research 2013, Book of Abstracts*. pp. 54-56. Bergen, Norway.

Johansson Britt & Anniqa Sandell Ring. (2010). *Låt språket bära: genrepedagogiken i praktiken*. Hallgren och Fallgren, Stockholm.

Krippendorff Klaus. (1980). *Content Analysis: An Introduction to Its Methodology*, chapter 12. Sage, Beverly Hills, CA.

Meunier Fanny & Gouverneur Céline. (2007). The treatment of phraseology in ELT textbooks, In: *Corpora in the Foreign Language Classroom. Selected papers from the Sixth International Conference on Teaching and Language Corpora* (TaLC6), University of Granada, 4-7 July 2004, Encarnación H., Quereda L. and Santana J. ed(s), Amsterdamm & New York, Rodopi, Language and Computers Series 61, p. 119-139.

Meunier Fanny & Gouverneur Céline. (2009). New types of corpora for new educational challenges: collecting, annotating and exploiting a corpus of textbook material, In: *Corpora and Language Teaching*, Aijmer, K. ed(s), Amsterdam & Philadelphia, Benjamins, p. 179-201

Passonneau Rebecca J. (2006). Measuring agreement on set-valued items (MASI) for semantic and pragmatic annotation. In *Proceedings of LREC*, Genoa, pp. 831–836.

Reda Ghsoon. (2003). English Coursebooks: Prototype Textsts and Basic Vocabulary Norms. *ELT Journal* 57(3): 260-268.

Römer Ute. (2006). Looking at *Looking*: Functions and Contexts of Progressives in Spoken English and 'School' English. In: Renouf, Antoinette & Andrew Kehoe (eds.). *The Changing Face of Corpus Linguistics.* Papers from the 24th International Conference on English Language Research on Computerized Corpora (ICAME 24). Amsterdam: Rodopi. p.231-242.

Singleton David. (1995). *Introduction: A Critical Look at the Critical Period in Second Language Acquisition Research*, In Singleton D. & Lengyel, Z. (Eds.), The Age Factor in Second Language Acquisition (1-29). Avon: Multilingual Matters, Ltd.

Vajjala Sowmya & Detmar Meurers. (2013). On The Applicability of Readability Models to Web Texts. *Proceedings of the Workshop on Predicting and Improving Text Readability for Target Reader Populations (PITR)*, ACL 2013

Volodina Elena, Ildikó Pilán, Lars Borin, & Therese Lindström Tiedemann. (2014). A flexible language learning platform based on language resources and web services. *Proceedings of LREC 2014, Reykjavik, Iceland.*

Volodina Elena & Sofie Johansson Kokkinakis. (2013). Compiling a corpus of CEFR-related texts. *Proceedings of the Language Testing and CEFR conference*, Antwerpen, Belgium, May 27-29, 2013.